Books by Rex Reed

DO YOU SLEEP IN THE NUDE?

CONVERSATIONS IN THE RAW

BIG SCREEN, LITTLE SCREEN

Rex Reed

people are crazy here

DELACORTE PRESS / NEW YORK

All of the following articles previously
appeared in *Esquire* Magazine, *Harper's Bazaar*
or the Chicago Tribune New York *News* Syndicate.

Designed by Ann Spinelli

Library of Congress Cataloging in Publication Data

Reed, Rex

People are crazy here.

1. Performing arts—Collected works.   I.   Title.
PN1623.R4   791.43'028'0922   73–22203

ISBN: 0–440–07365–0

For Margaret Gardner

Contents

Part II: Ignoring the Crazy Life

Part III: Digging the Crazy Life

*Picture sections follow pages 143 and
229.*

Introduction

I was having lunch with Katharine Ross in the MGM commissary. Outside, a funny little man who looked like Leon Errol was appraising the buildings, the hedges, even the parking lot for possible resale value. The greatest studio in the world was bankrupt, marking the end of an era and the end of a dream. MGM was the reason a lot of girls like Katharine Ross drifted into the movie business in the first place, and the symbol of perfection and glamor that made a lot of critics and journalists like myself want to write about it. Now it was dying and we were sadly listening to the death rattle. A few blocks away from where we sat, nostalgically swallowing the last of the Louis B. Mayer chicken soup, bulldozers were tearing down Waterloo Bridge, tractors were crushing Andy Hardy's house into a heap of rubble, and a shopping center was rising gruesomely on the gone-forever backlot where they burned Atlanta in *Gone With the Wind*. It was a sad day, watching magic turn into a space for ugly apartment buildings and laundromats, and Katharine Ross had more reason than most for personal lament.

She was appearing in the last movie to be filmed on the old MGM sound stages. It was a cheap potboiler that came and went without embarrassment, but her particular *angst* had nothing to do with the low quality of the picture. It had to do with the even lower taste of the men responsible, men who had no interest in the history or perpetuation of the movies as a cultural heritage. Since this was the last film on the old backlot before it was razed forever and sold off at auction along with Esther Williams' bathing suits and Clark Gable's raincoats, somebody had the bright idea of casting some of the old MGM stars in cameo roles: Ann Rutherford, Peter Lawford, June Allyson. And so Katharine Ross, a relative newcomer to the horrors of Hollywood, was trembling as she told with anger and resentment of the morning's activities on the set. It seems that June Allyson was supposed to play a Lesbian. Now June Allyson, the all-American heartthrob who sent Van Johnson off to war in more Forties cockpit romances than most people care to remember, didn't have the faintest idea what a Lesbian was. She came to the studio in her son's baseball uniform, but the director insisted something was missing. "Lesbians have a grim and menacing look," he said crisply to the star whose box-office grosses for 20 years alone could, if MGM finances had been managed by saner heads, have paid off the back taxes and rescued the studio from debt. But June Allyson was a good scout who aimed to please. She snarled like Lassie when he played a war veteran with amnesia. It still wasn't the right Lesbian look, said the director. Then he had an idea (usually indicated above the heads of the directors in the New Hollywood by an art deco light bulb supplied by the art department). He marched June Allyson over to the Tait College set where she and Peter Lawford danced the "Varsity Drag" while coins jingled in box offices everywhere during the success of the hit campus musical *Good News* in 1947. While Miss Allyson surveyed the scene of her happy past, the director picked up some rocks from the Wall of China, which had just been knocked to the ground as though *The Good Earth* never existed, and began hurling them through the window of the old campus library. The glass shattered, the director giggled, and June Allyson began to get the cruelty of the joke. The edges of her smile turned to helpless anger and a cloud passed over her clear gumdrop Technicolor eyes as they filled with tears. "That's it!" cried the director. "That's the Lesbian look!" Katharine Ross finished the story and we sat silently, unable to finish the Lana Turner salad. "People," she said, "are crazy here."

We live in a world of madness, suffering new brain damage daily. To what extent can artists influence the changes that erode our environmental well-being without being crushed and shattered along with the fissile balance of communal order? And yet they survive. I think you have to be just a little bit crazy to preserve your sanity in the face of paranoia, greed and the lust for power that robs nature of every last vestige of mystery in these demonic times. It's always the artists who recognize the quality of life, not only as it is but as it should be—entertaining the rest of us, acting as mirrors to our lives in critical times, making their voices heard above the din of despair. I used to think people in show business were crazier than anybody else. I guess I still do. The reasons they gravitate toward the unreal tinsel of a life that promises nothing but insecurity in return are hardly the criteria by which so-called stable people base their lives: the desperation for attention, the need to be recognized in a sea of faceless mannequins, the fear of mundane boredom and everyday routine, the terrifying belief that, even at the risk of making a fool of yourself, you have to shout "Look at me, I'm a person too!" in front of millions of people, or nobody will hear you.

These are the things I look for in my interviews and profiles—the eccentricities, ambiguities and irreparable ego damages that set famous people apart from the folks next door, make them controversial, and keep them dancing recklessly on the lip of the volcano. Roger Moore, the new James Bond, telling me in a voice far removed from the steel-nerved coolness of 007, that he faints at the sight of blood. Tuesday Weld, an alcoholic at 12, a has-been at 18, now basking in a new career as a dramatic actress, who packs her daughter into a rented car and drives up and down the Los Angeles freeways for days to keep from screaming. Joanne Woodward, who ripped out the palm trees in her Beverly Hills driveway with bulldozers, replaced them with magnolias to remind her of home, and pulled her children out of the Girl Scouts when she discovered Debbie Reynolds was the scoutmaster. Doris Day and her crusade for animals, holding a customer's place in line at the bank while he unties his dog from a parking meter. Carol Channing, who carries her own food into Sardi's in Mason jars because she thinks she's been poisoned by the bleach in her hair. Tennessee Williams, convinced he has breast cancer only a doctor in Bangkok can cure. Hollywood hostesses who keep ledgers on their guests, demoting them in the imaginary social caste system from *Group A* because they've attended more than two *Group B* parties in a row. Or Peter Bogdanovich and an Italian film crew, pouring dirt on the ancient Colosseum in Rome, trying to make a 2000-year-old ruin look old enough for a Hollywood movie.

Not that show business has any exclusive contract with madness. There are probably more crazy people in Washington these days than anywhere else—a generalization one glance at the headlines of any daily paper will quickly fortify. Fame (and the glow that bleeds over from the spotlight to warm the people on the sidelines) makes most people crazy. Athletes make the national magazines when they swap wives, writers jam the airwaves when they libel each other on television, and criminals on trial for murder are besieged by autograph hounds (the going rate for one Charles Manson right now is ten Winston Churchills).

That is the point of this book. People are crazy everywhere and there is no evidence to the contrary. We might as well enjoy it. I guess I can stand anything but mediocrity. I like them for their craziness. I guess that makes me just a little bit crazy myself. And proud to be.

Rex Reed
New York City

PART

ONE

Living the Crazy Life

A Compleat Guide to the Hollywood Society Game

THE SOCIAL CASTE SYSTEM in America did not die with Elsa Maxwell. It's alive and well and being lushly nourished in an artificial nursery called Los Angeles. Just living there guarantees the loss of a few I.Q. points each year, so you've got to do something to pass the time before you wake up by your kidney-shaped pool one day, as Oscar Levant used to say, and discover you're eighty. So Los Angeles has invented a society game as elaborate as it is vague. It's the biggest thing since strip monopoly.

Think of the Hollywood social scene as Vietnam—an expensive war game in which nobody wins. At the top of the military structure are the generals who map out the strategy. This is the impenetrable *Group A*, where all the action is (but not necessarily all the fun). Keeping the status going in *Group A* depends on how many times a week your name appears in either Joyce Haber's column or *Women's Wear Daily*. Nothing else counts.

Adjacent to *Group A* are the commissioned officers in what Beverly Hills hostesses jocularly call *The Fun Group* —those border neighbors who prefer not to belong to any group and couldn't care less about their social status as long as they're having a good time. *The Fun Group* often crosses over into *Group A* territory for periods of designated truce.

And finally, at the bottom of the scale, there's *Group B*, composed of enlisted men who try too hard, name-drop, social-climb, and seldom relax or enjoy themselves. *Group A* parties are held in a private upstairs room at the Bistro that looks like a leftover set from *Baby Doll*, catered by Chasen's, or prepared at home by sensitive chefs who are romanced to stay on at impossible costs. *Group B* is catered Chinese food and movies. Below *Group B*, you don't exist at all. You just stay home and read about it in the *Hollywood Reporter*.

Admission to *Group A* used to be based solely on money and power. A *Group A* hostess had to spend a minimum of $30,000 a year on clothes and $50,000 a year on jewelry. All that has changed. Denise Minnelli Hale, the doyenne of *Group A* who often hand-picks new members, says the only requirements are "a combination of money, power, achievement, savoir-faire, great connections throughout the world, wit, talent and charm." See how easy it is? She says clothes play only a small part. "If Audrey Wilder spends $2,000 a year, it's a miracle. Her mother makes her clothes."

If you want to get into *Group A*, these are the people you have to know:

The leading *Group A* hostess is Denise. The *Group A* millionaires are her new husband, Prentis Cobb Hale (he owns Neiman-Marcus and Bergdorf Goodman, for starters), the Alfred Bloomingdales and the Jerry Ohrbachs (of department store fame), the Armand Deutsches (as a boy, he was the originally intended victim in the Leopold and

Loeb kidnapping), and Doris and Jules Stein. The *Group A* stars are Kirk Douglas, Gregory Peck, and Robert Stack (mainly because of their wives, Anne, Veronique, and Rosemarie). The *Group A* actress is Rosalind Russell. The *Group A* producers are Ross Hunter and Ray Stark. (Rosalind Russell's husband, Freddie Brisson, another producer, is tolerated by *Group A*, but referred to as "The Lizard of Roz.") The John Waynes are border cases. The *Group A* director is Billy Wilder, because his wife Audrey is the *Group A* wit. (Before his divorce from Denise, Vincente Minnelli was a *Group A* director, but he lost his status when he started dating Lee Anderson, closet publicist for *Group B*.)

Nancy Sinatra, Sr., is the *Group A* martyr and Frank Sinatra is the *Group A* singer, but you can't invite the *Group A* martyr and the *Group A* singer to the same party. The torch gets so hot it melts all the imported candles. Paul Ziffrin is the *Group A* attorney (replacing Greg Bautzer). Irving Lazar and Sue Mengers are the *Group A* agents. Henry Kissinger is the *Group A* politician (but not his dates). Ronald Reagan is the *Group A* governor, and Zubin Mehta is the *Group A* conductor. Have I left anyone out? Oh, yes. Janet and Fred DeCordova (he's *The Tonight Show* producer) and Mrs. Tom May. Truman Capote and Aileen (Suzy) Mehle are the *Group A* visiting firemen; Joyce Haber is the *Group A* gossip columnist, and John Gavin is the *Group A* single man. There is no *Group A* single girl. It depends on whose husband is out of town that night. Joanne Carson (Johnny's ex) was the *Group A* single girl there for about ten minutes, after her pal Truman Capote sent an SOS to Hollywood to announce her arrival. Suddenly her phone stopped ringing. "I don't know what I did wrong," says Joanne, "but it's more fun being in *The Fun Group*. That's where the real people are." One *Group A* hostess claims Joanne was dropped because she dated Glenn Ford, who is positive *Group B*. Do you love it?

If you live in Los Angeles and don't get invited to *Group A* parties, some people think you might as well be dead. Take heart. You might fit in farther down the ladder. *The Fun Group* gets around and still ends up in Haber. This includes the Henry Mancinis, Burt Bacharach and Angie Dickinson, Esther Williams and Fernando Lamas, Cyd Charisse and Tony Martin, The Jack Beans (Mitzi Gaynor), George and Joleen Schlatter (he produces "Laugh-In"), Polly Bergen, Burt Reynolds and Dinah Shore, Natalie Wood and Robert Wagner, the Jack Lemmons. Occasionally Marlo Thomas, if *Group A* is meeting at Joyce Haber's house.

And if all else fails, there's *Group B*, composed of Cliff Lambert, Henry Berger and Ann Miller, Marsha and Larry Israel, Harold Robbins, Dorothy Strelsin, decorator Tony Duquette, and Wally and Seth Weingarten (when Wally's father, Walter Annenberg, American Ambassador to the Court of St. James's, is in town, she's temporarily elevated to *Group A* for the duration of his visit). *Group B* also includes all the "young execs" who are currently running the Hollywood studios, but who are considered flash-in-the-pans who haven't yet proved themselves to the Establishment—men like James Aubrey, Ted Ashley, John Calley, and Doug Netter. Also practically everybody in television.

A *Group A* hostess's Gucci address book is like a Dow Jones average. Columns of names are juggled and matched for best results at the dinner table. Sometimes the structure of protocol allows a couple of token *Group B*'s, but only if the party is for more than ten guests. The exceptions fall into two separate categories:

(1) *Group A*'s who decline the mantle by their own choice, not the group's. These dark horses are called "group recluses." They include Hal and Martha Wallis, Cary Grant, the Jimmy Stewarts, George Frelinghuysen (currently in disfavor because he has too many *Group B* guests) and Ali MacGraw, whose new romance with Steve McQueen has all but ruined her socially. Not to be confused with the genuine recluses who wouldn't be caught dead in any group—Loretta Young, Barbara Stanwyck, Katharine Hepburn, and Doris Day, who lived across the

street from Denise and Vincente Minnelli and didn't even know they had split until six months after the divorce.

(2) The one-time greats who are currently going through a fading process. One of *Group A*'s hot pursuits is seeking out new blood to avoid resembling a geriatrics ward. Since they see each other constantly, they have to do something to keep from boring themselves to death. One way is to slowly weed out the old-timers. Currently fading *Group A*'s include Jack Warner, Frances and Samuel Goldwyn, George Cukor, Jack and Mary Benny, and Edie Goetz (daughter of Louis B. Mayer and sister of Irene Selznick, who is *Group A* everywhere). One peculiar exception is Ruth Gordon and Garson Kanin. Not exactly *Group A*, but—like the gargoyles on top of the Notre Dame cathedral—hard to knock off.

How do you get into *Group A?* Nobody tells you the rules, because there aren't any. But there are a few guidelines. Forget about joining things. There is no such thing as a *Group A* country club. Donating to charity is not an automatic guarantee, but there are *Group A* charities. Contributions can't hurt. The only major organization in Los Angeles that means anything socially is something called "The Amazing Blue Ribbon 400," which supports the Los Angeles Music Center. This is the only fund-raising group in town (maybe even the world) where you have to be *invited* to donate money. The inviting is done by Mrs. Norman Chandler (her friends call her Buff), wife of the owner of the *Los Angeles Times*. She's so high up on the social scale, she'd fall right out of her Bentley if you even so much as suggested she might be a *Group A*, but if she asks you to donate money to the Amazing Blue Ribbon 400, you are probably *Group A* and don't even know it.

The three other still-fashionable charities (though socially iffy) are Cedars of Lebanon Hospital (it's chic to have your name on the committees, but uncool to volunteer nursing service of any kind—when Jennifer Jones sold candy bars at Synanon, she was banished forever), The Neighbors of Watts (Mrs. Henry Fonda is very big here), and something called the Frostig School. "What's that?" I asked one *Group A* mascot. Reply: "Oh, God, I don't know, but it's important." SHARE, Incorporated, is déclassé, and Thalians is as out as its chief supporter Debbie Reynolds.

Short of hanging out with Denise Minnelli (you're just going to have to break the habit of calling her that, because she's Mrs. Hale now, dammit!), the only other way to get into *Group A* is to captivate a *Group A* member at a *Group A* gathering where the other *Group A*'s can watch. A brief hello doesn't count. You have to engage an important *Group A* person in some kind of serious discussion for a minimum of thirty minutes. Then you are almost assured of a second invitation.

Now you're in. Your troubles are just beginning, because once you're in, it requires a very high energy level to stay in. Certain standards must be met. You must sit at the *Group A* tables at the Bistro, either upstairs, or downstairs at the front-room corner table, or at the two adjoining tables on the side. You must play tennis (preferably at Ingrid Ohrbach's court where Fran Stark and Rosemary Stack work out). You must have seen two out of three productions at the Los Angeles Music Center each year in their original form on Broadway. ("It was much better in New York" is a favorite *Group A* sentence.) And you must give inventive parties. One reason why almost all of the younger stars in Hollywood are scorned by *Group A* is because their idea of entertaining is smoking pot and sending out for pizza.

One thing you must never do is pick up a book and learn how to do anything. You have coaches and teachers for everything from baccarat to needlepoint. Marvin Hart is the *Group A* exercise instructor. If you walk into a Beverly Hills mansion and see a custom-padded Marvin Hart back-slant board, you know you are in the presence of *Group A*. It's all very incestuous, but you also don't steal anyone else's husband (that's why Mia Farrow is out of *Group A* forever). If you have an affair, it's with your tennis coach.

Group A "taboos" are blacks, *nouveau-riche* rock stars, going to three *Group B* parties in a row, being seated by the bar at Chasen's, wearing last year's Oscar de la Renta, and living in a house in Truesdale. *Group A* weekends are Palm Springs in winter and Malibu in summer (leave us not accuse this group of originality). The only exceptions are wealthy widows and divorcees who own ranches (Kay Gable, Mrs. Robert Taylor, Mrs. Dean Martin). Nobody in *Group A* lives in the San Fernando Valley, which leaves Bob Hope out.

Yugoslavian-born Denise Minnelli Hale says: "It is important to remember one thing, dalink. It's not the money that controls *Group A*. It's the women." She should know. When she was married to Minnelli, she couldn't afford servants, but *Group A* flocked to her house to devour her spaghetti, which she cooked herself. (She even mopped her own kitchen after they left.) She is the only *Group A* power who has automatically brought two husbands into the sacred ranks, and she's the only member of *Group A* who maintains her charter status from San Francisco. Denise says, "Kirk Douglas wouldn't be *Group A* without Anne. Ray Stark has the brains, but Fran has the savoir faire. Jerry Ohrbach is rich, but Ingrid has the charm. It's the combination that works, but the women run the show."

Group A ladies stick together, and maintaining the status quo is a unit project. They rise from their Porthault sheets at 10 A.M. From 10:00 to 12:00, in fashionable houses throughout Beverly Hills, *Group A* wives check for their names in Joyce Haber's column and decide what they will wear to the Bistro for lunch. This varies according to whether they feel like going hippie or mod or radical chic that day. If there's a man for lunch, they might wear something by Luis Estevez, the *Group A* designer (who is often also the *Group A* escort). Lunch is almost always at the Bistro. Occasional exceptions are La Scala Boutique, St. Germain, and Jerry Magnin's Greenhouse, but this is considered strictly slumming.

At 12:00, cars are waiting at the curb. Lunches are called

for noon, but it's always fashionable to arrive a half hour late. At 12:30, the Rolls-Royces and Cadillacs arrive at the Bistro. From 12:30 to 3:30, they sip white wine and carve up whoever isn't there that day. From 3:30 to 5:00, they shop for new things to wear to the Bistro for the rest of the week. Gucci for replacing leather bags and shoes they wear out schlepping in and out of the Bistro; The Staircase and Shaxted for Porthault linen; Amelia Gray (the only place they can buy Galanos); Georgio's and Saint Laurent Rive Gauche for clothes; RSVP for lucite jewelry to pay back other *Group A* ladies for dinner parties they've attended that week. And if you're wondering about the foundation for all that status couture, no *Group A* lady would consider herself anything but naked without her *Group A* custom lingerie from a place called Juel Park ($25 for bikini panties, up to $800 for nightgowns). Then they have their hair done by Hugh York (the *Group A* hairdresser), their legs waxed at Elizabeth Arden, and their false Juliet nails fabricked and splinted at Grace's. All serious *Group A* jewelry is ordered from the David Webb catalogue in New York. The *B Group* goes to Marvin Himes (because he's wholesale).

At 5:00, they return home, bathe (careful to wash around their individual eyelashes), cream their splinted Juliet nails, and dress for *Group A* dinners.

In the *Group A* glossary, "Dress informal" means dress to the hilt, but with secondary pieces of jewelry. "Dress casual" means Halston pajamas at $600 a crack. A "no-no" means someone who is dead in Joyce Haber's column (there's a two-month period of grace, reasonable excuses being: out of town, in Europe or working on a picture).

To end the day, they arrive at 8 P.M. for dinner parties called for 7:30, at which Jody Jacobs will hopefully be present with a photographer to take pictures for the *Los Angeles Times*. Nobody is quite sure what they do when they get back home at night, but there aren't many *Group A* babies.

Some words of advice: Charitable donations must not be publicized. Publicity is OK, but it can't be planted. And one last talisman to live by: You must never be hungry. Ambition they can handle, because they're surrounded by it every day, but desperation is too unpredictable. Above all else, *Group A* never does anything to cause perspiration.

It's all silly, meaningless, and exhausting, and has nothing to do with the actual work that is done in Hollywood, but it keeps 'em off the streets. Trouble is, after all is said and done, the final irony is that most of *Group A* in California would be *Group B* in New York.

2

Tennessee Williams

BABY, I'VE BEEN SICK." Tennessee Williams sits under a chandelier sporting a rosy suntan and a freshly thatched beard, having dinner at Antoine's. He is eating Oysters Rockefeller and sipping cold white wine and talking about life. If a swamp alligator could talk, he would sound like Tennessee Williams. His tongue seems coated with rum and molasses as it darts in and out of his mouth, licking at his moustache like a pink lizard. His voice wavers unsteadily like old gray cigar smoke in a room with no ventilation, rising to a mad cackle like a wounded macaw, settling finally in a cross somewhere between Tallulah Bankhead and Everett Dirksen. His hands flutter like dying birds in an abandoned aviary. Tragic flamboyance masks tortured sensitivity. At the age of sixty the world's most famous play-

wright stands precariously on the ledge of vulnerability, fighting like a jaguar and talking like a poet. "The carrion birds have tried to peck out my eyes and my tongue and my mind, but they've never been able to get at my heart."

He's been sick all his life. Diphtheria left him with a kidney ailment and a childhood paralysis that took years to cure. He had his first nervous breakdown when he was twenty-three. For the past ten years his bouts with alcohol and drugs have made headlines. In 1969 he found himself in a psychiatric hospital. "Baby, I was out of my skull. I could no longer remember how many pills I had taken, and the liquor I washed them down with had a synergistic effect. I woke up at two A.M. pouring a pot of scalding hot coffee all over my body. When I woke up my brother Dakin had committed me to the loony bin where I had three convulsions and two heart attacks in three days. They were unbelievably cruel to me. Sleep is absolutely essential to me if I'm to do my work. Four hours is adequate, but I became a pill freak because I wasn't even getting that. In the loony bin, they let me go as many as four days and nights without closing my eyes. I lost thirty pounds and nearly died. But I'm well now. I'm off the booze and I only take two Miltowns and half of a Nembutal a day. I had to give up phenobarbital. It had absolutely no effect on me whatsoever. If I still can't sleep, I take the other half of the Nembutal. I don't think I am going to die."

"Are you afraid of death?" I ask.

He stares at the swirls inside an empty oyster shell. "I think I've always been somewhat preoccupied with it. It appears in my plays as an excessively recurring theme. There have been evenings when I've been afraid to go to bed. The past few years have been suicidal. I was living a life during the Sixties that was virtually an obliteration of life, deep under the influence of pills and liquor around the clock. I don't know what I was doing if I wasn't trying to find an easy way out. Oh, I thought now and then how I would kill myself if I ever got around to it. . . ."

There is a gasp from across the table, where Tennes-

see's two friends sit quietly listening. They are a professor of English in a small liberal-arts college out West, who had come to see his old friend in New Orleans before he sails for Italy on another restless search for inner peace, and a young muscular beachboy named Victor Herbert Campbell, twenty-one, the latest in a line of secretaries and traveling companions. "You can call me Vic," says the young man, "it's short for Victor."

"Hah!" snorts Tennessee. "You mean, short for Victim." The beachboy blushes and returns to his steak. "I am sailing on the *Michelangelo* for Rome. George is going with us."

"How is George?" asks the professor, spilling sauce diable all over his white linen plantation suit.

"Not well," sighs Tennessee. "Last time we saw him he hadn't bathed for five weeks and cobwebs were hanging down from the garage over his car doors. The change will do him good."

"Have you seen Gore?"

"Of course not. I expect I'll see him before I hear from him. I was simply furious over what he wrote about me in *Two Sisters*. Young Victor here looks very much like Gore when he was young."

"Who's Gore?" asks Victor, swallowing a forkful of French fries.

"He's a writer, baby. He wrote *Myra Breckinridge*."

"Oh. I heard of that." Victor smiles triumphantly.

Tennessee turns to me: "This child doesn't know Carson McCullers from Irving Berlin. He's a product of the television generation, aren't you, Victor? At home in Key West, he stays up and watches the *Late Show* and then comes up to my room and tells me the plots. We should be home there now, except that I cannot live in Key West anymore, because I am too ill to live anyplace where I can't get medical treatment when I need it."

There are so many illnesses in the life of Tennessee Williams that after a while it is not clear just when one begins and another leaves off. I ask him about his most recent one. "I've had almost nothing *but* illness, I, yuh,

don't know which is the most recent. I did have an operation in Bangkok for breast cancer. When I consulted my heart surgeon, Dr. George Burch, here in New Orleans last summer, in the course of the examination he noticed a slight swelling in the location of the left mammary gland. . . ."

"I am here to consult *my* neurologist *and* my cardiologist," interrupts the professor.

"Breast cancer is a rare thing among men, isn't it?" I can't resist the question.

". . . yes, but baby, rare things have been happening to me all my life. Anyway, an acquaintance of mine, who shall remain anonymous for our purposes, was in the process of taking me to the Orient and my doctor told me if it was malignant, I shouldn't take a chance because the delay would be unfortunate, and he advised me to cancel the trip. My acquaintance said that would not be necessary because he, uh, knew the surgeon of the King of Thailand personally. I said the hell with it, I'm going to take this trip. Well, the swelling continued slowly but perceptibly to increase on the Pacific crossing so that by the time I reached Hawaii [he pronounces it Hi-wah-yuh] I was rather alarmed. I, yuh, believe I mentioned it to some members of the press who came aboard the ship. I told them I was going to be operated on by the King's surgeon in Bangkok. Well, when I arrived in Bangkok, the receptionist at the Hotel Oriental called me half an hour after I checked in and said there are a few reporters who would like to say hello to you. I went downstairs and they were passing out martinis to everyone, so I joined in . . . heheheh . . . and there was a hush and one of them spoke up and said, 'Mr. Williams, is it true you have come to Bangkok to *die?*' . . . hehhehheh . . . yah! . . . I laughed, of course, and said no, if I were going anywhere to die, I think it would be Rome. And that's how the rumor got started that I was dying of cancer last year. It's all over now, so I don't mind talking about it. It was performed with a local anesthetic and the dope wore off before the end so it was quite painful, but fortunately I had thought

to bring a bottle of sherry along with me. I didn't even
have a room reserved at the hospital, so I got up after the
operation and returned to my hotel in time for dinner.
Breast cancer develops more rapidly in a man than in a
woman, so I presume it was not malignant or I would be
dead by now."

"But you've had additional problems since then,
haven't you?"

"Physical problems? Oh, yes. It's been a long time since
I was physically well. I think my early years were very
wearing on me, the years before I made any money, terrific years of physical want and punishment that left me
exhausted. Along with that, I, yuh, had a good deal of
hypochondria. My sister Rose has been in a sanitarium
since she was twenty-seven years old. I suffer from claus-
trophobia. I was once put into a jail cell for driving without a headlight and the fear of dying in a damp, dark hole
with prostitutes and people screaming for help completely shattered my nerves. I went to a strict Freudian
analyst who attributed nearly everything to a . . . mis-
directed libido, shall we say? . . . hehhehhehyah wheeze
. . . I thought *that* was an oversimplification . . . hahahaha
. . . but ya know, I lived for years in an apartment on East
Sixty-fifth Street between Park and Lexington with one of
the tiniest elevators in the city. It said its capacity was five
people, but it was a tight squeeze with three. . . . I always
have trouble breathing in New York. The place most con-
ducive to work for me is Key West, where I have my
studio and swimming pool . . . the place is of no interest
socially or intellectually, although my friend James Leo
Herlihy lives there, as well as a few painters, but there is
nothing to do except work. But I may not be able to live
there much longer. During my stay in Bangkok, a terribly
vicious and scandalous piece about me was published in
The Atlantic, of all places, and while I was away my house
was bombarded with rotten eggs and rocks were thrown
in my swimming pool and now that I am back I have
encountered a great deal of hostility. Three weeks ago I
stepped into a fish pool while crossing an unlighted patio

toward an outside staircase. My back was lacerated by a low wire fence and I suffered a broken rib. I called four doctors in Key West and not one of them came or responded to my calls. I had begun to run a high fever and I could not get medical help, so I telephoned my doctor in New Orleans who said to take an aspirin. 'But I'm allergic to aspirin,' I said. 'You just think you are,' he said. So I took an aspirin and during the night my fever broke and I was cured."

"He's a saint," says the professor. "I saw him today and he said I could live to be a hundred. But the condition was I give up drinking. I guess I'll stick with sherry and settle for seventy-five."

"Anyway," says Tennessee, returning to his own problems, "this magazine also erroneously quoted me as saying I was one of the two or three richest writers in America, which is preposterous, ya know, absolutely pre—*pos*—terous! My total assets probably come to $750,000 including property I own. Fortunately I make a good deal each year from royalties. I have no particular anxieties about money. But *The Atlantic* had me *boasting* I was a multimillionaire, which I most certainly am not. They also said I cut my mother out of my will. She was never *in* it! I gave my mother Edwina half of *The Glass Menagerie,* my father gave her half of everything he owned when they separated, she is an independently well-to-do woman of eighty-eight years who lives in a suburb of St. Louis in an exclusive retirement home. My will provides for my sister after her death. She is older than I am, but she had one of the first prefrontal lobotomies performed on her brain in this country and is incurably schizophrenic and will no doubt outlive us all. I was most upset about the vulgar remarks about my sex life—now really, who cares about the sex life of a sixty-year-old writer?—and the tasteless implications that I abandoned my best friend Frank Merlo on his deathbed. My heavens, I slept in the study and gave him the bedroom until he went into the hospital for the last time before his death. I was with him continually, including the day he died. So many people knew the truth, but nobody came to my defense. My agent Audrey Wood knew the truth. The article made me out to be a monster! Now high-school kids, delinquents I imagine, race past my house in Key West in their cars at night shouting, 'Queer! Faggot!,' and young Victor here has to go out and see if his car has been stolen. The whole attitude of the island has distinctly altered toward me. When people meet me face-to-face, they are very kind. Society is becoming very permissive to one's inalienable rights to pursue whatever personal choices make one happy in life. But among the unsophisticated, there still exists a conspiracy to destroy the sensitive people of the earth."

I ask if he feels he has been personally persecuted because of his private life-style. His mouth forms a round opal, sucking in a tiny sigh. "In the theater especially, one is exposed to a kind of criticism which will use personal lines of attack. I've seen it done time and again."

"I thought theater people were very broad-minded in protecting their own."

"The actors, yes. I'm speaking particularly of people who *write* about the theater more than those who participate *in* it. I've read things that say Blanche was a drag queen, Blanche DuBois, ya know . . . that George and Martha in *Who's Afraid of Virginia Woolf* by Albee were a pair of homosexuals . . . these charges are ridiculous!" His voice becomes high-octane, bordering on hysteria. "If I am writing a female character, goddamnit, I'm gonna write a female character, I'm not gonna write a drag queen! If I wanna write a drag queen, I'll write a drag queen, and I *have* written one, as a matter of fact, which *will* be produced someday. The setting is right here in New Awlyuns and it's called *And Tell Sad Stories of the Deaths of Queens* and it's about a drag queen and I think it's quite funny. It's a paraphrase of that line from *Richard II*—'Now let us sit upon the ground and tell sad stories of the death of *kings*,' only I changed it to *queens* . . . heh-hehhehheh. . . ."

The professor has a good laugh, joining Tennessee in his

private joke. Young Victor almost chokes on his cherries jubilee.

"I have not always been mistreated by the press," he continues when he has caught his breath. "I had very good relations with Stark Young and Brooks Atkinson . . . . I've had pleasant relations with Walter Kerr. I think that Mister Kerr is the most brilliant *writer* among the critics, but I'm somewhat puzzled by a man of his obvious cultivation and learning and all, that he could expose some of the predictable prejudices and biases that he does. I think it has something to do with the fact that he's a Catholic . . . hehhehheehee . . . but the viciousness of the critics will not drive Albee or me, either, from the theatah . . . it can be very wounding and demoralizing, but it can't stop me. The critical assaults on my work had something to do with my period of maladjustment during the Sixties. I think some of my work was better than it appeared to be from the notices it received, although some of it was thrown on too hastily in the Sixties under circumstances that were not auspicious. *In the Bar of a Tokyo Hotel,* for example, was not as bad as the critics said it was. *Life* magazine said I was all washed up, finished as a playwright, and they even paid for space in *The New York Times* to reproduce this obituary. I heard some people took another ad to denounce that review, but if they did, I never saw it because Anne Meacham and I ran away to Japan . . ."

"To the bar of a Tokyo hotel?"

". . . to escape the brutality of the press, and my agent Audrey Wood never sends me anything good about me. My poor little dog Gigi landed in quarantine. We left in such haste I didn't look into her vaccination papers, so I had to rent a Japanese house and hire Japanese servants at great personal expense because that was the only way they would let my dog out of quarantine. Oh, it was a dreadful mess. That was the beginning of my breakdown. I had been disintegrating for years, but that was the final culmination of events. I went out of my mind."

During the above, the professor has fallen asleep. "The

professor accompanied me to the Orient and he was more
ill than I was. I think he has a brain tumor." Throughout
dinner, for which he arrived an hour late in a state of
dazed confusion, the professor has consumed an old-
fashioned, followed by a crème de menthe frappé, followed by a vodka on the rocks, followed by a stinger and
polished off with a bottle of white Pouilly-Fuissé. Now he
is dozing at the table, like Lionel Barrymore by the fire
in *A Christmas Carol.* "Your heart, baby. You're not as
young as you used to be."

Tennessee's voice, sharp as a snowflake on a sunburned
nose, wakes the professor, who has turned a glass of wine
upside down in his sleep. Two waiters fly over with wet
cloths to wipe the grape from the carpet as the professor
runs his hands through his fading hair. "I am not myself
tonight," he says gently. "I think I am suffering from a
terminal case of yellow fever."

"I know what you mean," laughs Tennessee in his soft,
maniacal giggle. "Those Oriental boys are pure poetry."

Victor lets out a puppy yelp. Tennessee shoots him a
thumbtack look. He retires to the men's room to smoke
a forbidden cigarette. Cigarettes are not allowed in Tennessee's house since his closest friend for fifteen years,
Frank Merlo, died of lung cancer. The subject returns to
suicide. "It would probably be something dramatic," I
suggest.

"No, I would never jump off of or under anything."

"You'll probably fall upon a samurai sword."

Tennessee lets out a shriek of pleasure at the thought.
"Nononono, I don't think I shall ever commit suicide. As
a matter of fact, I have been resurrected and come back
to life. Looking back on that black nightmare, I don't
understand it except that there had been disappoint-
ments in my professional career and the death of Frank,
the person closest to me in my personal life, and my life
was something of a shambles. When I got up in the morning after all the sedation, I gave myself speed injections
administered intramuscularly. It was the only way I could
write."

"Did it improve your work?"

"It gave it a momentum, ya know, during a period when I was in a clinical state of depression. It gave me a sufficient charge in the morning to get me to the typewriter to feel some interest in putting words down on paper. For four years, I had no love life at all. I was only interested in sedation and the shots and writing, that was all. It was a retreat from life, a protracted death wish that lasted roughly from 1963 until my release from the psychiatric hospital where I came within a hairsbreadth of death. That's when I fell in love with life . . . hehhehhaha . . . I didn't like the feeling of death being *that* close and tangible."

"I've had brain damage," says the professor quietly, not wanting to be left out of all this.

"I don't notice, baby," says Tennessee.

"I've just had an injection of Demerol."

"I will summon young Victor to carry us home to bed," sighs Tennessee. "Tomorrow we will both see a doctor. I have no strength. I become exhausted [pronounced eggs-zost-id] quite easily. Right now I am physically unprepared to continue our conversation and young Victor will have to see me to my hotel." Victor returns from the men's room, smelling of peppermints, and helps both Tennessee and the professor on with their coats. At the door, there is a flourish of starchy genuflecting as New Orleans' most famous expatriate makes his exit. His manner is unassuming: he could be a clerk or a wigmaker or a pornographic-movie director. I am beginning to think he is just an ordinary man when, by some rare occult vibration, he seems to instinctively mirror my thoughts in his glazed expression. "I am paranoiac, baby, so I hope you do not make the mistake of laboring under the false impression that you are talking to a sane person!"

Outside, under the lamplights of Antoine's, the beachboy and the staggering professor take their places silently at his side, like sentinels, and walk into the night. "I used to depend upon the kindness of strangers," says Tennessee, as though he were projecting across footlights into an

empty theater. "Now I depend upon the kindness of
friends."

What to make of this Halloween goblin? This gilt-edged
invitation to decadence, this life lived with constantly
recurring visions in a madhouse, laced with the beckoning
insinuation of champagne and flaming foods, of Oriental
rugs and dimly lit brothels, surrounded by exotic friends
like Anaïs Nin and Anna Magnani, who has publicly announced on several occasions she would like to marry
him? He has gathered his years slowly, savoring the lusty
taste of living, taking swooning delight in extravaganzas
of brocade, crepes suzette, and a mild scent of orrisroot.
High ceilings and dust on antiques fill him with a sense of
appropriateness. He has created a myth of himself. His
temple holds much ivy. He is shy, pursued by visions of
hell, and is blind in one eye. He has done everything and
seen everything. He has won every award there is, including two Pulitzer Prizes. There is scarcely a minute of the
day when he doesn't complain about either emotional
exhaustion or being physically assaulted by any number of
undiagnosed afflictions. One senses he is his own worst
enemy, that it is miraculous that he has indeed been able
to write at all. Yet, like the old dog that has survived many
seasons of distemper, he keeps coming back, a Phoenix
rising from the flames.

He was born old. His grandfather was an Episcopal
rector in Columbus, Mississippi. He was a delicate, introverted child who hated his father, an aggressive, brutish
shoe salesman. He was raised by a doting, genteel mother,
and fawned over by a protective, half-mad sister who later
became the model for Laura in *The Glass Menagerie*. His
father called him "Miss Nancy" and he retreated into a
world of Gothic books. At sixteen he sold his first story,
about an evil Egyptian queen who invited all her enemies
to a banquet and then drowned them, to a magazine
called *Weird Tales* for $35, but his father transplanted the
family from the charming protectiveness of the Old South
to an unpleasant row of dimly lit apartment complexes,

the color of dried blood and mustard, in St. Louis. To thwart his son's writing, he put him to work in a shoe factory where life became "a living hell." He worked all day and wrote all night until his health collapsed and he was sent to live with his grandparents in Memphis. There were painful years in various colleges, flunking ROTC at one, Greek at another; there were lean years of gypsy travel, during which he worked as an elevator operator in New York, a $17-a-week usher at the old Strand Theater on Broadway, a bellhop in New Orleans, a teletype operator in Jacksonville, a shoe salesman in Culver City, and a waiter and reciter of poetry in Greenwich Village. Years of indescribable torment and physical dissipation that taught him a way of life. Even now, he still wanders restlessly in search of the sad music in people, ordering a banquet for the spirit, and although he has always got what he asked for, the melody has often been in the wrong key and the meal served at inconvenient hours. And out of the loneliness and self-destruction and pain have come some of the world's greatest plays. Why do they survive along with him? Why does Tennessee Williams, already written off by the cynics in the obituaries they keep taking out and rattling whenever a new play opens, make more comebacks than Judy Garland? Because in an age so filled with nonappreciation and polite sensibility, a time of fatalism, nihilism, a certain destruction of the ideal of beauty, a replacement by wastelands and other sterile sanctuaries, he suffers the urgent need to bring meaning to life, to resurrect gentility and kindness. It is not necessary to understand him to appreciate his genius. One needs only to feel, and he *feels* magnificently.

Morning. The sky over the narrow streets that dive crazily into the New Orleans French Quarter is bronze marble, hard and brilliant. By the time I reach his hotel suite at the palatial Royal Orleans, he has been up for hours, hammering away at his portable typewriter. It is a daily after-breakfast routine. If he is excited about his theme, he may type for eight hours straight. Other times he may brood like a Thurber character, producing doodles. Today is a good day. He is reworking a scene from something new called *Two-Character Play,* which he describes as his "last long play." It will be tried out in Chicago and the prospect worries him. "Although I feel I am only fully alive when involved in a new production, I have great anxiety about this one: it was conceived and written when I was almost completely phased out, and rewritten several times after my release from the psychiatric hospital, but it is still the work of a very disturbed writer, and it is terribly personal and I don't know how much audience empathy will be engaged. I do know the play will be exposed to critics in Chicago who have been known to bring personal bias into their criticism and at least one of them, Claudia Cassidy, officially retired but still quite active, can be quite devastating. I remember, when *Night of the Iguana* came dragging its ass into Chicago, she dealt it a terrific clout, calling it a 'bankrupt play,' and we were barely able to complete our engagement despite the box-office appeal of Bette Davis, who had fired the director."

Victor is in the bedroom, reading a comic book. He comes in with some Polaroid color snapshots he has taken of the house in Key West, pert and sassy, like an art nouveau candy box, and Tennessee's pets—a Boston terrier bitch named Gigi who looks like a canine Colette, an orange tabby cat named Gentleman Caller, and an iguana chained to the front porch to scare off marauders called Mister Ava Gardner. "I feel the constant threat of hurricanes that will someday sweep my little frame house out to sea in a tidal wave, but it is really home to me. I went there after my first play *Battle of Angels* with Miriam Hopkins caused a sensation of the wrong sort and was closed down in Boston by the Theatre Guild in 1940. They gave me $100 and told me to go somewhere and write something else. In those days, it was possible to live on $100, ya know. So I went down to Key West and lived in a genteel boardinghouse of solid mahogany. That was

before Howard Johnson came along and ruined it. I
should be there now. I'm too weak to travel. I don't know
what I'm doing here, payin' $80 a day in the Royal Orleans
Hotel. I should have never come here. So many painful
memories. It was such a wonderful place to be in the
Thirties. Of course, I couldn't afford to eat anything but
grits then.

"I am one of the richest writers in the world now," he
says, contradicting his remarks of the night before, "but
there were many desperately poor years, even after I was
well-known. I started writing when I was twelve, but I
never made any money at it until *The Glass Menagerie*.
People think Audrey Wood sent me money to keep me
alive, but that is a myth. She was once instrumental in
procuring a $1,000 Rockefeller grant which she paid to me
in installments of $25 a week, so I wouldn't spend it all at
once, but I lived quite frugally at the Y. She *never* subsi-
dized me."

I ask him about his money, since he makes continual
references to it. "But you know," he drawls, like spitting
butter, "I have never written anything for money. I have
made a great deal of money and I've tried to invest it
wisely, but I have no head for financial matters. I have a
portfolio of stocks, in a custodial account. I don't fool with
them myself. I let Chase Manhattan handle them. I told
them do what you will with the stuff as long as you don't
invest in anything involving deforestation or jeopardizing
the ecology. I was once advised by a business associate to
put $50,000 into a Denver bowling alley. I sent my
brother Dakin out to look at it and he said it was mahvel-
ous, so I went ahead and invested in it. Shortly after,
another bowling alley, much bigger, was put up right
beside it and it went out of business. I lost the whole fifty
thousand, and then some. Dakin is notoriously ambitious.
He'll walk up to people on the street and say, 'Hello, my
name is Dakin Williams and I'm running for the United
States Senate. Do you know Tennessee Williams? He's my
brother.' In my life, Dakin has always been the one to
bring me bad news first. When I was in the loony bin, I

was just recovering from my heart attacks when Dakin presented me with that scurrilous piece in *The Atlantic.*"

It was also Dakin who converted his brother to Catholicism in 1969. "He attributes my recovery from madness to himself and God. I attribute it to *myself. And* God. Dakin did get me into the church at a time when he thought I was about to expire. It wasn't much of a conversion. I have never once been to confession. If I had a church like the St. Louis Cathedral here in the French Quarter, I might get into the habit. That is like going to the theater. I'm religious but I'm not a churchgoer."

He prepares for his walk through the French Quarter with glee. Victor, who has been giggling in front of a closed-circuit TV channel that shows the hotel guests around the swimming pool on the roof, emerges in a one-piece red jump suit. He waits silently by the door with his camera over his arm. "I've never thrown any of my plays away," says the writer, not yet ready to give the green light. "Although I have burned sections of them and I've had things disappear . . . hehhehhehheehee. . . . I started a novella on the long voyage back from the Orient called *Hang It Loose.* It's about a, yuh, hippie that I met on de boat. He had been thrown out of Japan. He was not allowed to go in any of the public rooms on de boat because he only had a pair of pants and a shirt, no socks, no jacket. . . ."

"How could he afford to be on this luxury liner. . . ."

"Well, he had to get out of the country and that was the only passage available. He had just enough money to get him to Hi-wah-yuh. . . ." He seems perturbed that I have interrupted his story, but continues. "He was persecuted on the ship. One thing I detest is the deliberate cruelty of one human being to another. He was a lovely person. Had long, golden hair, looked like a young Greta Gah-bo, yes that's it, a young Greta Gah-bo. . . ." He is obviously enthralled at the vision. "He was somewhat as I'd visualize Chris Flanders, the young man in my play *The Milk Train Doesn't Stop Here Anymore,* who was no Richard Burton, baby. I will eventually finish the novella, but right now

I'm concentrating on my last long play. I don't think I will ever have the energy, provided I do have the time, to write another full-length play."

I ask if he ever feels he has dried up as a writer. "Never really," he answers quickly. "I've gone through periods when I have reached a, yuh, *impasse,* when it was impossible for me to *express* what I wanted to express, but never when I had nothing to ex*press.* It's very egg-*zost*-ing. I never think too much about plots, ya know. Plots just sort of happen. I create the characters first and the rest just happens. *Milk Train* was the most frustrating experience I've ever been through. It was never a successful piece of work. I keep rewriting it all the time, but I've never gotten it right. Hermione Baddeley was quite, quite brilliant in the first production, but the part of the boy was never realized. Tab Hunter was hardly what I'd call an innocent, and poor Tallulah could no longer project her voice in the second production. Her physical strength was not adequate. That play reflected a great preoccupation with death, as did most of my work in the Sixties. I'm much more stoical now, hehhehheh. I regard myself as a failed artist. I'm as happy now as I've been in many years. I've come to terms. I don't mind being sixty, I get glasses stronger each year to compensate for failing eyesight. And I've learned how to deal with success. I once wrote an article about it saying security is a kind of death, I think, and it can come to you in a storm of royalty checks beside a kidney-shaped pool in Beverly Hills or anywhere at all that is removed from the conditions that made you an artist. It happened to me after my first success, *The Glass Menagerie,* turned me into an overnight celebrity. I moved to a first-class hotel and lived off room service. Between the moment when I ordered dinner and when it was rolled in like a corpse on a rubber-wheeled table, I lost all interest in it. Once I ordered a sirloin steak and a chocolate sundae, but everything was so cunningly disguised that I mistook the chocolate sauce for gravy and poured it all over the steak. Of course this was the more trivial aspect of a spiritual dislocation that began to manifest itself in more disturbing ways. I became indifferent to people. A wall of cynicism rose in me. Conversations sounded like they had been recorded years ago and were being played back on a turntable. I suspected everyone of hypocrisy; I still do. I hated my work and was in physical agony. I decided to have another eye operation to give myself a gauze mask to hide behind. I had been afflicted for some years with a cataract on my left eye which required a series of needling operations and finally a serious one on the muscle of my left eye. I was in pain and darkness and I ran away to Mexico, an elemental country where vagrants innocent as children curl up to sleep on the pavements, and human voices, especially when their language is unfamiliar, are soft as birds. My public self, that artifice of mirrors, ceased to exist and I learned that the heart of man, his body and his brain, are forged in a white-hot furnace for the purpose of conflict. That struggle for me is creation. I cannot live without it. Luxury is the wolf at the door and its fangs are the vanities and conceits germinated by success. When an artist learns this, he knows where the dangers lie. Without deprivation and struggle there is no salvation and I am just a sword cutting daisies."

There isn't much to say after that. We leave the hotel suite. A maid has left a tangle of vacuum-cleaner cords outside the door. "Snakes in the hallway!" cries Tennessee. Outside, he leads the way to a jewelry shop on Royal Street to buy a diamond ring. "It's only $125, a very good bargain," says the shopkeeper.

"A genuine diamond for $125?" gasps Tennessee.

"It's not perfect. . . ."

"Who *is?*" He buys it. Guided by the sun, he continues his stroll. "This place has so many memories. I came here in 1939 to write. I was heartbroken over my sister Rose's confinement in a psychiatric hospital and I suffered a breakdown myself. In New Orleans I felt a freedom. I could catch my breath here. See that bar over there? That used to be called Victor's. I lived just around the corner in a large room on the top of an old house where I worked under a skylight at a large refectory table writing *A Street-car Named Desire.* At that time, I was under the mistaken impression that I was dying. I didn't feel much like eating, but in the evenings after working all day my only close friend would bring me a bowl of oyster stew and in the afternoons I would go around the corner to Victor's Café and have myself two brandy alexanders. Without that sense of fatigue and that idea of imminently approaching death I doubt I could have created Blanche DuBois."

He talks as though Blanche is still inside him, trying to get out, a victim in the jungle without talons. His face is sad and old as he leads the way past antique shops, a flamenco parlor and a genuine voodoo shop, the owner of which claims to be a warlock who, in a former life, was a cat. The window is full of howling cats among the gris-gris, love potions and books on Marie Laveau the Voodoo Queen. He stops at 722 Toulouse, his first address in New Orleans, and the years cross his face in a shadow. "In those attic windows I wrote a short story about a tubercular poet throwing up blood—a recurring theme in my work. I used to do it myself. I stayed alive by hocking my typewriter and waiting on tables. It was a boardinghouse and I thought up a slogan—'Meals for a Quarter in the Quarter.' I'd go outside the old gray building with its green shutters and iron grillwork, hang up my sign with my own slogan, then I'd run back inside, and change quickly into my waiter's uniform just in time to serve the okra. One night I came home and found an old hag who lived in the place pouring boiling water through the cracks in the floor to scald the tenants to death. I escaped owing $50 by sliding down from the second story on a string of bed sheets to a trumpet player waiting below who promised to drive me to California in his jalopy to what he described as his uncle's magnificent ranch. It turned out to be a run-down pigeon farm where they took me in out of pity after the trumpet player deserted me, and I earned my keep plucking squab feathers. I still remember how I got paid. For every squab I plucked I'd keep tab by putting a feather in a milk bottle."

We pass stuffed mammies holding boxes of pecan pra-
lines wrapped for mailing. At the Cabildo, he crosses over
by the Jax brewery and walks along the New Orleans
waterfront. "This reminds me of the time I did *The David
Frost Show.* He asked me if I was a homosexual in front
of millions of people. I was so mortified I didn't know what
to say, so I just blurted out, 'I cover the waterfront,' and
the audience cheered me so loud he said he guessed he
better break for a commercial and I said, 'I should think
you would.' " We come to a sign advertising bayou cruises
and riverboat rides and I ask if it was true that Truman
Capote once tapdanced on a steamboat and painted flowers on jelly glasses. "I think that was just a product of
Truman's fanciful imagination. He always lived in a fantasy, ya know. When I first met him, he told me he had
a ring given to him by André Gide. But he was so amusing
in those days, before he discovered the Jet Set. I will never
forget we were coming back from Europe together on the
Queen Mary once and there was a mad Episcopal bishop
on board who kept following Little Truman around. Truman was very, very funny and kept us all in stitches by
telling this poor depraved bishop, 'You know I've always
wanted to own one of those bishop's rings for my very
own,' and the poor man kept saying, 'Oh, that's very difficult . . . you have to be a *bishop,*' and Little Truman said,
'Well, I thought perhaps I could get one from some de
frocked bishop!' . . .hehhehhee. . . . I always said Little
Truman had a voice so high it could only be detected by
a bat!"

He lets out a wild, weird cackle that causes people to
turn around in the street. "The only *real* writer the South
ever turned out was Carson." Of all the writers he's
known, Carson McCullers was the only one with whom he
established a lasting friendship. "She was no angel, ya
know. Or if she was, she was a black angel. But she had
infinite wisdom. Ours was a deep relationship that
spanned many years. I first met her when I went to Nantucket to die. I had read *The Member of the Wedding* that
year and I considered her the world's greatest living

writer. I wanted to meet her before I died, so I wrote to
her and she arrived on the boat, this tallll girl came down
the gangplank wearing a baseball cap and slacks. She had
a radiant, snaggletoothed grin and there was an immedi-
ate attachment. I seldom remember addresses, but this
was 31 Pine Street in Nantucket, an old gray frame house
with a windup Victrola and some fabulous old records,
like the *Santiago Waltz* and Sousa band numbers. A big
windstorm broke the downstairs windows and a pregnant
cat jumped in and had kittens on Carson's bed. This was
her last good year before her stroke. She did a good deal
of the cooking, mostly canned green pea soup with wie-
nies in it and an innovation called 'spuds Carson,' which
was mashed potatoes with olives and onions mixed in it.
She was in love that summer and mooning over somebody. Her husband Reeves had not yet committed suicide, but it was not him she was mooning over. She would
go out and buy Johnnie Walker and sit in a straight-back
chair at the foot of the steps and after my friend and I
went to bed she'd sit up all night mooning over this romance in her head. I'd come down in the morning and the
bottle would be empty. It was a crazy but creative summer. We read Hart Crane poems aloud to each other from
a book I stole from the St. Louis public library, and we had
a portrait of Laurette Taylor, who had just died, with a
funeral wreath around it, and the fireplace was always
filled with beautiful hydrangeas, and we sat at opposite
ends of a long table while I wrote *Summer and Smoke* and
she wrote *The Member of the Wedding* as a play. Carson
is the only person I've ever been able to stand in the same
room with me when I'm working. After her stroke, she
was incapacitated, but my sister Rose was in a sanitarium
near her house in Nyack and I would often stay with
Carson when I went to see her. She kept a room upstairs
called 'Tenn's Room' which was always prepared for my
visits. My fondest dream was to own a ranch in Texas and
have my sister Rose, my grandfather, and Carson, and we
would all live together, all of us invalids."

Williams saw a lot of McCullers in her last years. He sent

her money, refused to recognize her strokes ("Why
honey, you jus' been havin' a li' ol' psychosomatic breakdown") and transferred to her large doses of his stifled
affections for his sister Rose. He later used many of her
characteristics as the basis for the female lead in *Night of
the Iguana,* just as she based the old judge in *Clock Without Hands* on Tennessee's Grandpa Dakin. "She loved life
passionately and, even when in dire stress, always
managed to survive somehow. When her husband killed
himself, they lived in an old rectory outside Paris. Reeves
had a tree all picked out and two lengths of rope, insisting
they hang themselves together. 'All right, I can no longer
fight with you,' sighed Carson, 'but first let's have some
wine.' They stopped at a tavern, Carson stole out the back
door, got a bus ride back to Paris, and never saw him alive
again. There were only two great female writers—Carson
and Jane Bowles—both so vulnerable, and so mad. The
human body cannot hold that much talent. It has to explode. All the charming people I've ever known are a
little bit mad. I am very suspicious of people who appear
to be outwardly happy all the time and have always regarded them as somewhat simpleminded."

At the corner of St. Ann and Royal he is almost hit by
a bus named Desire. "Sad, sad," he shakes his head, "it
replaced the old streetcar years ago. You know I took
quite a bit of poetic license in that play. If you follow the
instructions in the play and take that streetcar, it never
went to a place called Elysian Fields, and even if it did,
you wouldn't be in the Quarter anymore. I used it because
I liked the name Elysian Fields." Past the gumbo shops
and windows filled with fig preserves, past the boarded-
up horse stables, across Bourbon Street, where, even at
midday, the sound of Dixieland jazz lifts toward the Louisiana sky where clouds never touch. "I wrote the first
draft of *Camino Real* in that house," he says, or, "Victor,
take a picture of me in front of old Andrew Jackson's
statue covered with pigeon shit." He is feeling his oats.

Just behind the Morning Call, where Tennessee spent
many early hours in the foggy predawn of New Orleans

drinking black coffee with chicory to wash out hang-
overs, stands the old streetcar named Desire which operated on the streets of the city from 1903 to 1935. The squat
little man standing in front of the iron railing that protects
it from invaders doesn't seem to know its motor has
stopped running and its electrical wires have long been
disconnected. Tears appear in his eyes. "Come on, baby,
let's eat," he says suddenly, breaking the mood as he scur-
ries from the site. "I'm so hungry I could eat moose pie."

He sips a vermouth cassis at the bar of Brennan's,
served by darkies who look like they just stepped off an
Uncle Ben's rice box. "How you, Mr. Wi'yums," they grin.
A wild, electrified woman flies at him with intense determination in her eyes, nearly knocking him off his barstool.
She is Mrs. Irving Stone, whose husband is in town pro-
moting a new book. "Mr. Williams, I just want to tell you
we are on a cross-country tour"—she unfolds a series of
eighteen plane tickets, each one representing a different
city, and throws them across his chest, causing him to spill
his vermouth cassis on his blue jump suit—"and this ticket
right here says New Orleans, which wasn't on the trip, but
I told them I don't care if it isn't a book town, I don't care
if people don't read books there, it's so much fun. I only
love two men in the world—Lawrence Durrell and
Tennessee Williams." She throws her arms around him,
gives him a wet kiss and flees to her table, where she is
joined by her husband, who does *not* come over and tell
Tennessee Williams he is one of the two greatest men in
the world.

"Who *is* that woman?" growls Tennessee. "And who is
Irving Stone? I hope he doesn't come over too, because I
don't ever remember reading anything he ever wrote.
What did he write?"

"He wrote a book about Michelangelo and a book about
Andrew Jackson and a book about Vincent Van Gogh and
now he's got a new book about Sigmund Freud. . . ."

Tennessee rolls his eyebrows. "Hmmm . . . can't think
of any original characters, eh?"

Our table is ready. People are staring at the world's

most famous playwright with a young man in a tight-fitting Tom Jones jump suit. "After lunch," announces Big Daddy, "we are going to purchase you a conservative blue suit, Victor. If you are to continue to be my secretary, you'd better start looking the part. These red Santa Claus suits you wear are fine for Key West, but they don't go over at the Edwardian Room of the Plaza hotel."

"Can I have a shoulder bag, too?" asks Victor.

Tennessee rolls his eyes toward heaven and strokes his beard, grinning a jack-o'-lantern smirk. "No need to gild the lily." He lets out a scream of laughter.

Tennessee studies his menu. "I'd like to order a Waldorf salad, but my doctor won't let me eat nuts. He didn't say anything about cannibalism, however. Hehhehhehheh-heehee. Although I'm sure it's very bad for the choles-terol." He settles for grits and grillades, a veal dish served with red-eye gravy. A waiter with a rather large behind passes the table. Tennessee reaches out and pinches it. The waiter hurls around, his fists doubled. "What the . . . oh, it's *you*, Mr. Williams . . . what are you doing in town?"

Tennessee looks innocent-guilty, like a choirboy who has just been caught sneaking a bullfrog into the collection plate. "We ah heah fo' Holy Week," he says, exploding with laughter. The waiter leaves, laughing too, and rubbing his derrière. "Don't you think I should become an actor? I am sixty years old, nobody in the world has a voice like mine, and with my new beard, I could play a lot of grotesque, decadent old Sydney Greenstreet parts. I'm a great ham, ya know, and a notorious publicity hound. When I was in London recently doing a poetry reading, Pier Paolo Pasolini, the Italian director, came up to me afterward and said, 'You know, Mr. Williams, you're really an actor!' and I said, 'Okay, got any parts for me?' It's much more fun than writing for the screen. I once spent several months under contract to MGM in 1943, making $250 a week, and I didn't write a goddamn thing except a thing for Lana Turner called *Marriage Is a Private Affair*. It wasn't bad, but I was writing for a *real* actress

and Miss Lana Turner could not say the lines, so they
finally told me they couldn't use my script because it was
simply beyond her abilities. When I saw the picture, they
only kept two of my lines. Then they asked me to write
a movie for Margaret O'Brien and I refused. I loathe and
detest child actors. Can you imagine Tennessee Williams
writing for Margaret O'Brien? It would be ludicrous.
Later, when I did the screenplay for *Senso,* Luchino Visconti used his old standby, some hack woman he keeps
around, to rewrite my script and when I finally saw *that*
one, only one scene of mine was left—a scene in a bedroom with two people waking up in a bed. There was a
line that went, 'There's always a sound in a room when
you wake,' and Visconti had a fly buzzing around. Of
course, that's not what I meant at all. When I wake up I
always start belching. There's always that sound of getting
rid of the poisons from the night before. I've never had
any success writing for the screen unless it is a film script
of one of my own plays.

"I might as well be an actor. I just paid my income tax
for last year. I paid $65,000 and I didn't write a damn
thing. Somebody is screwing me! Nobody ever tells me
anything. I didn't even know *Summer and Smoke* was
being done as an opera until someone in St. Louis wrote
me about it. I don't think anyone wants to encourage me
at all." His voice mounts hysterically and people from
surrounding tables turn around to stare. Uplifted eyebrows turn into knowing smiles when they recognize the
speaker. Tennessee settles down to his red gravy, dipping
it up in hearty spoonfuls, forgetting his outburst like a hen
in a barnyard whose feathers soften once again after being
knocked off her nest. "Anyway, I've made a great deal of
money during my life and I don't know where most of it
has gone. I own an apartment building here in New Awlyuns called the Patio Pool Apartments which is inhabited
by more than its share of dykes. Last time I was here, I
walked into the courtyard and screamed, 'All right, all
dykes—*out!*' There was a great banging of shutters. Property is an awful hassle, ya know. You have to pay for the

eviction of undesirable tenants. Actually, I've always had a great relationship with dykes. They don't frighten me at all. Some of my best friends are dykes. One is a notorious lesbian in the Quarter who draws people's pictures in front of the St. Louis Cathedral for a dollah." There is an enormous rustle of summer organza as solid silver forks go clattering into the china plates.

Another waiter passes with a tray of hot bananas foster. "He looks just like Marlon Brando. I first met him in 1947, when I was casting *Streetcar*. I had very little money at the time and was living simply in a broken-down house near Provincetown. I had a houseful of people, the plumbing was flooded and someone had blown the light fuse. Someone said a kid named Brando was down on the beach and looked good. He arrived at dusk, wearing Levi's, took one look at the confusion around him, and set to work. First he stuck his hand into the overflowing toilet bowl and unclogged the drain, then he tackled the fuses. Within an hour, everything worked. You'd think he had spent his entire antecedent life repairing drains. Then he read the script aloud, just as he played it. It was the most magnificent reading I ever heard and he had the part immediately. He stayed the night, slept curled up with an old quilt in the center of the floor.

"I have never indulged in any sexual encounter with any actor who ever appeared in one of my works, although there was *one* quite famous one who tried. I was at the roulette table in San Juan once when a waiter delivered a crystal goblet filled with cold milk. It was from a young actor who had sought me out to read for a part. He looked like a Midwestern basketball player and seemed totally unsuitable, but he read well and later got the part. He tried to follow me to my room to consummate the arrangement and I said, 'That won't be necessary—the part is yours because you read superbly!' Actors are such children. I am always very shy with them. I was so ill for years I don't remember anything about my opening nights; I was too drunk to know where I was. Estelle Parsons, however, was quite brilliant in *The Seven De-*

scents of Myrtle, but the poor thing had no help. José Quintero didn't direct her properly, so everything that happened onstage was her own invention. The film version of that play was perfectly disastrous. Gore Vidal wrote it, he said, out of friendship for me. Baby, with friends like that. . . . I have not had good relations with Sidney Lumet. He directed that flop as well as *The Fugitive Kind,* which was so dark and murky it looked like everyone was drowning in chocolate syrup. And Brando and Anna Magnani engaged in a clash of egos never before equaled. And I also didn't understand why Joanne Woodward had to be so dirty all the time. I also hated *Cat on a Hot Tin Roof,* although it made a lot of money for me. Elizabeth Taylor is not what I had in mind at all for Maggie the Cat. Maureen Stapleton I think is an absolute genius and one of the total innocents of the world, you know. Very self-destructive. She's a genius because her talent doesn't seem to come from anywhere. It just comes out of her fingertips and her toes and her kneecaps. And I loved Vivien Leigh. And Kim Stanley. Another case of too much talent to fit one body. Once she came running up to me at a party and began to beat me on the chest, which was not good at all for my breast cancer, ya know, and screamed at me, 'How *could* you write that dreadful play?' I never did find out which play she was talking about. The last time I saw her I gave a party for her in my rooms at the Plaza and she came three hours late. She walked in just as everyone was packing up to leave, all wrapped in swaddling black draperies, and sweating in the face. The next day she called up and apologized sweetly for her behavior, asking if there was anything she could do for me and I said, 'Baby, I'm out of Nembutal and I cannot sleep,' and she telephoned her pharmacy and they delivered by special messenger a whole supply of Nembutal, which got me through the next week and a half. I adore her. She has never been closely associated with my plays, but we understand each other. A kook likes a kook, baby. She once played Blanche DuBois in Houston, but nobody told me about it until too late and I never

saw her in it. I think she would be the best Blanche
DuBois in the world. The *worst* Blanche DuBois in the
world was poor Tallulah, although I must say she was
amusing. I'm sure that attack on Blanche DuBois being a
drag queen started when Tallulah played her. When she
came down to Florida she would say, 'I'm going to take a
suppository and do not become alarmed at anything that
might happen. I will soon become incoherent and leave
the room, but let the party continue.' Then she would
turn into a zombie and pass out in the middle of the floor.
I don't think anyone ever realized how desperately ill
poor Tallulah was. By the time she opened in *Milk Train*
in New York, she was beyond all help and her voice had
given out completely. She could no longer project beyond
the first row and I was no help at all because I was desperately ill myself at the time. Tallulah always blamed the
failure of that play on Tony Richardson and the goddamn
Chinese gongs, but most of it was my fault because I
allowed people to do whatever they liked with my plays
then. I'm much more protective now."

And so it goes, the wine flowing into the talk, with
Tennessee Williams never running out of stories, anec-
dotes, philosophical observations, on a lazy afternoon in
New Orleans. It is possible to think twice before taking
him home to dinner (he once stood up at one of New
Orleans' most distinguished tables and announced he was
an octoroon just to clear the room), but it is difficult to
dislike him. How can you dislike an honest man who
wears his trump cards on his sleeve like an epaulet? He
stands like a tiny troll in the revealing sunlight outside the
restaurant, not at all resembling a man who writes plays
about incest, rape, cannibalism, homosexuality and rape,
trying to say good-bye nicely so as not to hurt anyone, his
voice a furry caterpillar, sinuous and warm, wriggling into
all kinds of boozy shapes. "I must hurry now before the
store closes to buy young Victor his new suit. I saw a
notice in *The Village Voice* last week," he says from nowhere, "advertising exotic massages administered in a
bubble bath. Victor, make a note of that so I can try it on

my next visit; the only thing I've never done is take heroin, because that's the end, baby. Pills and booze are a
slow means to an end, but heroin is the end itself."

A Jesus freak selling religious pamphlets stops him.
"What're you pushing, baby?" he says. "I'm selling the
word of God in a book called *As It Is,* which teaches you
self-acceptance." Tennessee rolls his eyes, tugging on his
beard with glee. "I could use some of *that,*" he chuckles.
He pays the Jesus freak five dollars and says over his shoulder, "The hippie movement is becoming quite profitable,
I see." The Jesus freak gives him the peace sign, stuffing
the fiver into his dirty jeans.

Tennessee enters a curio shop selling rare antiques,
manuscripts and maps of buried pirate treasure. He is
complaining about the ring he bought that morning. "It's
not Victorian enough. I only look good in Victorian jewelry. I lost three diamonds in the ocean near Key West. I
lose all my jewels swimming. But this is not Victorian
enough. I think I'll give it to young Victor, here." Young
Victor is preoccupied with a drawing of a skull. A trompe
l'oeil: on closer inspection, the skull becomes a woman
looking into an oval mirror. It is called *Vanity.*

"Can I buy it, Tom?" asks Victor gently. Only Tennessee's closest friends call him Tom.

"Absolutely not," he cries, visibly upset by the skull. "I
will not have it in my house. It's all about death and I
cannot stand anything around me that reminds me of
death."

Gentleness, kindness, mixed with madness and contra-
diction—conflicting traits that define the man, occurring
in uneasy rhythmic patterns. Outside the shop, he is
merry once more. You don't know whether to laugh or
humor him. A man of shifting contrasts, like watermarks
on a desert horizon.

I say farewell at the edge of the Quarter. "Ya know, I'll
be all right. They've left me for dead, but I'll survive." He
searches the Tiffany-lamp sky of New Orleans, looking for
carrion birds perhaps, always nearby in his shadowy mind,
waiting to dive. Then his face breaks into a reassuring grin

and he is the mischievous imp once more, tapping his foot on the corner of Royal and Canal in a blue denim jump suit, blue tennis shoes and a long gray overcoat. "I told my friend Gore Vidal, I said, 'Gore, baby, I slept through the Sixties,' and my friend Gore, he said, 'You didn't miss a thing!' "

3

The Cockettes

THIS IS WHERE IT'S AT," said Truman Capote when he went to see the Cockettes, and he said a mouthful. The Cockettes are the most unbelievable American phenomenon since Martha Mitchell. They are the current sensations of counterculture show business, the darlings of the powerful underground press, a landmark in the history of new, liberated theater, and if you've never heard of them, there are some circles that would say you just aren't alive. Mostly they are hippie drag queens, but you have to be careful with the semantics, because although the group is largely composed of men in women's clothes, it also includes women, married couples, even babies. They refer to themselves and their work as "Sexual Role Confusion," and they perform Friday nights at midnight between Dick Tracy serials, porno

flicks and revivals of *Snow White and the Seven Dwarfs*
in a Chinese grind house called the Palace, in San Francisco's seedy North Beach. The Cockettes, named after the
abominable Rockettes at Radio City Music Hall, is not a
revue or an act; the only way I can describe it is a noctur-
nal happening composed of equal parts of Mardi Gras on
Bourbon Street, Harold Prince's *Follies,* old movie musicals, the United Fruit Company, Kabuki and the Yale
varsity show, with a lot of angel dust thrown in to keep the
audience good and stoned. Examine this:

It was a Friday night at midnight and in the streets
bewildered police tried to control 2,000 screaming, romp-
ing, bumping, grinding, flaunting, swishing, writhing and
staggering fans in front of a Chinese temple that looked
like Kublai Khan's opium den. Nobody paid any attention
to the SOLD OUT signs. They broke down the exit doors
and 300 more friends of the Cockettes stormed in free—
jamming the aisles and sitting on floors covered with
chewing gum, pistachio nut shells, cigar butts, candy
wrappers and styrofoam teacups—a floating carnival of
freaks in sequins, feathers, skirts, mesh hose, cowboy hats,
bras and panties. "I hope it's not like *Oh, Calcutta!*" said
Mrs. Johnny Carson in tennis shoes. There were street
violinists, spare-change freaks, Mrs. Sam Spiegel in a purple feather boa, chanting monks, black-tie socialites who
had just come from the opening night of Beverly Sills in
Manon, speed freaks, Hell's Angels, hairdressers, Chinese
coolies playing flutes, babbling children in Shirley Temple
curls, holdovers from Denise Minnelli's wedding in $2,800
Adolfo gowns. Even Denise Minnelli herself showed up in
emeralds but left when the cops told her there might be
a raid. "Dahling, I've seen the Cockettes already anyway," she said, stepping back into her limousine.

Inside, 200 transvestites in the balcony screamed, "Truman, baby, we love you!" as Truman Capote entered in an
orange sweater. A rainfall of rolled joints showered down
upon the orchestra seats and there was so much smoke in
the air you could get high just by taking a deep breath.
Women's Wear Daily was there, and the Jefferson Air-

plane. Billie Holiday was singing at the wrong speed from loudspeakers. Somebody passed a bottle of Southern Comfort for me to autograph. A beak-nosed Peter Lorre in a Garbo cloche, a white fur stole and his behind hanging out of a black crepe Harlow dress, paraded down the aisle, followed by Margaret O'Brien's double in pigtails and a moustache. Two bottles of cold wine were passed through our row and everybody drank openly, fearless of hepatitis. An enormous blond in tomato-red satin hot pants with biceps and a hairy chest where his cleavage should have been, held hands with an Indian maharishi carrying a Sun-Ra poster. "This is the only true theater," observed Capote, "where there is total participation from an audience that is part of the show itself." Three flappers with Band-Aids on chins cut while shaving applauded with glee.

The show began amidst a colossal stampede of applause, screams and foot-stomping. Onto the stage trooped the Cockettes—a spangled chaos of flesh, a seething mass of lurching bodies in lavish hock-shop costumes, doing their thing for freedom. The spectacle devised for this particular evening was called "Tinsel Tarts in a Hot Coma" and it began with a gigantic transvestite who looked like Birgit Nilsson, playing the Statue of Liberty holding a Halloween sparkler against a cardboard Manhattan skyline. This was followed by an elaborate Busby Berkeley number called "Depression," in which fourteen Floradora girls and a naked man with a tiny photo of Franklin D. Roosevelt covering his genitals sang a song about the stock market. Mrs. Johnny Carson turned white. Vetta Viper, a syndicated gossip columnist who looked like Linda Darnell, delivered campy patter about the stars while doing a reverse strip, naked from the waist down, squeezing hairy legs into a floor-length formal. The crowd went berserk. Then the entire company boarded a cardboard train to New York while other Cockettes danced by the windows dressed like telephone poles. A villain in a fur loincloth tied Pearl White to the tracks and the Cockettes saved her. The Marx Brothers glided across the stage

singing "Paddlin' Madeleine Home" in a rowboat made
out of a huge Chiquita Banana. Everyone mounted the
footlights for the big "College Rhythm" number in a
prancing holocaust of cigarette holders, mascara, wedgies
and chiffon see-through gowns with their sex organs exposed. A photographer from *Vogue* fell out of her seat.

Next, what looked to my bloodshot eyes like the chorus
from *Aida* came down the aisle, stepping over stoned
bodies, dressed like flaming Christmas trees while a frantic Hollywood-type director raced about the stage
screaming "Cut!" This entourage of lights and tinsel disappeared into the wings and a heavily veiled Hedy La-
marr type in a mink-dyed fox leaned over my shoulder
and whispered, "This is a dream sequence." I hadn't seen
anything yet. A topless pregnant Betty Hutton in a tank
suit, pearls and a Carmen Miranda hat sang "I need a little
hot dog on my roll" while the audience threw weenies on
the stage. Before the song was finished, all her clothes
were ripped off and the singer was seized, dragged to the
floor still clinging to her microphone, and, as the British
put it, "interfered with." The audience stood on their
seats, whistling and shrieking with approval. "This is the
most outrageous thing I have ever witnessed," said Truman Capote, roaring hilariously.

And on it went in a delirium of hysteria. A long-legged
chorus girl who looked like a pubescent Betty Grable and
a Harvard sophomore wearing earrings danced a Fred
and Ginger pas de deux with castanets, bringing down the
house. A beefy contralto with quarterback feet stuffed
into size 6A pumps and a bouffant hairdo sang "Midnight
in Manhattan" at a lonely bus stop while two Cockettes
dressed like hatcheck girls kept the beat with cocktail
shakers. There were curb-service waitresses dressed like
the Andrews Sisters singing "Yes, We Have No Bananas"
while all sorts of unprintable sexual activities occurred on
platforms, stairways and the bare floor. Bare-chested cho-
rines missed cues, came on too early, then tiptoed offstage
again to deafening applause. A husky "Mame" hung from
a tipsy moon. And when we couldn't yell anymore be-

cause the tears were running down our faces, there was a wild psychodrama of a finale with naked women, groupies, angels with wings and halos, Plaster Casters, rock musicians, babies running across the stage, and even some of the audience, belting out a rousing chorus of "C'mon along and listen to, the Lullaby of Broadway. . . ."

A mind-blowing experience, a new concept to replace the advent of the rock concert in the 1970s? That's how some critics and culture mavens are describing the Cockettes. They started out as a hippie commune on Haight Street who stepped from the pages of old copies of *Flair* and *Harper's Bazaar* and found themselves too beautiful and talented simply to stroll among the stoned and weary, but thought they should be onstage for all the world to see and love. So the press in San Francisco lionized them and they became masters of satire, parody and nostalgia. They range in number from twenty-two to sixty-five, depending on who's in town with a new costume, and vary in age from the older Cockettes like Goldie Glitter, Hibiscus, Scrumbly and Dusty Dawn, to the youngest Cockette— Dusty Dawn's thirteen-month-old baby son, Ocean Michael Moon. They used to perform free, but now they're such a fantastic success on the pop scene, they've generated into a business flourishing with commerce. They recently completed their first movie, *Tricia Nixon's Wedding,* made for $4,000 in two days, which features the Cockettes as Pat and Dick, the Kennedy Sisters, Martha Mitchell with a beard, and a riotous Mamie Eisenhower who keeps falling into the wedding cake. The movie got rave reviews and is making a fortune, so now they're into their next film, *The Gospel of Jesus Christ According to the Cockettes.* Then they plan to reopen Fillmore East and invade New York on Halloween night. They already have an 800-seat theater lined up in Paris and offers are pouring in from other European capitals.

Like all other show-biz successes who work up to the big time, the Cockettes are now in danger of becoming slick, polished and promoted into something they aren't. Blasé New Yorkers will probably come to their show expecting them to be part of the Andy Warhol scene, to which they bear no resemblance. The Warhol people are largely decadent and meaningless, while there is no brittle self-loathing or nihilism about the Cockettes. They are joyous people who love the old movies and political celebrities they parody. You can be at the beach or hiking in the woods near Frisco and suddenly there they are—their turbans and ragged kimonos in bright prints getting caught in the brambles as they swing along in their outlandish hairdos, warbling songs from old MGM musicals in their baritone falsettos. Overexposure and quick success could result in a loss of innocence. And strangely enough, there is innocence in their grotesque arrangements of homosexual, bisexual, asexual and quadrisexual parodies of Women's Lib, old movies, politics and Unisex that you'd never find in the more professional transvestite revues of T. C. Jones or London's Danny LaRue.

On the other hand, maybe they won't change at all. Backstage, they served champagne and banana cake, hugged Truman Capote around the waist, and tried on Mrs. Sam Spiegel's purple feather boa. "I'll probably never have a real one," sighed Goldie Glitters, whose wig was slipping over her left sideburn. "Still, my philosophy is it's better to be a Tinsel Queen than a Golden Toad."

4

A Last Night at Joe's Place

T'S A DUMP!" I looked around, half-expecting to see
Bette Davis, but the social observer at the next table
who had just made the remark about Joe Namath's
saloon, Bachelors III, turned out to be a tall, skinny chick
with freckles drinking vodka and cranberry juice in a
black Halston wet suit. She was the only attractive girl in
the bar, and she was absolutely right.

It was about a month after Joe's tearful press conference and still two weeks before he announced his return
to football. And it was 11 P.M. Much too early for Broadway
Joe. Most of the curiosity seekers and autograph hounds
and tourists, who had walked over to the bar at Sixty-
second and Lexington from their hotels because they had
read about Joe's troubles with Commissioner Pete Rozelle
of the National Football League over the gamblers and

47

bookies and Mafia czars who were allegedly hanging out there, were still out in the street standing in line. There was plenty of room inside, but to keep the hicks out Lenny, the "official greeter" at the front door, was telling them there would be at least an hour's wait for tables.

"This place got more newspaper coverage than the Judy Garland funeral," said the chick in the Halston wet suit. "Everybody wants to meet this guy. My date's in the john but when he comes back, want me to fix it up so he can introduce you to Joe Namath? He knows him. He's going to introduce *me* when Joe comes in."

"Do you come here often?" I asked.

"God, no. It's a dump. It was a dump when it was called the Twilight Zone, it was a dump when it was called the Leaves, it was a dump when some Wall Street brokers bought it and named it the Margin Call, and it's a dump now. Look, pal. Nobody comes here to look at the wallpaper. The only reason anybody comes here is to see Joe Namath. When he's not in town, the place is so full of gangsters you gotta beat 'em off with a stick."

I looked down at the lampshade on my table. Somebody had scrawled "Ronald Reagan Pees Fresca" on it. Then I made my way through air the color of coffin nails and asked the girl behind the bar for a spritzer. Her name was Mickey and she wore a costume that looked like a Kleenex with hormones. She had never heard of a spritzer, but she mixed one helluva Dewar's and soda, pouring three glasses at once without ever setting them down on the counter. I looked around and got the message. The first thing I noticed when my eyes adjusted to the darkness and smoke was how square everything was. The men looked like Square City junior execs from second-rate advertising agencies that handled medicated foot-powder commercials. The girls looked like hookers with hotel rooms down the block who had missed their checkups that month. It was definitely not the "swinging singles" Maxwell's Plum crowd in its Paraphernalia clothes. These girls wore stretch pants and see-through mesh midriffs and their jewels were by Coro, not KJL. But they all had one thing in common—they had all come to see Broadway Joe. These were Joe's People, and they were waiting for his entrance like it was the final race in the Virginia Gold Cup.

"Is he comin' in tonight or not?" whined the spitting image of Linda Darnell, in the first peasant blouse I'd seen since I was a sophomore in college.

"He was in here every night last week."

"I saw him at *Oh, Calcutta!*"

"What would Joe be doing at *that?* He could rewrite that show and teach people more about swinging with his eyes closed."

"What did Leo Durocher say about Joe's quitting?"

"I didn't like the way he cried at the press conference —it was like Nixon losing. No class, you know what I mean?"

"Man," said the bartender, "one night he was on the *Dick Cavett Show* with Tom Jones and they came in here after the show, and we had girls lined up all around the block. Tom Jones had an armful and Joe had an armful and man it was too friggin' much—Joe's got so many broads he gives 'em away for Christmas presents."

The bored, the lonely, the sleazy late-night East Side watering-hole voyeurs, the Nowhere People. All crowded into one hot, smoky, damp room that smelled like urine and stale beer and looked like the inside of a Hershey's syrup can, waiting for their hero to come down from that great big football stadium on Olympus, smile, maybe touch them if they are lucky, and make their lives richer for a few minutes between headlines.

Joe had been looking for a bar for a long time. Two years ago, he and Robert Vannuchi, who likes to be called Bobby Van (no relation to the Bobby Van from MGM musicals), almost became partners in a hangout called the Jet Set. Then Joe almost bought The Penthouse Club on Central Park South, but it cost too much ($200,000) and besides it was fifteen stories high and Joe likes to be down on the ground with the truly trues. So Joe settled for a dark little hole in the wall which has been losing money with one name or another as far back as anyone on Lexington Avenue can remember. Joe and his roommate, former Jet teammate Ray Abruzzese, each contributed $7,500 toward the total purchase price of $50,000 and along with Bachelor No. 3, Joe Dellapina, who handles the books (the ones with dollar signs, not the ones with horses), they had themselves a bar.

Joe took over the place in October, 1968, pulled down the wall decorations of stock-exchange tapes and framed WALL STREET LAYS AN EGG front pages from *Variety*, and replaced them with photos of himself, his buddies and several bosomy stripper types. The liquor license was officially transferred from the former owners and the bar opened for business on November 11, 1968. Joe's troubles were just beginning. In February, 1969, he and his coowners applied to the State Liquor Authority for permission to sell a one-third interest to Bobby Van, who by this time had moved into a pad in Joe's apartment building and was acting as the club's official "host." Permission was held up on the grounds that Van had been previously employed by several unsavory dives the police files term "trouble spots." Crackerjack law-enforcement agents began investigating Joe's place for the NFL, whose job it is to protect gullible and immature football players from corroding influences. They discovered among the regulars at Bachelors III, such stiletto superstars as Tea Balls Manusco, Harry the Hawk, Varmine "the Snake" Persico and Johnny Echo. Bobby Van is still one of his best friends. Bad Guy? "Not so," scoffs Joe Dellapina, the club's general manager. "If you print our names here, they'll really think it's a Mafia hangout. We're all paisanos." Joe Dellapina. Lenny Giancola on the door. Joe Abruzzese, Bobby Vannuchi, and the phone ringing every five minutes behind the bar for somebody called Tommy Mannino. The only thing missing was Nancy Sinatra. "Look," said Joe, "things get all twisted, you know? When we opened this place, we went to the DA because we knew with Joe as the center of attraction we'd get a certain number of undesirables in the place. We asked for help. Nothin'. Then we went to the Football League and asked for a list of undesirables so Joe wouldn't get in no trouble and at the head of the list was both *me* and *my lawyer!* They had me fronting for some underworld outfit *myself!* So Joe told 'em to go stick it. I mean, he's loyal, you know what I mean? I'd stake my life on him. So he's loud and he likes to get drunk and get laid. He's twenty-six years old, he's entitled. He's worth millions to the Jets and to the League. They treat him like Caesar's wife! Without him, they know instead of NBC givin' 'em $75,000,000 they'll only get $25,000,000. His name is an investment to everybody. At the beginnin' of the season we announced this package deal, see—forty-seven season tickets to the Jets home games. Buy a season ticket, you get to come here before the game, have breakfast and we furnish free transportation to the stadium. Since Joe got mad at Pete Rozelle and said he'd rather quit football than give up his bar, I haven't been able to sell one ticket! I may have to eat 'em. I mean, Joe don't want nobody tellin' him what to do, you know what I mean? So he quits and everybody suffers."

A gum-chewing Goldie Hawn type with a polka-dot bandanna around her head chimed in. "I read in Earl Wilson that they had enough evidence against Joe to close *ten* joints."

"Malicious lies. The press is against Joe. A couple of years ago he even beat up one reporter so bad that he put him in the hospital. Now they are saying we're runnin' a bookie joint. So we got three phones in the basement. What am I gonna do? Yell 'Naughty, naughty!' every time somebody uses the phone? You can't ask everybody who comes in to use the phone what business he's in. They lie anyway."

It was midnight and the place was filling up with so many old Johns with young chippies on their arms it was beginning to look like a fathers' weekend at Smith. Everyone at the bar was joining in on the discussion. After all, discussing Joe Namath, getting in on a tiny slice of his life, touching the edge of whatever spotlight he happens to be standing in, is what it's all about at Bachelors III. "Let's be realistic," said one Kilimanjaro-topped cigar smoker. "There's a good reason why Rozelle wants Namath to sell this place. If the wrong people in here heard Joe talking, they could throw points. I mean, take the game the Jets played in the Super Bowl against the Baltimore Colts. The Colts were known as a rough team to score on. They had a great defense. The Jets were better known as a team which scored the most points through passing and receiving. The Colts were a ground team, the Jets were good as a passing offense. That's Joe's claim to fame—the man with the golden arm. . . ."

Everyone agreed, even Tough Mickey behind the bar. "Man, his arm's like a bullet," she explained.

The man continued. "Let's say before that game the gamblers hanging out in here found out Joe had a sore arm. The Jets' scoring power would've been off because their game was off. If a gambler knew this, he'd pass the word around that the Jets wouldn't be at full strength that day. All those bums gotta know is your weakness and then you got a new set of odds, baby."

"Rozelle's right," pitched in the only man in New York still wearing a 1951 crew cut. "Gamblers work on points. If you wanted to bet on the Jets in that game, you had twenty points going in. If Namath and his boys had to play a ground game, you wouldn't have had as many points.

"Jim Brown used to get up out of a tackle like an old man. He'd almost crawl back off the field before the next huddle and everyone said, 'Jim, why do you do that?' He never answered. It wasn't until after he retired that he told. 'Because,' he said, 'I didn't wanna give the other team the edge of knowing whether I was hurt or not, so I faked an injury every time.' You gotta protect yourself all the time and never let anybody know too much."

"Honey," nudged his date, "you didn't tell me that you knew Jim Brown."

A man in pink pants and a suede Cardin jacket, who looked like he had been searching for the men's room at the YMCA and wandered into the wrong doorway by mistake, chimed in: "Also ask yourself why the underworld should start hanging around Joe Namath. For friendship? Don't kid yourself. There's always a motive. This club wasn't built for Namath. It was here before. So why should all of a sudden this creepy joint become a big syndicate hangout? Why should undercover agents and Pete Rozelle's private investigators suddenly tap the phones? It's a real downer, but I think somebody tipped them off that Joe was a dupe. I think he's being taken for a ride by his so-called friends. Football players haven't much sense. It's the little punks who tell the gamblers everything—it certainly isn't stars like Joe Namath."

Joe Dellapina wiped his forehead nervously and sent a flying order to turn up the air conditioning. "You can't throw Joe. He's clean. There's even one idiotic rumor going around that he threw a game for $10,000. What would a guy like that need a measly $10,000 for? He makes $100,000 a year just from football alone. He's on TV. He's on the Braniff commercial."

"Look here!" An elderly lady at the bar got so excited she knocked over her Manhattan. Her husband picked up her cherry from the bar and ate it, stem and all, as she took from her purse a page from an old New York *Daily News* showing Namath circled by a couple of models in an ad for Lady Schick leg razors. At the very top of the ad, in big black letters, were the words JOE NAMATH HAS SOMETHING FOR THE GIRLS. What the little old lady forgot to mention was a bitter column next to it, typical of the kind of razzing he was getting from sportswriters, a column called "Ward to the Wise."

"He don't need this place, man. He don't need no Schick ad. He don't need nobody. He's gonna be a movie star. I don't know the name of the picture. I don't think they even named it yet. He's gonna play an Indian."

"Bill Russell's gonna quit basketball and be a movie star."

"Mickey Mantle oughtta be one, except he's got that awful Oklahoma twang."

"Joe don't wanna be no movie star," argued Joe Dellapina. "He loves football more than anything else in the

world. But he don't want nobody pushin' him around,
you know what I mean? He hasn't done anything
wrong. The doctor already told him to give up the
game—three operations on his legs already—can't bend
them under the table even. He's paid his dues to football with his own blood. He doesn't owe anybody anything—not his fans, not Pete Rozelle, not the team,
nobody."

"How about Joe's teammates quitting because of Joe?"

"If Joe walks, his buddies walk. All for one and one for
all."

"Such stupidity," said the one in the pink pants. "How
the hell do they think they're gonna make a living? Those
guys don't have the brains of a canned sardine. I had no
idea football players were so e-*mo*-tional. . . ."

"How about the president of the New York Jets, Phil
Iselin? He's also the president of a racetrack. Does that
make *him* an undesirable? Pete Rozelle isn't making *him*
sell."

"Yeah. And Louis Cordileone, with the New Orleans
Saints, has a joint down in the French Quarter. Pete Rozelle ain't said nothin' about *that*, man."

"You outta your tree, man? Louis Cordileone's a
shrimp, Joe Namath's the whole goddamn seafood special.
He's an example."

"I think that they've been more than fair. According to
every rule in football and the NFL's own constitution,
Namath should never play again. . . ."

"It's my opinion that Joe's being framed."

"I hear the Mafia controls every banana in the port of
New York. Why don't they worry about all the murders
they commit and not about whether they're using Joe
Namath's telephone. . . ."

"What he does in his spare time is his own business. If
he wants to pal around with gangsters, so what? He
shouldn't sell."

"He'll sell if he gets his asking price. He wants three
quarters of a million dollars plus an option on the stock."

"It's a dump!" said the chick in the Halston wet suit.

At one-thirty, a roar went up in the street outside, and
a hush of clammy anticipation fell over the bar. Frank
Sinatra was singing "My Way of Life" on the jukebox and
the shoulder-to-shoulder-pad mob in Bachelors III was
facing its moment of truth. "He's here . . . it's him . . . Joe's
coming. . . ." And there he was, grinning that Aw Shucks
grin in his blue windbreaker and unpressed Daks, and the
bar went wild. "Oh my God, it really *is* him," wailed the
chick in the Halston wet suit, "I think I'm going to faint."

"Joe baby!" yelled the bartender pouring a generous
Johnnie Walker Black.

"What're you givin' me Black for?" demanded Broadway Joe. The bartender turned the color of prune juice.
Everyone stared at him with enough hate to burn another
Reichstag without the aid of matches. The bartender
poured a Johnnie Walker Red in a whiskey glass with no
chaser, smiling hysterically. His hands were shaking.
(Broadway Joe drinks only Johnnie Walker Red.) Then the
bartender poured the first drink down the sink while
Tough Mickey stared hard at some creep who kept asking
her to cash a $100 check so that Broadway Joe could sign
his autograph on a $100 bill. "He pours me Black, and then
he pours it out!" said Broadway Joe. His pals and his fans
and his hangers-on all roared on cue. The bartender's
head shook like a coconut on a stick.

Billie Holiday swung into a lazy jazz waltz on "Crazy
He Calls Me" as Broadway Joe lumbered into the back
room, sipping his drink. The catastrophe was over and the
crowd moved with him, pushing and shoving to get up
close and touch him. Although the service I was getting
from Tough Mickey at the bar had improved so much
since she saw me talking to Joe Dellapina that she had
even given in and tried to mix a spritzer (Bachelors III
must be the only bar in New York that makes a spritzer
with white wine and 7-Up), I decided to desert my post
and case the back room myself.

Beyond the jukebox, away from the tourists and the
gawkers and the squealing hookers, the back room is
where the regulars sit. The girls are slinkier here. Their

hair looks shampooed, their nails are cleaner, and the smell around them switches from Kiss Me Quick to Detchema. The wall photographs are bigger too, and the frames more expensive. There's a touch of irony: Joe settles down under an enlarged blowup of the fighter Frank DePaula, another of the club's regulars, who was suspended May 22, 1969, by the New York State Athletic Commission after a federal grand jury indictment charging him and his manager with the theft of $80,000 in copper from a New Jersey pier.

Twelve tables with red tablecloths are grouped together in a huddle formation, all occupied by Joe's friends. Nine fake oil lamps hang from beamed ceilings. Dark blood-red carpets melt into dark blood-red walls. In one corner, a fireplace with a copper mantel is filled with leftover wood from the winter before Joe's discontent. The strippers and movie stars have been replaced on the walls by Joe's idols—Reggie Fleming, the pro hockey star; Carmen Basilio; Babe Ruth; Joe Pepitone, first baseman for the Yankees; Joe's coach Weeb Ewbank, who had stood beside him at the last closed-door conference in Pete Rozelle's office; Bill Hartack; Lew Alcindor; Sugar Ray Robinson. This is Broadway Joe's kingdom. His throne is usually shared by his most frequent girl, a pretty blond dish named Susan Storm. Susan didn't make it on this particular night, but one of Joe's admirers, sensing the call of duty, was playing "Stormy" by the Classics IV on the jukebox as a sort of tribute to the fact that somewhere in the world she exists.

Suddenly fifteen Negroes feeling no pain enter in a flourish of renewed excitement. Joe starts pushing tables together. The women all wear sequin collars and carry beaded princess bags. "It's so ethnic!" squeals the chick in the Halston wet suit, who has somehow managed to get a table close to Joe so it will be easier for her date to introduce her.

A jockey at a corner table empties a whole bowl of sugar cubes into his date's handbag to carry back to Monmouth Park to feed the horses, complaining, "All they have at the track is powdered sugar."

The Negroes are all hugging and kissing Broadway Joe, and one, who looks especially like the mother in *Raisin in the Sun,* is introducing him to each member of the party. Joe Dellapina pops a champagne cork as Broadway Joe Namath yells, "Did Ray Abruzzese teach you that?" This is obviously an "in" joke, for the initiated spectators all laugh and nod approvingly at his keen sense of humor. A couple at the next table goes into a passionate soul kiss. Joe grins wider.

The fat Negro woman presiding over the cushy champagne party announces: "I been a mother and a wife and a grandmother, and now I am gonna swing, Daddy!" Her escort throws his white carnation at her. "Clam up, Pearl Bailey!"

Downstairs, past the three controversial telephones with phone numbers written all over the walls, on my way to the men's room, I passed the chick in the Halston wet suit, who was so stoned she was caressing the wall. "The ladies' room in this dump has a broken handle on the door and no towels. This joint caters to men only, just like the Playboy Club." I found the men's room in somewhat better condition. The walls were fabricked and instead of the usual rubber machine, the dispenser on the wall offered Canoe. Two men who looked like commuters from Larchmont were talking animatedly at the urinal. "Well, why the hell don't you just walk up to him and ask him for the goddamn autograph if it means so much to you, for Chrissake." "It's not that it means so much to *me;* personally I think the guy's a phony. Up to his eyeballs in hoodlums and Jesus knows what else. But what can I tell ya? My kids think the sun sets in this guy's ass. . . ."

It was 2 A.M. and Broadway Joe's party in the back room was just getting started. On my way out, Joe Dellapina looked tired and deflated, like an old cowpoke who has clipped his last barbed-wire fence. "See that painting behind the bar? That was done by a real wacko—a drug addict—a real junkie—just did it from a newspaper photo —Joe never even posed for it—he never got paid—never *wanted* to get paid. People big and little come here to see Joe. It makes 'em feel good."

One of the waitresses who was blowing her nose into a
red napkin agreed. "We got a good thing here if somebody don't screw us up," she said, plunking a quarter into
the jukebox and playing "Aquarius" three times in a row.
"We turn away five, six hundred people a night and we
never had a minimum or a cover. We're also open for
lunch, do between seventy-five and a hundred lunches,
but when the papers write it up, they never mention the
food. American Airlines had a press conference in here,
and they loved the place. Did you try one of our hamburgers? You don't get just a little London broil with some
Gravymaster thrown over it. Over at Allen's, you go in
there this time of night the cooks have everything
cleaned up. You come in here, you can still get a good
steak at four in the morning. Joe's always here then." And
the black Perle Mesta in the back room? "Oh, that's Joe's
maid. . . ."

Outside, the hot acid night licked the salty faces of the
people who couldn't get into Bachelors III. They stood
patiently, waiting with their autograph books, watching
the chick in the Halston number, who by this time had lost
her cool entirely and was busily throwing up on Lexington Avenue while her date, who turned out to be a nean-
derthal with arms so beefy they looked like football padding sticking through the sleeves of his Robert Hall
wash-and-wear suit, was trying to hail a cab. A block away,
I could still hear them. "You dragged me all the way
across town to this dump for nothing" . . . "You said you
knew the sonuvabitch. . . ."

And inside the Hershey's syrup can, the band played
on.

5

Marcello Mastroianni

MARCELLO MASTROIANNI'S MOTHER—eighty years old, almost totally deaf and mad as hell about it—sat under a flowering cherry tree waiting for her son. She was paying a rare visit to the set of *The Priest's Wife,* a new movie filming in English that is giving the Roman Catholic Church an itch that has nothing to do with the starch in its clerical robes. In the film, the Italian Clark Gable plays a devout priest who falls in love with Sophia Loren, a rock-singing bobby-soxer, and leaves the motherly sanctity of St. Peter's dome to take up the swinging good life. It's the kind of movie a Catholic mother likes to look in on.

Except for the duenna-like tapping of Mama Mastroianni's foot, it was a peaceful scene. The ancient villa near Padua that was being used as the schoolhouse where the priest teaches was bathed in soft, lazy sunshine. In the background, an old peasant crone, hired for the day, walked a gaggle of geese back and forth, in and out of camera range, enticing them with a pan of corn. "They've been seduced so many times today with that corn, you might call them 'quackolds,' " quipped a press agent. Suddenly Mastroianni appeared, looking pious and sad (or sad-pious, if there's a difference). Cameras turned as he walked among the children playing among the beehives and grapevines and slowly announced to an elderly understanding Dorothy Dix–type priest that he had decided to leave the church for Sophia Loren. A Scottish dialogue coach crouched behind a tree and whispered the words to Mastroianni in English, which were then whispered to his mother by her companion in Italian. The old lady belched in confusion but instead of handing her anything so sensible as an ear trumpet, the companion just smiled broadly.

They broke for lunch and a typical Italian movie-location siesta, and Marcello frowned. "It is very boring being an actor—you need great patience. I don't think I will ever speak well the English." While he escorted his mother to her car, ignoring her protests to stay for lunch, his dialogue coach said, "Actually, his English is improving. I record the lines on a casette tape recorder and he recites them back while he's shaving. His accent is charming, but sometimes he's unintelligible because he mumbles. But we're coming along."

With his mother safely on the autostrada on her way back to Rome, he headed for his trailer, where he unbuttoned his priestly cassock, lit up a black cigarette and plunged into a bowl of cold, greasy spaghetti served by a surly assistant who looked like a Marseilles gangster. "That is Fred. He goes with me everywhere." Fred snarled menacingly like an Italian Mike Mazurki. "Fred does not like to see me dressed like a priest because it is sacrilegious. This film is a *scandalo*—try and understand me if possible, because I invent words—because in Italy the church is popular and the priests are public gods. I'm not interested in the church, but as a man, I understand priests who want to marry. They all have sex anyway, so why shouldn't they marry? Oh, they make them exercise and feed them things to keep them from wanting sex, but a man is a man. . . . The church has more strength in Italy than in other countries, but I do not think the Italians are so superstitious anymore. Only the peasants are close to the church. When you get a little money, you break away from religion. As a parent I no longer feel the need to send my daughter to church. My mother raised me in the church and it had a very bad influence on my life. When I was a boy we had no discotheques, no money to buy motorcycles or go to the cinema, but it cost nothing to sing in the choir, so we went to church to pass the time. I used to take communion twice a day because it was like a game. I was playing a part. My daughter Barbara and her friends are so busy they don't have time for St. Peter and madonnas and mysterious religious symbols and philosophies. They find a Divinity, like God or Buddha or Lenin, in themselves. Now they go less to priests and more to psychiatrists. Church is old-fashioned. Today kids don't want to be told they can't go to bed with their boyfriends. To them the only sin is denying themselves pleasure in life. The Italians are stupid people, but they are changing."

Such opinions have not earned him any recent garlands of praise in his native country. When he won the Best Actor award at the recent Cannes Film Festival, it was the Italian press that crucified him in print. They don't like to see him appearing in English and they don't like the stories, well publicized in the American press, of his affairs with Faye Dunaway and Catherine Deneuve. In Catholic, monogamous Italy, you can be arrested for adultery. In addition to that, Mastroianni has a wife whom the Italians respect and admire, a nineteen-year-old daughter who would be publicly disgraced by a scandal, and 500 years of Italian punctilio to buck. It's not easy to be a married Don Juan in a country where journalism is aggressive rather than accurate. Result: The shunned Italian press is currently conducting its own war against him. No Italian photographers are allowed on the set and Marcello will not speak to any Italian reporters. So they stay away and attack from the rear.

On the set, he is funny and amiable, mainly because he and Loren have made so many films together and are such old friends that he often breaks her up in the close-ups with four-letter Italian swearwords only the two of them understand. He is an interesting combination of sartorial elegance and the smell of fish, and when he talks he is so gentle and faraway he often gives the impression of being half asleep. He often refers to himself as "tormented" and there is about him a lumbering, harassed air that opposes his juvenile dimples and choirboy haircut. When he looks at you, his eyes are the wide, troubled agates of hungry children—seeing everything, but without depth or wisdom. "What attracted me most to him," says John Boorman, who directed him in *Leo the Last*, "was his plastic side." Mastroianni likes that description. "I am very lazy, passive man—an observer, not a man of action. I am a man at the window, looking out at others. I am a very negative man. In *La Dolce Vita, 8½, Leo the Last, The Stranger*—all my good films—I played all men who don't act but *react*. I feel more comfortable in parts like those.

"The Americans think I am Rudolph Valentino, because they are very romantic. But look at my films—in *La Dolce Vita* I was a lover, OK, but also a victim. In *8½* and *Bell' Antonio* I was impotent. In *Casanova 70* I couldn't make love unless I was in danger. Anyway, a latin lover doesn't make sex, he just talks a lot. I played Valentino on the stage in a big musical in Rome called *Ciao, Rudy!*, but even in that we showed Valentino as an ordinary man, not this miracle of sexuality the Americans imagine. Joe Levine and David Merrick have both asked me to take the show to Broadway, but I am too lazy. There were, in this show, all my dreams—I always wanted to be Bing Crosby, Gene Kelly and Fred Astaire all combined into one man. As a child I saw all their films, so I put all this into *Ciao, Rudy!* and I sang and danced and it was an enormous success. But I don't know if I could do it in English."

Two years ago, he didn't speak enough English to make a simple transaction at the five-and-ten, but it's improving, even though every other word is that old four-letter job beginning with *f* that you still can't print in *The New York Times*. "It's the first word I learned in English," he winks mischievously, "and it's a good one. It covers just about everything. I began to speak English only to make money. Two years ago I was without money and Carlo Ponti asked me to go to England to make a movie in English, but I could say only 'good night' and 'hello' but Ponti said, 'Don't worry, *I* am the boss!' so they didn't fire me, they got me a teacher and I learned to say the lines phonetically. The film was *Diamonds for Breakfast* with Rita Tushingham. Terrible! But I did learn a few words of English, enough to give me courage to do *A Place for Lovers* with Faye Dunaway. Ridiculous! Why an Italian accept invitation from a dying woman? Why? If I knew she was sick, I would not make her have sex. It was a stupid movie. Also, I'm too old to be a latin lover. I am forty-five years old. At my age, if you have sex then you go to bed and rest for three days."

He has several unreleased films—*Sunflower* with Loren, *The Voyeur* with Virna Lisi, and a silly sex comedy called *Drama of Jealousy* with Monica Vitti about a *ménage à trois* between a street worker, a flower girl and a pizza cook—and he is down on all of them. "They give me the prize at Cannes for *Drama of Jealousy* but it is not important. I make eighty films in my life, but only ten of them are any good. *Bell' Antonio* was my favorite. And the things I made for Fellini—but he is a genius. Antonioni is something else. He hates actors. I understand that. For his kind of cinema, he doesn't need actors. The only good thing about *La Notte* for me was meeting Jeanne Moreau. She is a total woman—a prostitute one moment and a mother to a man the next. Fellini is my favorite director because he has the enormous ability to see inside people and use their faults. Actors are always good in his films because they don't play roles, they play themselves. In *La Dolce Vita* he even named the character Marcello. I would make another film for him in a minute, but I don't want to stay in Italy. It is easy for me to go on making films here because I know the mentality of the workers, the psychology of my own people—but I feel I've had the most success I'll ever have here. I want to do things that are different. Otherwise, I get bored. I never had any curiosity about the world before. I was content just to eat spaghetti and speak with my hands like all Italian peasants —oh yes, I am really a peasant—but now I must go on, meet other people, learn new countries. I don't want to waste any more time with my life and the only way to do it is through the cinema. So I am trying to learn English, but I can't be pushed. I am very slow to learn. I have the Italian philosophy—*domani, domani*—put everything off until tomorrow. It's part of my Italian nature. Sophia is more ambitious. Sixteen years ago we made our first film together. She couldn't order an egg in English. But she went home every night and study. I'm different. At night I want a plate of spaghetti and a bottle of wine and my friends."

He sipped his capuccino slowly, remembering his child-hood. "I have a very modest background. I was born in Fontana Liri, a hamlet in the mountains . . . poverty has been my daily bread most of my life . . . until I was twenty-five I accepted poverty as a natural condition to accept and respect. All the houses in my town were made with pieces of rock. . . . I remember chimneys and homemade wheat bread and walking so much in the streets that my shoes were always full of holes and my father would fix them with pieces of aluminum and when I walked I sounded like a horse . . . bing bong like a horse . . . ha ha. My friends called me 'Skinny Paws' because my poor arms hung down out of my uncle's hand-me-down clothes. My father was a woodworker who died before I ever became successful. He went blind from diabetes and never saw me act. He went to the cinema and heard my voice in the first two films I made, but he couldn't see me. My mother loved actors, she always wanted me to be like Nelson Eddy. She goes to all of my films now because it's the only way she ever gets to see me. I am not so kind to my mother. When I do films in Rome, I often look up and see her in the crowd of onlookers, but she never waves or calls out.

"At first I wanted to be an architect, but the war interrupted my studies and I ended up drawing military maps for Mussolini's retreating armies. When I was nineteen, I was captured by the Nazis and escaped to Venice, where I drew the Bridge of Sighs on handkerchiefs and sold them for food. After the war, when it was safe to return to Rome, I got a job as a bookkeeper and acted with an amateur group at night. Visconti saw me there and I applied for a job in his production of *Streetcar Named Desire*. Visconti and his assistant, a young man named Franco Zefferelli, met me in a tearoom and said they'd give me $3.50 a day to play Stanley Kowalski. It was a big success, so I went on for ten years on the stage. I was very lucky. It was a hobby; I always thought I'd go back to being an architect someday. It all just happened. In the movies it was harder. Only little roles at first. Taxi drivers and carpenters, you know. My interest in movies only started in Visconti's *White Nights* with Maria Schell and by then I had already made thirty-five films. Nothing important. The next thing I knew Fellini called me. I remember he said, 'I need a face with no personality in it—like yours.' He was very cruel, but I agreed with him. He had already turned down Gerard Philippe as 'too much of a musketeer' and Paul Newman, whom he thought 'evoked an athlete with the Colgate smile of the Actors Studio.' Well, I didn't think I was as good an actor as either of them, but I didn't want to sound like I didn't want to work for him, so I just asked to see the script. 'Impossible,' he said, like I was crazy to ask for a Fellini script. Then I said, 'Well, just send me a page describing what the role will be like,' so he sent me this package and when I opened it there was this cartoon inside showing a man on top of the sea with his sex organ going to the bottom of the ocean floor with mermaids dancing around it. I become red in the face and I never to this day ask Fellini to see a script or even an idea on anything I've ever done for him.

"Fellini made me a star but I'm not sure it was a good idea. This is a terrible life. When I'm bored I pretend I have another profession. I want to build something with brick, cement and wood . . . it is so marvelous to build a house to touch, something with a life of its own. In my spare time, I draw plans for houses. I never go to premieres or cocktail parties. I never was *à la mode*. I am not on display, I don't go around with cinema people. Every time I go to a restaurant with ten people, they cut off the other eight and suddenly I'm in the papers having an affair with the girl next to me in the photo. I am a victim. My mother is very proud of me but I have not been able to give her anything. 'A car and chauffeur? Marcello, don't be an idiot—what would the neighbors think?' I have a certain tenderness for my daughter, but I seldom see her. In the business I have chosen I have never felt anything solid. And from this lack I have developed this incredible passion for things that can be mixed with cement and earth in a pail to last a lifetime. From time to time I think of old age and I don't picture it as a happy time for me. I earn money now, but somehow I just can't put any of it away for my old age. It's strange. Somehow a person who has been poor all his life should know how to put money aside for a time when it will be needed, but all the money I have ever earned I have just spent like water, as if it didn't belong to me. I am a very bored man. They come for you in the morning in a limousine; they take you to the studio; they stick a pretty girl in your arms; sometimes they earn something off you and give you some of the profits. They call that a profession . . . come on.

"The future for me will probably be lonely. I will continue to make films for money, but architecture will always be my first love. I own a yacht and six houses. I don't need them, but it's a game. It's an expensive game, but better than spending all my money in Monte Carlo. I don't read anything—I hate books—so I will continue to draw plans for houses and study English and then I will make a film in New York in which I play an Italian who speaks bad English. Everybody knows I'm Italian and ev-

erybody knows my English is bad. OK. So why not make
a movie where I speak like myself? It would be more
charming, more realistic, yes? Look, they made *Johnny
Belinda* about a girl who didn't speak at *all.*"

But now it is time for him to speak once more the lines
of a horny priest in love with Sophia Loren. They are
calling him to the set. Outside, in the sunshine, Fred appears like a thundercloud, handing him two of the latest
Italian scandal magazines. He becomes furious. Lines
crease his forehead. The cameras must wait while he
reads about his latest bedroom capers. "See—this is what
I mean. A victim! They never leave me in peace. Read this
headline." It is in Italian. "I translate for you. It says:
MARCELLO PREFERS PORK AND BEANS TO ACTRESSES!"

"That's not so bad. . . ."

"And see here is a photo of Faye Dunaway and me
entering a private apartment together. There were eight
other people with us but they were all cut out of the
photo."

"Can't you sue?" I ask.

"In Italy, there is no protection from these rats. The
judges are against me. They never expose the Mafia or the
Vatican or all the corrupt politicians. It's always Mastroianni! I'm an automatic target and there are two *scan-
dalos* a day. Me, I don't care, but it's cruel to my wife. The
reporters call her on the phone and pretend to be friends
to get a story from her and the paparazzi follow my
daughter around in her car and try to take her picture.
They dug up a woman who was my mistress seven years
ago and followed her son to school and made such a *scandalo* he had to leave school! Listen, you have just been in
a movie yourself. They will make up terrible lies about
you, too. What will you do about it?"

"You just have to develop a sense of humor. . . ."

"Ha! When they print an article called I MARRIED A SON
OF A BITCH signed by my own wife? This article said first
I was afraid to go to war because I was a coward. Then it
said my parents were Fascists who supported the Nazis.
Then I was a homosexual who was in love with Fred here

—you saw this ugly animal?—that my daughter followed us to my yacht and begged me, 'Don't go with this man, Daddy!' Then my wife came to visit us on the yacht and slept with both Fred and me! Oh, I tell you it was something *fantastic!* Life is hell for me, sometimes I stand in front of my mirror and cry. . . ."

Suddenly they were around him—taking the cigarette from his mouth, trying to adjust the white collar on his black cassock and leading him away to face the cameras like a sexy Tartuffe. Grumpily, Fred picked the magazines up off the grass and went back inside the trailer.

Sally Kellerman

JUST WHEN EVERYBODY at the 1970 Cannes Film
Festival was about to give up and go home—at
some point, I believe, between the movie about
Hungarian falcon hunters and the one about a rock break-
ers' strike in Tunisia—Sally Kellerman arrived and people
stopped yawning. "M*A*S*H EST SMASH," yelled *Nice
Matin*'s headlines, and so was Sally. The bored paparazzi,
tired of photographing actors from movies about peasants
trying to save enough money to buy a tractor, followed
her like hound dogs because in a festival full of true al-
legorical grit, the girl they called "Hot Lips" was pure
Hollywood gold. She came on like a hippie Venus de Milo,
waving her arms around her body like Carole Lombard,
smiling like Veronica Lake and walking like an anchovy.
For three days the flashbulbs never stopped flashing.

On the day of the prizes, the jury was locked away on
a yacht in the harbor, but by 4 P.M. everybody in the
Carlton bar knew *M*A*S*H* had won the Grand Prize.
"Well, whaddya know?" said Sally in a voice that sounded
like a furnace on the blink. Crowds applauded when she
slinked down the beach in her Levi jacket without a bra.
"Mercy bouquet!" grinned Sally, flashing the peace sign
with her fingers. Then she did some shopping. "Showez-
moi some—what's the word for watches in French? Trav-
elers checks ici? Bon? To buyez with, oui?"

"I speak English," sighed the clerk.

"Mercy bouquet! It's for my man. In California. Let me
tell you about my man. He has a gaucho moustache and
a very nice Jewish face. Do you have any butch watches?
He's very butch, my man."

There was a great flourish as everyone in the shop said:
"Qu'est-ce que c'est butch?"

Then she acted out about a hundred great parts, leaning
on all the counters munching chocolates and putting out
her Juicy Fruit gum in a silver ashtray. By the time she
left, all the clerks were waving: "Au revoir, Sally!"
"Mmmm, tray bon, y'all!" She flashed the peace sign again
and clattered away in her ankle-strap shoes like a crack of
sunshine on a foggy day.

An hour later, she collapsed on her bed at the Carlton
with her arms full of French postcards, a $75 Omega
watch that was very butch and $10 worth of marzipan
lobsters. "I'm too tired to be interviewed. This Cannes
Festival is wild. All yachts and hookers in bikinis and I've
never had less sleep or eaten more rich food in my life.
I've always been a compulsive eater, which means you
take a bag of cookies to bed and watch the *Late Show*,
right? But here I have twenty croissants for breakfast and
300 courses for lunch all covered with mayonnaise and
585 things for dinner and I look like I'm pregnant
. . . . *M*A*S*H* is the second-highest grosser in the world,
they told me yesterday as I was being photographed on
some bicycle on the beach, so I said '*Wow*, what's the
first?' and they said *Airport!!!* God, can you believe it?

When you're second to *Airport*, makes you wonder how good your own picture is, you know? I need some sleep."

She crawled under the covers in her clothes. Then she leaped out of bed, picked some chewing gum out of her bathing suit and wandered about the room folding clothes, flushing the john, throwing panties into suitcases. "I've got to have my house in order before I can talk . . . the only thing I can't do is wash a car . . . I'm going to take all these postcards home and then everyone I didn't send one to will get one . . . this is going to be a *muted* interview because I've been telling all these French reporters terrific things for days and they didn't understand a word I said and now I'm too tired to talk. OK. What do you want to know? My background before *M*A*S*H?* I have no background. Where were you the first day I got here? OK. I was born in Long Beach and I always wanted to be an actress and now at thirty-two—oh, God, you found out how *old* I am—listen, I was a late bloomer. Took me eight years to get my first job on TV. Discovered right away, heh heh."

Ring. "Hello, Gig? Isn't it great? Yeah, I'm sitting here being dissected . . . will you give us the award tonight? Yeah, I can't speak French either . . . hello, bonjour, bonjour. . . . He hung up. That was Gig Young calling to congratulate me . . . he's giving out the awards with Candy Bergen. God, nobody has a right to look as good as she does in the *daytime!* Sweet guy, Gig. I used to date him. I've gone with so many guys, but I won't tell you their names, because they're all famous and they're all married . . . where was I? *Oh* yes. When I got out of Hollywood High, I studied with Jeff Corey and went to college on the side just to please my family, but I failed everything except choir . . . I was already five feet ten and a half in grammar school, so there I was, terrible in college, no ambition except to be a movie star and too tall to see in the mirror to even put my lipstick on . . . so I decided to concentrate on something worthwhile . . . . I got a job as an elevator operator that lasted a week because I got carsick. . . . I was a waitress for one day

.... I was a mess because I couldn't wear starched napkins and high hats, they made me look like the Jolly Green Giant.... I taught swimming!... I got a job as a secretary on a Friday and learned how to type over the weekend .... I was just never together. But in *class! I* was the one everybody said would be a star. *Aaagghh! !"*

She leaped off the bed to show me the piece of marzipan she was eating from the $10 box. It was covered with green mold. "And then, folks, in the middle of this terrific interview, Miss Sally Kellerman dropped dead from poisoned candy. Can you believe the way they rook the tourists with this stuff? ... Then I got a job playing the school dyke in *Girls Reform School* with Edd Kookie Byrnes .... I should get an award for just having the courage to go *on* after I saw *that.* ... I didn't work again for three years. In all that time nobody ever thought I was any good except Hugo Haas. I couldn't get myself together long enough to even have my picture taken.... Do you know I don't even have a single publicity photo? ... Then I did a play, *Enemy of the People,* on La Cienega Boulevard and one critic wrote, 'Although her fresh beauty was a delight to the eye, her wooden portrayal leaves her with no potential at all. She should quit the business before further damage is done.' ... I toured with Ozzie and Harriet in *The Marriage Go Round,* then I did a TV show that was so bad they didn't release it for six months .... I didn't work one day during that period.... I became totally negative.... I've been depressed every day of my life until *M*A*S*H* ... anyway, for a while I played cold rich women who shot monsters in outer space.... I looked like Lizabeth Scott and I played girls who got beaten up a lot ... for a girl five feet ten and a half I've gotten beaten up more than anyone I know ... then I did my first really big picture, *The Third Day,* and I thought, 'Get ready, here comes a big movie star' ... one of the worst movies ever made.... I wrote George Peppard dirty letters and got killed in a car wreck in the first scene ... just awful .... Warner Brothers hated me so much they wouldn't even give me a standard contract ... so my manager walked into my singing lesson and said, 'Jeez, with your personality you should be a variety star! We'll take you out to the topless room at the airport and get you a singing job!' "

There was a knock and Robert Altman, the director of *M*A*S*H*, came in thrilled and she threw her arms around him. "Hey, we won! We don't have to be nice to anybody in French anymore!" Altman gave her a gift—a stone eagle sculpture—and she burst into tears and he left, embarrassed. "See, that's why I don't like to talk about the past, because I was a jerk then. *Now* is what's happening, man. I was a Fifties child who grew up on Jo Stafford singing 'See the pyramids along the Nile.' . . . I was just doing what was expected of me . . . they said 'You're sexy' I tried to play sexy parts, they said 'You're sophisticated' I tried to play deadly Nina Foch parts . . . . I was going to auditions in Chanel suits, man, when I met Bob Altman . . . now I feel like I'm a woman all of a sudden, I mean I feel like *me* . . . anyway, I got into *Breakfast at Tiffany's* on Broadway. . . . I went to see David Merrick at the Beverly Hills Hotel and I had my dog, whose name was Holly, with me and my cat, J.R., and they ran all over the room and I guess he thought I was crazy because he said Mary Tyler Moore was playing Holly but I could play Mag Wildwood and when I left he said, 'By the way, where did you rent the dog and cat and what are their real names?' I went to New York, oh God, some of the worst days of my life there in hotels with athlete's foot on the rug and costing $360 a minute, but David Merrick walked me to rehearsals and he was just fantastic and I didn't have an affair with him or *anything!* A new phase of my life was beginning and I was going to be a singing Broadway star, but it turned into a nightmare. . . . I really liked Mary Tyler Moore, God was she a pro and the rest of us were afraid to walk out in the curtain calls for fear we'd be murdered by the audience . . . anyway, *she* was great, but I feel threatened by girls like Doris Day, you know? I mean, I couldn't stand being second bananas, even though Edward Albee was writing

scenes for me and David Merrick liked me, but then our
names got linked romantically in the papers and he got
very upset although I swore it wasn't me who did it and
everything was collapsing around us and I never got to
open in New York so nobody except the hostile preview
audiences knew how good I was and I was neurotic and
awful and caused a lot of trouble and everybody *loathed*
me so I came back here. . . ."

"Here, in Cannes?"

"Oh, aren't we in Malibu? I don't even know where I
am . . . let's see. . . . I went to an analyst for two years and
had a lot of affairs and I had to find out who I was because
I was in serious trouble. . . . I was $10,000 in debt, so I did
The Boston Strangler playing the victim who lived to tell
about Tony Curtis. . . . I was the one tied to the bed with
black eyes and I looked just awful, but I think it was the
first time people really thought I could act . . . then I
played Jack Lemmon's wife in *The April Fools* but it was
the same old stupid blonde routine with only seven lines.
I was so desperate after that I went to see Bob Altman
about *M*A*S*H* and I said, 'I'll do *anything!* I can be
funny, I can break loose, just let me *try!*' and I think I had
hold of his pants legs or something because he took a long
look at me and jumped up and yelled, '*Hot Lips!*' I was
there to see about the role of Lieutenant Dish. I didn't
know anything about any Hot Lips, but for the first time
in fourteen years somebody had responded to me, so I just
said, 'Oooh, yes, Hot Lips!' and I ran right out of the
meeting and practically ripped that script apart looking
for all the lines belonging to Hot Lips . . . on page 40 I
found one line, on page 70, another line . . . fourteen years
and at the end of the rainbow a nine-line part of a soldier
called Hot Lips. . . . I cried for three days. . . . I screamed
at my agent, I yelled at my manager, I told Bob Altman
I hated him, I hated his stupid script and I hated his stupid
movie and most of all I hated Hot Lips and they could all
take their stupid little project and go @/?*@ themselves
. . . . Well, Bob Altman must have known what he was
doing, because he said, 'Don't worry, you'll have more to

do than it says in the script, because I plan to make up this
movie as we go along,' and what did I have to lose? . . .
it was a gamble . . . I could've lost everything . . . but
Altman is the first director I ever worked with who didn't
make me afraid . . . he was a great audience . . . the things
in the movie everyone thinks took a year and a half were
totally spontaneous . . . we were a family . . . the people
you see the most of in *M*A*S*H* were the ones who
worked the hardest . . . the assistants didn't even yell,
they'd just say, 'C'mon, Sally' . . . even my analyst said it
did more for me than a man could. . . . I'm not kidding
. . . it was like a two-month paid vacation . . . that's what
the new renaissance in films is all about, feeling *good*
. . . it was the first time in my life I'd ever had a real family
. . . from the first day, Bob told me, 'If you worry about
what you look like, you're fired!' and now people are asking me if I minded playing a poor lady who gets knocked
around by all the men because it is such a blow to
Women's Liberation . . . oh, *no*, man . . . I was a stiff, rigid
Victorian when I got into *M*A*S*H* . . . Hot Lips changed
me because she was the only character in the film who
was allowed to change . . . she ended up gaining from the
degradation . . . she was a pill, she needed shaking up, just
like me . . . she was an uptight bitch, but she ended up part
of the family, yelling for the guys in the football game
. . . the M*A*S*H unit for her was like the movie crew for
me. . . . I'm not a Women's Liberationist anyway. . . . I
think people should be allowed to do whatever they want
to in life without outside intimidation . . . otherwise, I
think they're more like Hot Lips was at the *beginning* of
the movie . . . most of them look like bull dykes. . . . I want
a man to run my house and make my decisions, man
. . . when a burglar comes, I want *him* to be the one to
go downstairs."

Sally was next to do another film for Altman, *Brewster
McCloud,* as "the fairy godmother of a boy who tries to
fly off the top of the Houston Astrodome. That's all I know,
except that I have been told I may also be a birdwoman
from a foreign planet and I have bird-wing scars on my

back and wear a trenchcoat. . . . I haven't read it yet, but it doesn't matter because I would do anything for Bob Altman and I won't have to wear Army fatigues . . . then I'm going to do a rock album and I just did a cut on an album of music from *The Adventurers* in which I fake twenty orgasms to music. . . . I don't want to get locked into anything and that's why it's hard for me to give interviews because I can't be typed as either a comedienne or a siren and I'm sorry I've had so little to say in this interview but you should catch me on a good day. . . ."

By 8 P.M. she was on her way to the gala at the *Cinema Palais* singing Laura Nyro songs and looking like an Aztec choirboy who had just read his first J. D. Salinger. She was wearing white high-heel sandals, a Lois Lane shoulder-strap purse and an Indian headband. "Say, I've been thinking here we are at the Cannes Film Festival, man, and it's all so unimportant, we gotta go home and fight, man, and carry on the revolution. . . ." Then she was swept into the army of paparazzi that descended like ravens, baffled maybe, but breathing heavy.

I saw Sally three years after that interview was written. I had just come from a screening of *Lost Horizon,* sort of a *Brigadoon* with chopsticks. Nine million dollars and it looks catered by Trader Vic's. We had a steak in her room at the Drake Hotel. She wasn't too thrilled either. She was the same treetop-tall blonde with the voice like a Honda in need of a thousand-mile checkup. In *Lost Horizon* she plays a *Newsweek* photographer who travels ten million miles to the top of the Himalayas just to give up smoking. She was still a bit crazy, but the thing about Sally is she's the first to admit it. She married the man with the "butch watch," writer-director Rick Edelstein, and divorced him, too. "So now Rex Reed catches up with Sally Kellerman three years later, folks, and guess what? She got thrown out of her house, lost her man, and doesn't have a baby on each knee but she's still in there swinging. Want some french fries?"

She doesn't smoke real cigarettes, "just dope, man,"

and eats candy by the jar. The room was decorated with Raisinettes, three bottles of vitamin C, scattered fan mail, some wilting Easter lilies and a book on yoga. Columbia Pictures had flown her in to plug *Lost Horizon,* the multimillion-dollar bomb, but it was clear that all she wanted to talk about was her other new movie, a daffy murder mystery called *Slither.* "It only cost a million three thousand or maybe it was a million and a half, I don't know, but it was terrific because in *Lost Horizon* we were just servicing a script, man, and in *Slither* we were servicing ourselves and turning out a groovy movie and I just love it and I don't think critics should review *Lost Horizon* anyway because it's not a movie for critics. . . . I mean, you know what it is going in, man, and no critic is gonna dig it but Ross Hunter has made maybe forty-eight movies and forty-seven of them made money and he's never got a good review in his life so why bother? I did it because I wanted to sing in a movie and I think Burt Bacharach is a genius and I made a very good friend out of Liv Ullmann who writes me letters from Norway and it was worth it. We worked for five months and I was locked in that airplane for three weeks with all those guys and parkas and snowshoes and hot light bulbs and it nearly drove me bananas and you could see what kind of movie it was going in but what the hell it was an experience. . . .

" . . . and this has been a rotten year for me and I'm feeling pretty sad right now because I got a divorce and my father died and I'm taking care of my niece right now and although I set out to make my marriage work with some ivy planted and some fruit trees and dinner on the table I just couldn't cut it, man, and now I'm trying to cope in my own way. . . . I've got a two-story Cape Cod house with a badminton court in the backyard and a pool and an orange tree and Bud Cort above the garage in the guest room and I'm getting my act together, man. . . . I live at my shrink's and it's saving my life because he tells me to remember back to the time my sister died and I say 'Listen, you creep, I'm telling you something important and you bring up something from the past I have no feelings about whatsoever I was only seven at the time and I'm blowing this scene' and suddenly I'm crying for three days and it's all coming back and you realize that if you can hit one little pocket of memory it's worth it like right now I'm in this terrific suite and what do I overlook but a lot of dirty windows and it reminds me of the six months I lived in New York doing *Breakfast at Tiffany's* on Broadway and everybody thought I was having an affair with David Merrick only it wasn't true and I was living in fleabag hotels with athlete's foot on the rug that cost $300 a minute and I can't see why you live here . . . . First day in California I was jogging . . . and now I'm turning down all roles for a while to get myself together and concentrate on my singing and hope somebody buys my next album because nobody bought the last one but it's because the material was lousy and I shouldn't sing hard rock. . . . Neil Diamond dropped by the other day and said I should get my own band together and that's what I'm gonna do and I met this terrific piano player who learned in a Baptist church in Georgia and the man who's gonna produce my next album is the guy who produces Gladys Knight and the Pips . . . and I've got big eyes to do a movie about a jazz singer, man, you know, something where maybe I can sing 'Lover Man.' "

She was suddenly on her hands and knees on the floor trying to stuff a floor-length shawl under a heavy chair. "Listen, can you give me a hand with this? James Shigeta who is in *Lost Horizon* got robbed in this hotel last night and they wiped him out and we're on our way to London to meet the Queen for the royal command performance and I even learned to curtsy so I'm going as long as I don't have to talk about the picture and I gotta leave in five minutes for the *Mike Douglas Show* and before I go I just want to hide my favorite crochet shawl cape under this chair in case they break in while I'm gone and clean me out they don't get this . . . and listen, about this interview, you don't have to write anything at all if you don't want to because I haven't really said anything on account of I'm feeling pretty rotten today and all, man, so why don't you just have another french fry and wait a minute while I go to the the john and then you can walk me downstairs to the lobby and then if you wanna forget the whole thing I'll understand. . . ."

It's nice to know some people never change.

7

Grace Slick

A FEW BLOCKS FROM San Francisco's poorest low-housing district, in a run-down neighborhood that once knew elegance, stands a seedy white three-story mausoleum supported by four decaying Doric columns. Ancient white-lace curtains blow lazily in the breeze behind its open cut-glass windows. Its paint is dappled with age, like an enormous pastry crust that has been too lightly dusted with confectioner's sugar. A tiny patch of dead zinnias nuzzles the walk that leads to a sagging front porch where a broken toilet seat leans, cracked and peeling, against the door. Enrico Caruso once lived there, but now its former glory has fallen into a state of disrepair, like a noble countess violated by an army of callous invaders. This is the home of the Jefferson Airplane.

I pressed the bell next to a red heart that said "Stop the War." An upstairs window slammed open and a girl with a scrubbed Ivory Soap face and long curly hair leaned out. "Yeah? What do you want?"

"Is Grace Slick in?"

"I'm Grace. I'll be right down."

I had only seconds to recover. She doesn't look anything like her photographs. There she is, on the album covers and in the rock magazines and underground newspapers, looking like a dark purple menace—long straight black hair falling seductively about her face and shoulders like raven's wings, deep pools of darkness signaling world-weary insouciance from eyes like ripe olives. And here was this girl in neatly tailored slacks and a Mexican poncho (I later learned she was pregnant), cautiously opening the beaded glass doors for a stranger like a fourteen-year-old kid whose mother was gone for the day.

"I just wanted to make sure you weren't the FBI. They're always hassling us, trying to run us in for dope. I guess they think because we're rock musicians we have some kind of orgy going on here all the time. The FBI is always phoning us up and threatening to come over and talk to us and we just say, 'Yeah, well call our lawyer first —he's Mayor Alioto's lawyer and he'll have something to say about that,' and they leave us alone. Crosby, Stills and Nash live here when they're in town, and the Grateful Dead, so there's always some kind of hassle going on with the cops. Everybody in the group has been busted for dope except Jorma Kaukonen, who plays guitar." (Jack Casady, the Airplane's bassist, had recently been picked up by the San Francisco police while sitting in a mud puddle, stoned on pot.) "And me," she added. "I guess I've been lucky. The last time the group was busted down in New Orleans I had just left the room to go wash my hair. Come in."

Inside, it was about as cheerful as the interior of an Egyptian sarcophagus. Dark mahogany walls rose twenty feet high in a room the size of a dance hall. Light filtered through stained-glass windows above a massive winding

staircase, like a Barbary Coast brothel in an old Marlene
Dietrich movie. There was no furniture except a pool
table over which hung the dangling mammoth skeleton of
a dinosaur. Through a carved rosewood doorway, we entered the living room. The walls were covered with velvet
the color of raspberry sherbet. White columns supported
raspberry ceilings inlaid with gilt-edged cupids who
grinned dopily down on huge marble walk-in fireplaces
that hadn't been used since the San Francisco earthquake.
We walked through this room quietly, which is about the
only way you can walk through a room like that, as if not
to disturb the séance that seemed certain to commence
at any moment. Beyond was another enormous room that
was also empty, except for a statue of St. Theresa with a
San Francisco police badge on her bosom. "She was
kicked out of the church or something, so we like her,"
Grace explained. "We used to eat all our meals down here
like a family, but it's hard to keep heated in the winter,
so now we just sort of go out for pizzas and stuff."

She led the way into the Jefferson Airplane's kitchen at
the back of the house, also empty except for a king-size
stainless-steel freezer with pornographic comic strips
pasted on the door and walls of cupboards full of cat food
and underground newspapers, separated in the middle by
a dirty window overlooking the backyard, where I could
see the rotting hull of a fishing boat. "Let's go up to my
room," she said. "We can talk better up there." I followed
her up the turn-of-the-century staircase, dodging model
airplanes hanging from Tiffany lamps. David Crosby (of
Crosby, Stills and Nash) came bounding down the stairs,
almost knocking over a treetop-tall antique replica of Nip-
per, the old RCA "His Master's Voice" logo, with an arrow
through its head and a sign reading "Keep the Indians on
Alcatraz." "See ya later," waved Crosby. "Later," said
Grace. "Dave's been sleeping in my bed the past week
and the place is a mess."

The second floor contains the Airplane's office and
Grace's bedroom and the third floor is devoted to all the
pads of the other members of the group, their friends and

girls. In the office, Jack Casady was talking on one of a myriad of phones while an admiring circle of teenage groupies sat on a sofa covered with an American flag sipping organic apple juice. There were rows of filing cabinets and junk shop furniture; I totaled forty psychedelic posters on the walls before I stopped counting. "You gotta see this," laughed Grace, pointing to a gallery of high-fashion photographs and magazine covers of beautiful girls in elaborate Adolfo hats and Dior gowns, beautiful girls strolling through country flower gardens, beautiful girls in bathing suits, beautiful girls in panty girdles and Supphose, beautiful girls smoking mentholated cigarettes. All looking as though they had just stepped out of *Harper's Bazaar.* "Who are they?" I asked, doubtful that they could be friends of the Airplane. She roared. "They're all *me!* That was my modeling period. Boy, was I freaked out then. That's before I found out where my head was at."

The rest of the house is a blur to me now. I remember only a sensual assault of strobe lights, burning incense, psychedelic revolving sculptures, half-naked men with long hair roaming in and out of bedrooms, a room in which the entire floor consisted of a water bed pumped full of water that shook and revolved when I sat on it until I was seasick ("We all lie on it stoned and listen to music," said Grace), ceilings hung with parachute silk, cash registers, a floor-to-ceiling poster of Trotsky with a dart in his forehead, old Christmas trees, modern canvases filled with nails, airplane propellers and tree trunks.

Grace's pad is like Norma Shearer's bedroom in *Marie Antoinette:* Tad's Steak House wallpaper, Victorian satin drapes, flowered carpets and flowered ceilings, cupids and roses and cornucopias, gilt-edged chairs with the bottoms falling out, purses made of pheasant feathers hanging on wall sconces of melting candles, musical instruments, and suitcases everywhere with clothes hanging out. We sat on boxsprings covered with red velvet and when I looked up at the ceiling over her bed I found myself staring into the horror-filled eyes of a battalion of

naked women being plunged to some unspeakable desti-
nation in a chariot drawn by rabid wolves with fangs drip-
ping blood. It's the last thing Grace Slick sees when she
goes to bed at night.

A mortician's pall cloaked the room. She was waiting for
the interview to begin; I was waiting for Banquo's ghost
to appear. The surroundings didn't faze her. She was
cheerful as a bluejay. "Why are you looking at me
strangely?" she asked, puffing on a True.

"I guess it's just that you surprise me. I was wondering
what an all-American girl-next-door is doing in a place
like this."

She made a funny face, half smile, half yecch. "Black
people say *we* meaning their black brothers and sisters. I
say *we* meaning hippies because I'm thirty years old and
I've been in this freaky clothes and long hair scene for
twelve years. I may not look like a hippie, but I do identify
with these people because the musicians, writers and
painters of today are all called hippies by a stupid society
that doesn't understand them. I'm one of the noncon-
formists, so I'm a hippie too, I guess. I never get hassled,
but those guys out there in their crew cuts and their
button-down shirts never leave the guys in the group
alone. They can't stand to see these guys with long hair
and all these beautiful chicks on their arms making more
money in ten minutes than they do in ten years. So they
call them faggots and they won't cash their checks and we
have a terrible time finding hotels to stay in. People come
up to us in airports and sniff at us and say 'What a smell!'
and it is so incredibly stupid, because we bathe every day.
But it's a life-style, not the length of the hair or the clothes,
and we have fun and I'm much happier now than I ever
was working in a department store. So I don't mind being
called a hippie because it gives me an identity with a
group of people I dig and then after we get the hippie
label, we get more attention and more people listen to our
beliefs. Right now rock musicians think the same way
about the Vietnam situation as a lot of other people, but
we're the ones the kids listen to. The whole point of the

rock revolution is to take care of business in the time we live in. Rock musicians get into the bloodstream of more young people than anyone else in this time, man, so they have more influence and power over them than even the politicians or the clergy."

I put down my list of prepared questions. Grace Slick is not into forms and formality; formal interviews are out. One does not *interview* her; one *raps*. So we rapped. "Then you think rock has generated into something more meaningful than casual entertainment with a beat for dancing? A more serious social comment on our times?"

"Well, you can't hear the lyrics anyway, so I suppose it's dance music to some people. But it's never impersonal. I mean, that's what killed opera. Opera should've been more *current* if it was to survive. It should've gotten to the people faster. As it is, those guys just told stories. Every century's got that stuff happening. People got tired of trying to *relate* to something that wasn't saying anything. Crosby, Stills and Nash are now doing a song about Kent State. It's *now*. I think of rock musicians as journalists, as musical reporters. The better the journalist the more fandangos he can pull off. The cake's always there, it's how you put the junk on it. In order for people to warm to something, it has to hit them *now*, and that's what rock does. *Scientific American* says the female fruitfly needs to hear the male fruitfly at 150 decibels to make it with him. If he sings any lower, she won't listen. That's approximately the volume we play in. That's out-front sex. You can just enjoy it for that and that's OK too. It's all groovy. Sometimes we get audiences that are uptight and don't respond. We just play for ourselves. It's like guys who come up against a chick—or another guy, or a *dog*, I don't care—and they get no sexual response and they keep working at it. Leave it alone is the Airplane's motto. I remember a town we played once called Grenell, Iowa. All these kids came, man. The girls had on 1950s dresses and corsages and the guys had crew cuts to prove their masculinity, and it brought them down to see their way threatened. They couldn't believe what they were *seeing!*

They just sat there and didn't move or applaud or *any-thing*. So two years later we went back and they were naked in the mud, totally freaked out on LSD. The whole country is changing, becoming more involved, and rock is the music that is changing them."

"Have you deliberately tried to inject social comment in the songs you write?"

"Not really. Your music has to come from your own experience. Mine was not a ghetto experience. I guess the closest I came was on the recording of *White Rabbit*. I read *Alice in Wonderland* as a child and it wasn't until later, after I had tried drugs, that I began to get into it. I like Lewis Carroll because it was obvious he was into opium."

"Lewis Carroll was into opium? Hmmm. . . ."

"Oh sure. *Alice* has never been for kids, it's for adults. But I know adults read it to their kids, so the point of the song was to warn parents Carroll was into the drug scene, so don't put your kids down because they're into it. It was snide, I suppose, but I've always had a sarcastic mouth. The girls in high school used to say, 'Grace, you're the rankest chick we know, so why don't you shut up.' I never did learn to do that."

"But what I don't understand is why the kids need drugs to dig rock. It seems to me that if you need to get stoned to appreciate something, it must be flawed in the first place."

"Well, it's like if you had the dough and the custard but no chocolate, you'd be missing part of the eclair. Drugs help the way aspirin helps get rid of a headache. Because we're still killing people we haven't figured a way to love each other, so drugs help. Pot is a very peaceful drug. The Airplane condones the judicious use of drugs, but that doesn't mean we want people to harm themselves physically or blow the tops of their heads off with LSD. It's up to the individual to decide whether he should or shouldn't. I used to take acid myself because it was a wonderful, groovy experience, but I haven't been on a trip in a long time. I can't take drugs while working. One joint puts me to sleep, then I've gotta take speed to wake up and then that's like rotting your brain out too early. I can't handle fifty things at once. The only time I get stoned now is when I'm writing music. It depends on the individual needs. I know people who don't take *anything* and they're more stoned than I am. Van Gogh, Salvador Dali, people like that. They're crazy already, so they don't need it. I tried peyote and I was amazed at the amount of concentration I could put into or get out of a leaf. I sat in a room for four hours and I got more interested in textures and fibers than ever before. But I've never seen telephone poles turn into snakes, or anything like that. What I've noticed the most is air. I could see it happen, feel bunches of wind swirling around outside, and I could walk out of them and back into them. It was really *wild!* My main advice to kids about acid is don't drive, because you won't notice when the lights change. The steering wheel starts waving and you stare at it and everybody starts honking behind you. The only time acid is really harmful is when it is preceded by fear. If you are afraid you are going to have a bad trip, you probably will."

"I guess I'm not convinced."

"That's cool. You're not into that scene. I don't put that down. The best thing about the rock-drug scene is that nobody tries to force anything on anybody. That's why Peter Townshend of The Who hit Abbie Hoffman over the head with his guitar onstage at Woodstock. It wasn't the time to try to force anybody into politics. I don't think I'm narrow-minded about music just because I sing rock. Listen, the only two records I owned for eight years were Grieg's *Peer Gynt Suite* and Irving Berlin's *Say It with Music.* On my recording of *Rejoyce* I even patterned one horn section after Gil Evans. I used to play all the arrangements he did for Miles Davis over and over. I nearly drove the Airplane crazy when *Sketches of Spain* came out. I played it about eighty times a day. Now I don't listen to much of anything. I don't own a TV set, a telephone or a record player. The group usually buys a good record as a business expense, so I know I'll get to hear it somehow.

Crosby, Stills and Nash are around the house singing everything anyway, so who needs to buy records? I like
every kind of music, except country and western. Anything is good if it's done well. I like to eat Doggie Diner
Hamburgers, too, and that's dog food. I wasn't always into
rock, you know."

True. She comes from a very straight, middle-class
background that would probably consider her music
noise. Her real name is Grace Wing. She was born in
Evanston, Illinois, in 1939, her mother was "a pop singer
—very square—sang 'Tea for Two' a lot," and her father
was an investment banker in mutual bonds. She attended
high school in Palo Alto, then spent a year at New York's
fashionable and exclusive Finch College studying costume design and merchandising, and a year at the University of Miami majoring in art. The revolt against formality
and the Establishment was beginning about that time. "I
hated all those rich debutantes at Finch," she says. "What
a weird scene. Tricia Nixon is a good example of what they
turn out. I was invited to her birthday party at the White
House. They sent out these little engraved invitations to
the alumni and accepted unbiasedly the first ones who
responded. So I called Abbie Hoffman and he slicked
down his hair and put on a blue suit. He looked like a
karate-chopping pimp. It was a gas. So we showed up at
the White House and got thrown out as 'security risks.'
Boy, were they right, because I had 600 micromilligrams
of LSD in my purse that we were going to put into the tea.
Can you hear them now? 'Wow, the President's daughter
is freaked out drawing dirty pictures on the White House
walls!' The security guards were criticized in the press.
People wrote: 'How ridiculous—not letting someone in
because she's a rock singer.' Well, it's not ridiculous, because I really would have done it. I figured the worst thing
a little acid could do to Tricia Nixon is turn her into a
merely delightful person instead of a grinning robot. But
we were aiming for the Old Dad, hoping he might come
down to the party and have a cup of tea. Far out. I figure
if they can shoot us down, we can get them high, right?"

After two years of college, Grace dropped out and returned to San Francisco "to find out where my head was
at." She had already studied classical guitar and found it
a bore, so she started hanging around the hippie folk sing-
ers in Haight-Ashbury and learned how to accompany
herself on the guitar and sing ballads like "Barbara Allen."
She hadn't yet broken entirely with the Establishment.
She married a photographer named Jerry Slick and
helped put him through school at San Francisco State
College by modeling designer clothes at I. Magnin. "I was
nowhere. My old man was very square, I hated my job. I
made extra money by growing pot in our backyard. We
had a next-door neighbor who used to hang over the fence
and say 'Hey, Gracie, how's your plants?' She used to
water them for us when we were away. She never knew
what she was watering. Haight-Ashbury was a friendly
place when I lived there. That was before it got over-
crowded and violence broke out and the hippies started
killing each other. It's dead now, a terrible scene. You
cram a lot of rats in one place and they panic and start
fighting each other."

Eventually she quit her modeling job, tried LSD,
bought a steel-string guitar and some cheap sound equipment at Sears, Roebuck and started singing with a group
called the Great Society. "I looked around and saw how
bad the competition was, so I decided what the hell." She
heard the Jefferson Airplane in some of the places she
sang and they heard her and in October, 1966, when their
lead singer left to get married, Grace joined the group.
The Airplane had made a small dent in the rock world
already, but it was the addition of the little broad with the
go-to-hell grind in her voice that put them on the map. In
less than six months after she climbed aboard, they were
making $10,000 a night and more, depending on the gig.
Their albums and singles sold in the millions and Grace
became a celebrity. She insists that although rock has
become big business, she is not in it for the money. "Everybody thinks we're rich, and I suppose some of the rock
groups are, but although they tell me the Airplane has

made millions of dollars, we are all broke. We have never
been businessmen, so none of our earnings have ever
been invested and all of our money has been tied up in
legal hassles for years. We have no idea how much money
has been stolen from us by bad managers, insensitive
managers, crooks. Each member of the band gets $250 a
week to live on and everything else we make goes back
into the group for expenses, sound equipment, lawyers.
Nobody has any money in the bank. This house is all we
own. The money from royalties and publishing and all
that is tied up in an old contract and we never get a dime
from any of it. We are always in trouble with the government over taxes. We're fighting it out in court to get some
of our money, but we've lost four times already. The only
extravagance I've noticed is cars. Paul has a Porsche and
some of the other guys have Cadillacs."

Grace owns an Aston-Martin DB-4 which she bought
with the royalty money paid to her from an old contract
with the Great Society before she joined the Airplane. "I
was walking down Van Ness Avenue, where the foreign
car agencies are, and I walked into the showroom with my
hippie clothes on and suddenly all the salesmen started
running away. I thought, 'Gee, I don't look that awful,' so
I followed them all into the back room and said, 'What's
happening, baby?' and this salesman stared at my hippie
clothes and my bare feet and sniffed, 'It's the new DB-4
just arrived' and I said, 'How much is it?' and he just
smirked like he was really into putting me down, man,
and I said, 'Like, how much *is* it, man?' again, and he said
it was $18,592 plus tax and I said, 'Far out, I'll take it.' Then
I took two ten-thousand-dollar bills out of my pocket and
paid him. I think he's still lying on the floor. It's a groovy
car, but it's been in the shop four weeks now. It takes like
two years to get a part. I don't miss it. Material things are
unimportant."

She has been married to Jerry Slick for ten years, but
they seldom see each other. "I don't think my marriage
is odd. What I think is weird is when people stay together
all the time. I'm in love with Paul Kantner, who plays

rhythm guitar with the Airplane. I love him, I live with him and I sleep with him. My husband digs it. It's cool with him. We're still married because we don't have the energy to go through all the paperwork. I can't see telling some fifty-year-old judge I want a divorce because—why? Because I don't like my old man anymore? I like him fine. He's one of my best friends. He's one of the few people I know who can be totally objective. He's very amusing. He'll nail up a newspaper headline: '4,000 FROGS IN THAILAND GO MAD!' or something wacky and when all his friends read it, he takes it down. I just outgrew him and got into something else. We'll get around to getting a divorce someday if our tax situation gets messed up any more than it already is. But I could let it slide on forever. I'm not into legal papers and documents and contracts. That's not where my head is at. I let people like my family worry about the stupid things in life."

She has said some harsh things about her family in interviews, so I asked her if she was still on friendly terms with them. "They think I'm nuts. They've lived for sixty years now assuming that a certain method of conduct will net you certain rewards—the rewards being a house, a freezer, a mortgage, an electric kitchen, the Episcopal church. Those don't happen to be *my* rewards or the needs of my generation, but you can't wake these people up to that. You can't go backwards. It's like Ronald Reagan—he probably would've been a good governor in 1930, but it's gonna take a bloodbath to wake him up now. My mom keeps scrapbooks on me, but she still can't understand why I want to bomb buildings with nobody in them. I tell her it's a reminder to stop killing people, stop being fools. I don't want to blow up anything with people inside, but after they're gone for the day, I'm all for it. It's a warning to the government and the Establishment: 'You keep killing our people, we're going to have to keep bombing your banks!' All that, of course, goes against what I was raised on. But what my parents don't understand is that all that junk I was taught has nothing to do with my life. I used to fight with them but I don't anymore. My little brother's in jail for smoking dope. He used to be their only hope—'Well, the chick is nuts, but maybe the kid'll be OK'—well, now they know they can't hassle his life either."

So what are you into now, Grace Slick, with this new freedom? Ecology? "I would've been into it fifty years ago, but it's too late now. Nobody's going to give up their cars. Space is the only thing left, and there's not much of that. That's why Haight-Ashbury's dead. One cantaloupe rind doesn't smell as bad as forty rotten cantaloupe rinds. All the hippies are moving into the mountains now."

Women's Lib? "It's pretty dumb. I mean, in the face of other things that are more important, it's flippant. It's like a lotta chicks suddenly decided, 'Hey, I don't like to cook!' and they're making a lotta noise about it. Well, there's a lotta things chicks can do that won't force them into a home. I been around a lotta guys, not one of them ever asked me to *cook!* I say, 'Hey, I don't cook, man, I do *this!*' and they say, 'Cool.' I've never had some guy come up to me and say, 'Hey, how come you can't tell me how to tear apart a car!' I don't care if they can't sew, either."

Religion? "I believe there's a lotta stuff going on out there, whether it's molecules or mud or whatever. But I don't believe in all that God junk. I've never talked to spirits, either. Never had any flashes. Man is the only animal that knows he's going to die, so we invent a Heaven to keep from going crazy. Most people are hypnotized by organized religion from childhood; only a few really have the stuff. I don't think it's Billy Graham who has the stuff, though."

I asked her if rock had taken the place of religion in the society of the young. With drugs to keep it going, wasn't it creating a new style of worship through the same hypnotic effect on the minds of the young that she had just accused organized religion of doing? "I don't want to get philosophical about rock. It's just entertainment. Thirty years ago they went to the Copacabana with their drug, which was cocktails, and they turned on for a few hours. We're doing the same thing. The one thing rock does is promote peace. The Airplane is doing the same thing Jane

Fonda is doing, only she is one person and we're an organization of thirty people. We have six in the group, plus our staff, the guys who transport and run our light show, and by the time you add all the groupies and girl friends and all, it takes a lotta money to move that much tonnage across the country. So we put all our money back into the group. If I go out and demonstrate with Abbie Hoffman or Jane Fonda, twenty-nine people sit around on their cans. So we stick together and promote peace through publicity, our interviews and our music."

"Do you think rock will survive?" I asked.

"Well, the hardest thing about surviving is the outside influences, the dumb censorship from executives, and all the Right-Wing jerks who get uptight about nudity and dirty language and all that junk. The cops and even the record companies figure we take drugs and fornicate all the time, so they watch us pretty closely. RCA Victor has hassled us a lot. One time we got this idea for an album cover where everyone would draw something at the recording session and we'd put all the drawings together for the cover. Paul was eating a cupcake, so he took the holder and traced around it with a pencil and RCA wouldn't let it go through because they said it looked like a woman's sex organs. Idiots! We're always going to the head of the RCA record division and saying, 'Show us proof that somebody is going to make trouble. Send us the letters and we'll answer them.' Adults all think it's a bunch of noise and the kids don't care anyway, so who do they think they're kidding? We had the four-letter word for defecation on *Eskimo Blue Day* and RCA had a fit. We left it in. Nobody ever complained, man. We're talking about leaving RCA to join up with Crosby, Stills and Nash and the Grateful Dead to form our own record company, the way the Beatles did when they left Capitol and formed Apple. The good thing about the Airplane, and the main reason we've outlasted most of the other rock groups, is that nobody plays God or tells anyone what to do. The boss is whoever has written the song we're doing that day. It's like a family, built on mutual trust."

Grace has had many offers to be a star at ten times the

money she's making now. She's not interested. "I don't know one entertainer I would ever watch for more than two songs. That whole Judy Garland package is a bore. Even Streisand—one or two tunes and I say, 'OK, I've heard *you*, baby!' Three hours of Sammy Davis, Jr., would be like *They Shoot Horses, Don't They?* So I wouldn't want to look at Grace Slick for three hours, either. Some joker said, 'I'll make another Edith Piaf outta you!' and I said, 'OK, great, why don't you just put a knife in my back?' "

The only thing left dangling was the future. "You can last longer in rock than you can in something like opera because so few technical demands are made of your voice. Also, the fans don't judge you as harshly. If an opera singer hits the wrong half note, she gets murdered. If they took out my vocal cords altogether, they'd probably say, 'Oh wow, far out—she's singing through her ears now!' But I've had three operations on my vocal cords already. Janis Joplin yelled her head off for years and she had no trouble. My vocal structure is weaker. I can't sing as long as I used to and my voice gives out fast. Five years ago, I could go over a song fifty times in a recording session. I can't do that anymore. I used to sound like Joan Baez, now I sound like Louis Armstrong. My voice gets lower all the time— it gets used, abused, knocked around. My days are limited. But if I blow it completely, I'll just do something else. Rock is not my life's work. I've been drawing lately and writing a lot, too. If I stop singing it won't mean a thing to me. I'll get into another scene, man."

Like what? "I'd really like to do a film. The Airplane was in a Godard movie, but I'd like to do a project of my own. I was sent a script for a movie called *Big Fauss and Little Halsey* but it stank, so I said no. Now I learn Robert Redford and Michael J. Pollard are in it. Damn! I blew it. But I still don't want to do anything that means backing up. Mary looks at John, John kisses Mary—that's bull. Too many other things to say and do. That's why nobody slow dances or writes love songs anymore, because people are getting killed, man, so who cares if John gets Mary in the end?"

I don't know who will get Grace Slick in the end, but as we rode an electric wheelchair down a back staircase, it occurred to me he might have his hands full but he'll never be bored. "I'm crazy," she was saying at the door, "but I'm at peace with myself. The way we live in this crazy house, we're all nuts, man. But it's fun. We're too lazy to hassle anybody, even each other. That's why I don't shoot heroin. I'm too lazy to get into it. Like paying taxes. I just don't bother to keep receipts. I guess I'm also a bit old-fashioned. I still drink liquor, which is probably a throwback to the Establishment. It's legal and easier to fool with than dope. Either way, I know where my head is. This is where I'm at."

There was a noise at the front door and two hippies came in looking like the gravediggers in *Hamlet.* The one with the red beard did all the talking. "Hey, Grace, we got a parade permit from the mayor's office to celebrate the Age of Aquarius. We got a ton and a half of acid and we're gonna drop it on everybody in the street and we want you to be in the parade!"

She shot me a look: "Do you believe this, man?" Then she turned back to the hippies. "Far out, but we'll be on the road then. Try the Quicksilver Messenger Service or the Pacific Gas and Electric."

Crestfallen, they shuffled past the broken toilet seat on the front porch and headed off down the street. They didn't want the Quicksilver Messenger Service or the Pacific Gas and Electric. They wanted Grace Slick.

Frankly, I don't blame them. But give her time. If I know Grace, she can start her own parades.

8

Merle Oberon

MERLE OBERON BREEZED into New York last week with a new movie, a new man and a new life. Breezed is the wrong word. It was so hot and humid the birds were falling out of the trees in Central Park with sunstroke and the glamorous Merle went to bed with a cold, sighing, "I don't know how you people live in this hot, noisy, filthy place. Nobody goes to Hell anymore. They just go to New York." She didn't get an argument.

The new movie is *Interval*, a Mexican soap opera about a widow, recovering from a nervous breakdown after running her husband down with an automobile, who falls in love with a struggling artist in the Mayan ruins of ancient Yucatan. It's pretty awful, but she said she was prepared for bad reviews. "Joe Levine spent a lot of money releasing it and he said all along the critics wouldn't like it. They seldom like anything. It's very close to me and it hurts if people don't like it, but I hope they treat it with some respect. Even when I wasn't making films I would read reviews of other people's films and my heart would fill with pain. After all, they just made a bad movie. They didn't try to murder anybody."

The reason that *Interval* is so close to her is that she produced, edited, partially financed and starred in it. You can't blame her for wanting to get some of her money back. "I haven't worked in a film since *Hotel*, six years ago. The government-owned Mexican studios had always wanted to do a film with me and I got excited about the idea of working again, but I couldn't find a script.

"One night I was having dinner with Gavin Lambert, who wrote *Inside Daisy Clover*, and we were talking about it and suddenly I said, 'Why don't you write it?' Every time I picked up the movie page I'd get cold feet because everything was sex and drugs and violence and I felt the world had passed me by, so I told Gavin the only thing I could play at my age was a spinster. So he tried it and it didn't work. I guess I just didn't look like a spinster. What eventually evolved was a part very much like me— a woman who loved nature, who regarded love as something sacred between two people, a bit old-fashioned in places, but high on life. I'm always telling the servants in my house in Mexico not to kill the snakes. 'Don't bother them and they won't bother you,' I say. That explains the scene in which the woman asks her young lover not to kill a poisonous snake. There are many personal qualities like that in the film that came out of my talks with Gavin, so the film is somewhat personal."

She eventually became producer, too, but not because it was planned that way. "I tried everyone I knew. One producer became ill, then Dolores Del Rio's husband backed out to do a film with her instead of me. Then Vincente Minnelli backed out after script disagreements with Gavin and somebody just had to take over. Five Italian businessmen put up most of the money, but I sup-

plied the rest. Then I saw the first assembly of footage and
it wasn't the film I intended to make, so I cut it myself. I'd
never been in a cutting room before. In the old days of
Hollywood, everything was done for me. I learned everything from scratch. I sat on a concrete floor for six weeks
looking at miles of film in a Movieola until my back killed
me and I had to get rubber shoes and a rubber cushion.
Then I selected the music and learned how to splice it into
the sound track, and I learned about looping and mixing
and all kinds of technical things. I would never do it again.
From now on, I just want to be hired by someone else."

The new man is Robert Wolders, a thirty-six-year-old
Dutch actor who is young enough to be her son. It's the
Forty Carats theme, carried to dazzling fruition, and
Merle never looked better. If she's had plastic surgery, as
rumored, I didn't see the scars, and in the dresses Luis
Estevez has designed for her that famous size 6 is enough
to turn Twiggy green. "He called me yesterday to see how
the premiere was going," she laughed, "and I said 'Luis,
all they ask about is my age and I'm beginning to feel like
a freak.' He said, 'You *are*.' " The reference books all say
she's sixty-two, but she says she's only fifty-six because
"when I first went to England, a shy girl from Tasmania,
you had to lie about your age or you couldn't get a job."
Regardless, she is the most beautiful creature you could
possibly hope to imagine. "I love her because she has the
wisdom of maturity and the body of a twenty-five-year-
old," says Wolders, and I'm prepared to believe it.

As the wife of Italian multimillionaire industrialist
Bruno Pagliai, Merle has long enjoyed a deserved reputation as Mexico's most captivating Jet Set hostess. An invitation to her villa in Acapulco has been referred to as the
same thing as an invitation to join the *Social Register,* and
through the years she has entertained kings and presi-
dents and Noel Coward and the Henry Fords and Prince
Philip and just about everybody else who counts. Now the
house is up for sale and Merle and Bruno are legally separated. Quo vadis? "Well, I'll tell you, quite honestly, I
never wanted that life in the first place. I moved to Mex-

ico because Bruno had lived there for thirty-five years. I
never planned to make it home. It just happened that
way. We built a house in Acapulco and called it Ghalal,
which means 'to love' in the language of the Tula Indians,
and suddenly visitors started descending on us from all
over the world. If I gave a dinner party, it always got into
the papers, but not because I wanted it that way. I never
invited photographers or newspaper people. It was always one of the guests who gave out the story. The house
wasn't even finished yet when *Look* magazine called and
asked to take pictures. I didn't know how to say no, so they
came. The next thing, *Vogue* called. I couldn't say yes to
one and no to another, so before it was over every magazine in America had publicized the house, even *Architec-
tural Digest.*

"I won't walk away from my life there with no regrets,
because I do love that house. But I was very lonely there.
It was eight thousand feet high and the climate and alti-
tude never agreed with me. I often needed an oxygen
mask to breathe. And I found myself alone, running a
glamorous boardinghouse. To some people, that would be
sufficient, but Bruno was never there and I wasn't really
happy. I never planned to fall in love. I don't believe in
extracurricular activities in a marriage. I think husbands
and wives should be together, and Bruno and I were
never together. And then I met Bob through Noel Coward and while we were making the picture, it just happened. My husband did not hear about it from gossips. I
told him myself. We are very good friends. I received a
telegram from him today wishing me happiness. I hope
we will always be friends. If you live with somebody
fifteen years, you don't stop loving the person just because
you start loving someone else, unless you're a monster.
We've been very good for each other and I think he un-
derstands my new life. It's been very civilized."

The lady has lived. The daughter of a British Army
officer who died three months before she was born, she
went to Bombay when she was six years old to stay with
her godmother, then lived with an uncle in Calcutta and

ended up in London working as a dance hostess at the
Café de Paris. Hungarian director Alexander Korda discovered her and married her in 1939, Samuel Goldwyn
brought her to Hollywood, and she starred in a series of
classics, including *Wuthering Heights, The Scarlet Pimp-
ernel, Dark Angel* and *The Lodger*. After Korda was
knighted, he deposited a quarter of a million dollars in her
bank account. She divorced him in 1942 and married
cinematographer Lucien Ballard three weeks later. That
lasted six years. Then she fell in love with Count Giorgio
Cini, a married Italian nobleman who died in a plane
crash, and told Louella Parsons, "My life is finished."

Now it's beginning all over again. She has two adopted
children, fourteen and fifteen, who will attend boarding
school in Arizona, and Merle and Bob have taken a Malibu
beach house. There's a problem with her dual British-
Mexican passport that allows her to spend only a certain
amount of time each year in America, but they'll probably
work that out. And the age difference doesn't seem to
matter. In fact, it's Bob who has trouble keeping up with
Merle. "I'm very healthy, still as vital as when I was
twenty-five. Air is as important as eating and I am militant
about getting fresh air. New York is killing me. I swim in
the Pacific Ocean every day and never feel the cold."

Joe Levine is interested in starring her as Mahatma
Gandhi's wife in Robert Bolt's screenplay of *Gandhi*, to
be directed by Richard Attenborough. A fourth marriage
is on the way. With meringue-white skin and almond-
shaped eyes, she looks and feels younger than ever. Lotte
Lenya said: "Age is just something they stamp in your
passport," and Merle Oberon proves it. "Sag will come
someday," she winks. "Everything comes if you wait
around long enough." But the smile has a challenge in it
and if I were sag I wouldn't want to mess with Merle
Oberon.

9

Kay Thompson

CONTRARY TO WHAT you might think from watching the *Six O'clock News*, there are still a few original things in this seemingly joyless world. Things there are no other things like. Some of them are: koala bears, Harold Arlen songs, country tomatoes served with fresh dill, St.-Jean-Cap-Ferrat at four in the afternoon when the sun bounces polka dots off the fishing boats, any house Gloria Vanderbilt lives in, Concord Bridge bathed in the lemon of mid-October, the smell of gingerbread baking . . . and, of course, Kay Thompson.

If you don't know who Kay Thompson is, please turn the page. You just flunked pizazz. Legend has it that she invented the word. In the 1940s she was the forty-carat referee at MGM who put the kicker in those champagne Technicolor musicals with her stylish vocal arrangements

for everybody from Frank Sinatra and Gene Kelly to Lena
Horne and Judy Garland (who later made her Liza Minnelli's godmother!). In the 1950s she sang with Audrey
Hepburn and danced with Fred Astaire in *Funny Face*,
making movie history as a dazzling fashion editor like
Coco Chanel crosspollinated with Diana Vreeland. In the
1960s she revolutionized children's books by turning out
four more sophisticated *Eloise* classics. But probably
more than all that, she is best known for her legendary
nightclub act "Jubilee Time" with the four Williams
Brothers—an act so innovational every major nightclub
star has tried unsuccessfully to copy it ever since. In classy
circles people still talk about seeing Kay Thompson's act
if they saw it, and hearing about it if they didn't. When she
opened at New York's posh Directoire in 1948, Constance
Talmadge, William Randolph Hearst and Maurice Chevalier were sitting ringside. After the screaming died down,
they turned to Chevalier and asked, "Well, Maurice, what
do you think?" "I don't know," he said, puzzled. "I've
never seen anything like her." Years later, the world still
agrees.

"Boodle-dee-bopbop-bum-swee-bop . . ."

Fingers popping, she scats into the Oak Room of the
stuffy old Plaza Hotel like a magic ray from a voodoo
moon, wearing pants. Not just any old pants. Chamois by
Halston, with a black-ribbed Italian scoop-neck sweater,
a black belt with a big silver Pilgrim buckle, no makeup,
black sunglasses on her head. She looks like a cross between Isak Dinesen and a rhythmic condor as she folds
gingerly into a leather chair like crushed chiffon. "This
isn't going to be one of those 'And then I wrote' pieces,
is it? I don't like looking back. Let's keep it crisp as let-
tuce."

Original? "Well, I've always had a sense of line. In
clothes, I started a uniform look. Because of my height
and sharpness, I didn't need ruffles, bows and bracelets. I
was the first to wear pants and simple shirts because they
were easier for my arms to move in. I've always been a
long drink of water. I think it was the tempo and move-

ment they responded to that made the act such a great success. In show biz, people always did certain things. Esther Williams swam, Fred Astaire danced, Xavier Cugat played the maracas. Suddenly along came Kay Thompson, who did all the things people had done before, but it was totally different. The act started at a birthday party for Roger Edens. I got some of the kids together— Judy, Cyd Charisse, Peter Lawford and songwriter Ralph Blane—and dressed them in costumes from *Show Boat*. Bob Alton, the MGM choreographer, said, 'I think you've got an act!' I said, 'What's an act?' The world soon found out. The ingredients were joyous purity, energy and five voices that hit them in the stomach."

Energy is the key word in Kay's computer. She has a trumpet where her heart should be, an abundance of energy that does not come from a bottle, and even if she's walking through a revolving door, she does it with fanfare and a drum roll going on inside. "Fatigue is a stranger to me. It's caused by monotony and a lack of interest in things. It has no place in a creative mind. People with nothing to do and nowhere to go bore me. Cary Grant in a hotel lobby after a long trip is like four showers and a glass of shampoo to me. Whenever I'm tired, I just think about the glorious colors of butterfly wings. It's refreshing. I mean, butterflies never get tired—or if they do, we never hear about it. Enthusiasm and imagination can carry you anywhere you want to go without Vuitton luggage."

Dramatically tall (actually five feet five and a half inches, looks more like seven feet), reed-thin (110 pounds of unharnessed hydroelectric power) and limber as a Haitian dancer, Kay has her own solar system to feed her peculiar sunburst of energy. "I go along with a low-sugar diet, which means nibbling a lot of times during the day. In the A.M., an egg and a piece of orange. Two hours later, two ounces of Gorgonzola cheese and some cold roast beef with maybe a chunk of grapefruit. Two hours after that, a small portion of beautiful fish with watercress and lemon. Everything in tiny portions. I never eat much after 9 P.M. Maybe a peach before bed. Nothing heavy before sleep, unless you want to dream about dock strikes. An occasional B12 shot if I feel tired, which isn't often."

Kay isn't big on cosmetics. "I use a moisturizer from Orentreich's, a pale light powder from Kenneth, Chinese lily pink lipstick, and Ivory Soap." And in spite of her reputation as a fashionaut, she says she only owns seven dresses and fifty pairs of shoes. Crazy for shoes. "I only wear three designers when I do dress—Norell for sweetness and elegance; Giorgio de Sant'Angelo for marvelous, wild fun, turkey feathers and shells; and Halston for glorious fabrics and uniform-like casualness. No ball gowns. Just give me a prison shirt and prison pants, a four-yard long scarf tied around my head, and I'm ready to go."

Her unwillingness to be saddled by conventional formulas, her ocean-spray zest for living on the wind, and the aura of Garbo mystery that surrounds her (nobody knows how old she is, or how many times she's been in love) have made her a welcome face in every port. "My life has been *sic transit*, and now I'm sick of transit. No point in saving memorabilia—somebody always steals it. I own an orange tree here, a rattan chair there, and the rest is in storage in Rome."

To Kay, "home" is Rome and New York. In Rome, it's the top floor of an elegant house owned by the daughter of the Infanta in the Villa Torlonia, an aerie containing leopard rugs, Baccarat crystal and a piano with the legs cut off so you have to sit on the floor to play it. In New York, it's an autumnal suite at the Plaza where people often call and ask, "Is Eloise in?" and the operators all know to put the calls right through to Kay. Some people say she lives at the Plaza rent-free, but even the Plaza won't tell. "She's as much a part of the hotel as the palm trees," says a PR lady there. "She moved in two years ago to do some publicity for the *Eloise* books and we've just never asked her when she plans to leave."

People give her go-power. Noel Coward kept a spare piano in his Swiss chalet in Montreux for her to compose songs on. In Rome, it's photographers and art gallery owners. In London, it's Stanley Donen and John Gielgud. In Paris, it's lunch at Maxim's with Roger Vivier, who makes shoes. "I'm stimulated by whoever is around—queens, dukes, dishwashers. If the tailor is attractive, it's him for a week." She prefers hanging around in furniture refinishing joints with the smell of banana oil to New York parties, and says her greatest ambition is "to sit at Picasso's feet and clean his brushes with turpentine."

She's passionate about privacy, pedicures, Portofino, and Porthault linen; detests heat, Caribbean islands, suntans, flies, mosquitoes and wasps (living or dead), fads, phonies, drunks, loudmouths and Miami Beach. Loves: whales, pug dogs, films, fashions, fettucine, feathers, furs and fuss. Hates: plastic hair curlers, air conditioning, laundromats, people who have heavy furniture, smelly trains, broken sidewalks, hibiscus trees and plays by Edward Albee and Neil Simon ("Both overrated and nobody can tell you why").

Twice married to men she doesn't talk about, she's been single since 1947. "I love love and I believe in divorce. Two great things. I've lived with quite a few men and alone is better. That doesn't mean I'm a loner; I just don't like to ask permission." Psychiatry: "All for it. Got a problem? Talk to somebody and get it fixed. We are what we think. I've never been to a shrink myself, but I've dated a few." Female friends? Her face becomes a dried apricot. "I'm not much of a gossip. I don't like to get angry. It's unhealthy. I refuse to waste energy on anything that will pass tomorrow."

Ditto the future. What happens next depends on mood, temperament, laughter in the tarot cards and the best invitation. "Reality has left the building. Nothing is simple. The streets are the stage and we've got a whole new set of actors. My philosophy about work is the dream never passes, only the place you act it out in. I'm not sentimental about the good old days, but I see no genius coming out of show business now, either. There are good people, but there are too many of them and they're all alike. Elvis was unique, so why copy him with imitators?

Nothing Mick Jagger does is new. It's all copied from blacks. Bob Dylan is Leadbelly. The law of progress always carried me on to the next plateau and the current pop stars will go on to new plateaus, too. Let's all go out and be ourselves. Theaters are being sold, the record business is being choked by its own lack of imagination, and in about ten minutes rock and roll will be finished. Everyone's looking for something different. What next? Somebody who looks like Louis XIV in sweet little heels? I think it's going to be something elegant. Maybe the clavichord will come back. Originality will return, but it might take a revolution to do it."

Meanwhile, Kay Thompson is turning out her fifth *Eloise* book, *Eloise's Wit and Observations,* due soon, and designing and merchandising Eloise rag dolls, wigs, clothes, luggage and toys. Next, she might do a TV special. Or she might just stay home, like Eloise, and pour Perrier water down the Plaza mail chute. Whatever she does, she'll do it with pizazz.

"Boodle-dee-bopbop-bum-swee-bop . . ."

And suddenly she's gone, doing a time step to the unwritten melody in her head as she wafts through the door to get on with her life.

10

GONE WITH THE WIND
Hits the Stage

HAD TO SEE it to believe it. Darkness fell over the narrow stone street crammed with a traffic jam of Rolls-Royces, American Cadillacs, taxis and vegetable trucks in front of Covent Garden. Fruit peddlars and flower vendors in shirt-sleeves sipped ale in front of the pubs, people pointed from upper windows, and crowds milled aimlessly in front of the old Drury Lane, where a mighty cannon pointed toward the sky, cockney actors sang "Dixie" in Confederate war uniforms and British debutantes in hoop skirts greeted the arriving celebrities and critics by passing out Confederate flags while a Dixieland band played "Old Black Joe." It was the opening night of *Gone With the Wind*, and the single biggest night in London since the end of the blitz.

You also had to see *Gone With the Wind* to believe it.

Certainly I can remember nothing in my theatergoing history I consider a bigger disaster. Champagne flowed freely in all the bars, flashbulbs popped and Noel Coward said it was a return to the fabulous old days of the Drury Lane, when Ivor Novello sank a ship onstage. *Gone With the Wind* sank, too, like the *Hindenburg*.

The London critics, who are less demanding in their musical tastes than Americans who have seen everything, hailed the visual aspects of Joe Layton's production. Let me tell you about that. The curtain rises on the barbecue at Tara. You know it is Tara because there are two white shutters at the corner of the stage that suggest a plantation stands somewhere in the wings. But what you actually see is a mass of swamp moss made of hanging ropes and what looks like shreds of green toilet paper, under which dancers stumble through some poor man's Agnes De Mille choreography on a lawn of Woolworth grass, beyond which stands a covered bridge used for each character to make an entrance ("There's Ashley Wilkes." "Who's that?" "His name is Rhett Butler," etc.). Scarlett O'Hara must not only sing while being strapped into her corset, but is also forced to raise the curtain as well. There is never enough time in the show's three and a half hours for her to change, so she is always being dressed onstage, a trick that makes it impossible to concentrate on the songs she sings.

The biggest problem, of course, was how to get the passion and scope of Margaret Mitchell's book onstage, to capture the sweep and energy of the Civil War and to include all the plots and subplots of a famous movie everybody in the world has seen, without making the audience wish they were at the movies instead. It was a problem of condensing, and it was solved. General Lee declares war in the middle of Mr. O'Hara's song about how he built Tara. The whole war is symbolized in a tableau played against a backdrop of an enormous Confederate flag as a line of silhouetted soldiers falls each time a bugle plays. If you could see the fragile cockney chorus boys who play the Confederate soldiers, you'd stop wondering why the South lost the war.

There isn't a genuine southern accent onstage. For some unexplainable reason, Melanie trims her Christmas tree at the Atlanta train station while a locomotive puffs onstage blowing real smoke into the coughing, wheezing audience (then backs offstage backward). All the dying and wounded soldiers rise up from their stretchers and sing "We're Just Passing Through" in one of the show's more hilarious accidental moments. As Prissy runs away to fetch a doctor for Melanie's baby, Belle Watling's whores do a dance number and sing "This is the time, boys, your time for love" while Melanie writhes with labor pains. "Kiss me farewell like you mean it, I'm off to war now," sings Rhett Butler as Atlanta goes up in flames. The biggest show-stopping moment on opening night occurred as Scarlett tried to drag a horse with stage fright across the swamps back to Tara in the wake of war. "I will go!" she kept shouting, but only the horse did. The audience screamed with laughter and applause as the poor nag filled the stage with fresh manure. Then the mad soldier who tried to attack Scarlett from behind a tree fell dead from her gunfire under the curtain line. "I'll never go hungry again," wept the brave actress who played Scarlett (mostly from embarrassment) as the corpse, seeing the first-act curtain falling, rolled over to keep from being killed. Naturally, he rolled right into the horse's major contribution to the evening amidst a holocaust of hysteria and chaos among the stagehands.

That was only the first act. This is a *Gone With the Wind* that never seems to end. After Atlanta burns, everything else is anticlimactic, but it was already 11 P.M. and there were a lot of people left to kill off, so everything moves pretty fast in the second act. Scarlett's second marriage to a sawmill owner, her husband's murder, her marriage to Rhett, the birth of Bonnie, are all quickly disposed of. To suggest a passing of time, two Bonnies of different ages hide under Scarlett's hoopskirt and appear when needed in the middle of the same scene. In a big production number called "Bonnie's Here," what one redheaded Lilliputian is required to do is nauseating. Looking like Shirley Temple playing Aunt Pitty Pat, this poor midget clowns, lisps, belts and kicks its way through a dreadful spectacle of unbridled confusion until you want to call in the representatives of England's child-labor laws to tranquilize it and put it to bed. Happily, she dies quickly and in a tableau called "Bonnie Dies," Melanie sings "Peter's halo's kinda dusty, David's harp is kinda rusty." Before you can say "cornpone," Melanie grasps her heart in a deathly seizure and expires, too. Scarlett is left alone, back on the Woolworth grass at Tara, lamenting, "Tomorrow Is Another Day." I was, to put it briefly, underwhelmed.

Joe Layton manages miraculously to get all the cannons, muskets, swords, flags, flames, firecrackers, horses, trains and waltzing crinolines across the stage without everyone stepping on each other. Horton Foote's libretto has a southern feeling about it, although it seems spoken in comic-strip bubbles without much time for revelation, Harold Rome's score is, to be charitable, quite modest. Harve Presnell, the Hollywood actor who plays Rhett, is a good singer, but his acting is so flat and wooden one London critic said during the burning of Atlanta he expected Rhett Butler to go up in flames, too. The only real performance in the show is given by June Ritchie as Scarlett. She's only a fair singer, but her portrait of a vain and cunning bitch is tempestuous and triumphant.

Her acting comprises many elements of contrasting excitement, from cold fortitude to sensual gaiety to unquenchable survival power. Scarlett is one of the most demanding roles ever written for a woman and, even in this truncated form, it shines and keeps the audience from falling asleep. Miss Ritchie does an admirable and intelligent impersonation of Vivien Leigh.

They're talking about bringing *Gone With the Wind* to Broadway. They must be kidding. Even if they rewrite it, recast it, restage it, rescore it and stop feeding the horse before he goes onstage, they'll still be bringing in a wake.

Bette Midler

SHE'S FIVE FEET ONE INCH HIGH, downright homely, absolutely dizzy and rarer than a home-made honeybun. She's crazy Bette Midler (one syllable, just plain "Bet") and she's got a star-bent tiger by the tail and can't let go. You've seen her on all the talk shows, and you're going to be hearing a lot more. Show-biz crystal-ball gazers say she's going to be the biggest thing since Streisand. Up from the stygian depths of New York's steamy, seamy night-spas Bette is emerging like a nymphet Lorelei, singing and tempting her eclectic audiences right onto the comfortable-rare rocks of laughter and sentimentality. No matter where this deliciously insane creature performs, she leaves her fans standing and screaming for more of her special, zany brand of entertainment. Where Bette has performed is even more unusual than where she was born, which was Honolulu.

Honolulu? "Yeah, I know, me and Don Ho," shrugs this *zaftig* waif. "I left my family in Hawaii, came to New York and started singing. I got the role of Tzeitel in *Fiddler on the Roof*, but after that nothing much happened. Until this nut, Stephen Ostrow, came along and asked: 'Honey, I just hired the chic Richard Orbach to redecorate the Continental Health Club, and I'm thinking of putting in entertainment. How would you like to sing in the baths?' Do you believe him? The baths! As in Turkish! As in boys! Sure, I said, what've I got to lose? It's better than being a go-go girl in a Broadway bar, which is what I was doing at the time. So here I am, but I swear it's my last time here in 'the tubs.' It's time I started singing for audiences with clothes on."

Bette Midler is always threatening to leave "the tubs," which is how she refers to the baths. This little Jewish Jeanette Macdonald has made more farewell appearances at the Continental Baths than the famous Wagnerian soprano Kirsten Flagstad ever made at the old Metropolitan Opera House. Her fans won't let her go. "Actually, playing to this . . . do I dare call this place a house? . . . has been the best experience in the world. I mean, you have to be good to keep the guys fascinated. Gawd! The moment I bore them, well, they could go upstairs and . . . uh . . . shower?"

Bette giggles and grimaces and lights a cigarette all at the same time, like another famous Bette. "But they are loyal. Loy-u-yul! I played more glamorous places than a steam bath. I had a two-week booking at the Downstairs at the Upstairs, and the guy who owned the joint was in love with me. What he really loved was my fans. They came in droves and practically stood on the tables cheering. My two-week gig turned into ten weeks. Listen, you think the baths are the pits?" (This is Midler jargon for "the worst.") "Next week I'm playing Raleigh, North Carolina, in a place called the Frog and the Nightgown. Who do you think lives in *there?*

"I did seven Johnny Carsons and I'm going to Las Vegas on the same bill with him in April. I can't wait. Imagine

Miss M in Vegas? I think it's the Sahara, I'm not certain. I'm also cutting my first album with Atlantic Records, but it won't be out in time for my concert at Carnegie Hall. That's on April nineteenth. Another first. The first time anyone has ever played the revered Halls of Carnegie without having made it big on records. From the steam baths straight to Carnegie Hall. Can you dig it?

"My family can't take this scene. They are freaked by all of it. I think they wanted me to become a social worker or something. They came from Paterson, New Jersey, originally. My mother still talks about High Street. We were the cleaning establishment Midlers. My mother's biggest claim to fame is that she learned English in high school from Allen Ginsberg's father. I was an ugly, fat, little Jewish girl who had problems. I was miserable. I kept trying to be like everyone else, but on me nothing worked. One day I just decided to be myself. So I became this freak who sings in the tubs. Now, I dunno, it's a whole other world. Gawd, I don't know how long I've been here. It seems like forever, but I know it can't be, 'cause I'm still so young. Ver-r-y *young*, have you got that? Tonight is my last night, really. I mean it. No, it's the lousy sound that makes my voice bounce off the tile walls. It's just—well, I'm on my way, and like Thomas Wolfe, I feel you can't go home again. Lissen, you better get outta here. I've gotta dress for my final 'farewell performance,' and besides, my rear can't take this seat any longer."

Startled from the spell her rattle-tattle New York jargon has cast on me, I jump to my feet and realize that this entire conversation has taken place with Crazy Bette Midler sitting on the john. The only empty seat in the house.

In a city where nightclubs are shutting down faster than a row of stand-up dominos can tumble, there are 3,000 people waiting to get into the Continental Baths to see the freaky Miss M. Inside, the huge lower floor features a dance floor, snack bar, no booze, living room, swimming pool and a tiny stage. The crowd resembles a Baggie filled with water—contained but giddy and intractable in its enthusiasm to fill every inch of available space. Everyone is friendly, chatty and terribly helpful finding rooms for coats, elbows, yoga-bent knees and their "rears," to quote Bette. Most of the audience is on the floor and half of it is dressed only in towels. The only reason anyone is dressed at all is that when Bette sings, ladies are invited. There are even celebrities in the crowd, for word is out that she's the best show in town. Men wander in from the steam rooms upstairs and rub wet elbows with chorus girls, Andy Warhol superstars and reporters from *Women's Wear Daily* who are doing a two-page photo layout on Miss M. It's a circus, with all the acts in the sideshow.

The lights lower. Silence settles. In the dark, off to the side, a door slowly, insidiously opens. A lovable Zasu Pitts appears, and the crowd goes wild. A tight-fitting Garbo cloche is pulled down over her brow, pinching her eyes into glittering green venetian blinds from which stars are shooting like emeralds. She shuffles over the rolling half-nude bodies uttering long moans that sound like bovine pleas for peace: "Oooooohhh, ohohohoh." She sags into her mike, a vision of scrambled caricatures of past comediennes. Cass Daley, Charlotte Greenwood, Zasu Pitts, Martha Raye, Fanny Brice, Kaye Ballard—she resembles them all. With perfect timing, she accepts the bravos thrown from the crowd and begins her theme song, "You Gotta Have Friends." The applause echos like thunder off the walls. She does have friends. Now a new vision of personalities tumbles to mind: Streisand, Laura Nyro, Joe Cocker, Bessie Smith. (Yes, even Joe Cocker, because she is spastic, often seizure-ridden, while singing.) Bette is that talented. And outrageous.

"Oh! Oh! You're all mad. M-aaa-d, I say. Gawd, it's steamier than usual tonight. Wait 'til Marlo Thomas and her sister Terry play this room. Way-i-it." She has shed her chubby fur and pulled off the Garbo hat. Her hair is red as a pomegranate, parted down the middle, a swirling mass of frizzed boop-a-doop curls surrounding her grotesquely beautiful-ugly face. Her lantern jaw glides into a smile with the ease of a bulldozer pushing sand. When she smiles, the crowd smiles. You can't help yourself. She wears humility and vulnerability as nattily as she wears her funky Forties clothes. Shedding her puff-sleeved, shoulder-padded, pink-and-cherry-printed satin jacket, she wipes her damp forehead. She is a ganglia of nerve ends which can't stop twitching, clenching, jerking, moving. Always moving. She is deep into a number. The trashy old bubble-gum hit of the late Fifties, "Do You Wanna Dance?" But Miss M sings it in a soft, sexy, bossa nova style, throwing out knowing smiles to the men in towels over milky-white shoulders. Her black-velvet shirt is slit to her waist. Hubba-hubba! Her bosom is formidable —two lovely melons slung bralessly into a swath of tie-dyed chiffon with a life of their own.

She moves fiercely on tiny feet strapped into the highest platform wedgies since Carmen Miranda. Then she disappears for a second and returns to lay the audience low with a Carmen Miranda impression on the naughty old song "Marijuana." Finishing, she sheds her tutti-frutti hat and suddenly she's the Andrews Sisters reviving "Boogie Woogie Bugle Boy." Her energy and talent is so expansive, she turns into all three—Patti, Maxine and Laverne—all at once. Then, back into the blues with a new Joni Mitchell song. Many facets, all dazzling. The crowd goes wild. A man in a towel almost falls down on Helen Gurley Brown, who has been digging from the sidelines. Some of the men in the crowd look like those *Cosmopolitan* girls. Nobody cares.

"Remember the bouffant BMT subway hairdo of the Fifties?" asks their funny star. "Remember AM radio? Oh, my dears, AM. That's where it was all at. You didn't have to think, just listen. What fabulous trash. Remember girl groups? The Shirelles, Gladys Knight and the Pips? Okay. I'll be the leader, and you be the Dixie Cups." Boys in towels and bathing suits, women in mink coats, their rattled husbands, everybody joins in singing. Liberated Dixie Cups, supporting Miss M as the Queen Popsicle.

She sits on a stool looking down at the grinning, adoring mess of people at her feet. They sing along with her, rocking to and fro. "We're going to the cha-a-pel. Gonna get ma-a-a-ried. Going to the chapel, honey . . ." Magic is in the air. Magic that removes the violence of the cold, dark streets. The insecurities, the hates, the fears, the prejudices outside vanish in a haze of camp. It's Mary Martin asking if we believe in fairies. Yes. We do. Clap harder. And the Jewish Tinker Bell is right there in front of you. Twinkling, glittering, making soft musical chimes of peace. One boy gets so carried away his towel falls off and he stands there, unshattered in his nudity. The crowd does not faint. They join in the friendly laughter.

That's what Bette Midler does to her audience. The boy clutches his towel and says: "With Bette Midler, the world can overcome anything. Anything." Today, the tubs. To-morrow, the world.

12

Carrie Snodgress

WHO IN THE HELL IS Carrie Snodgress?
I'm sure I don't know, but I like what I see:
a jumping grouse of a girl, eyes like clear
gumdrops, staring giddily from behind plum-tinted
granny glasses, high-hurdling her way through a bland
little suite at the Drake with *Diary of a Mad Housewife*
posters Scotch-taped over the picture frames, hypoed
with enough vitamin C to get the first man on Venus
without a spaceship. She is about ten times prettier than
she looks in photographs or on the screen in *Housewife*.
Her hair is soft as corn silk, not that long, stringy straw
mattress stuffing that stares out from the pages of *Vogue*
on girls who look spray-lacquered for the day, but
ginger-peachy spry and bouncing up just above the shoulders of her gingham shirt. She has a precocious pink

mouth that always seems to be on the verge of saying
"Ooohh" and when she moves she floods the room with
midwestern sunshine that seems about as out of place on
East-Fifty-sixth Street as peonies in December. And the
voice, the voice. It's the kind of nutmeg-and-vinegar voice
most actresses spend years drinking good scotch to culti-
vate. Half 'Margaret Sullavan, half Sally Bowles after a
prairie oyster.

She doesn't have the vaguest idea how to give an interview (a refreshing innovation right there), but watching
her breathlessly leaping around the room with her bare
feet sticking out from under her blue-denim midi, going
through those halcyon hurdles called "the star treatment," with too many phones ringing and too many press
agents popping in every five minutes and too many ap-
pointments, it doesn't matter that she's a virgin at interviews. She is so dazzling I can't remember what I've come
to ask her anyway. "Oh man, this is just all too incredibly
un *real*," she croaks in that basso bravura voice Elizabeth
Ashley used to use in *her* interviews when *she* was still
new at the game. "I've got a chauffeur and a car and I've
been up since five this morning. I did the *Today* show and
then I met the people from *Look* magazine because they
wanted to see if I was interesting enough to write about,
then after they spend the whole day with you they come
back some other time for the interview itself—I mean, it's
like you've gotta pass this test or something—and then I
did a radio interview and David Frost and the Chicago
Tribune and some lady is coming in a few hours to do a
cooking column and I've got to find a recipe. And all
because of this movie, *Diary of a Mad Housewife!* ! They
don't know you're alive and then suddenly everybody's
saying 'Brilliant, terrific, the new Bette Davis, bla-bla-bla!'
and I was freaking out under all those trips and suddenly
my brother said 'Hey, leave some room for failure, too.'
Not that my ego is in that much jeopardy, but it's the only
way I can survive all this Drake Hotel and chauffeured
limousines and press agents and being dealt with like
some kind of super human being. The responsibility of all

that is frightening. You get scared that you can't fail or they'd take all this away . . . you just have to say 'Hey, man, I never wanted any of this in the first place' and just enjoy it for what it is and nothing more. This is the kind of unreal excitement that exists only in New York. The freakiness doesn't happen in California, where I live. This is some town, man. I mean, people are really vicious. I went to some fancy restaurant last night and this waiter started in on me, 'So how does it feel to be a star overnight and earning all that money?' I learned he was an actor. It's this incredible jealousy. I mean, what money? I was a Universal contract player when I got *Diary* and I made $500 a week all the way through the picture. Big deal. And now you'd think 'Oh wow, scripts flying in through the windows!' Well I've got nothing, man, no movies coming up. The only two things I've been offered have both been movies about girls shooting heroin up the arm. I asked this one director 'Is this a love story, or a story about heroin addicts?' and he said 'It's a love story about heroin addicts!' Can you dig it? When those people do *that*, they don't feel like making love. I just didn't believe it so I turned it down. Who would believe me, the way I look, as a dope fiend?

"I don't want to follow *Diary* with just *anything* because it was a pretty good movie, you know? But I'd like to make another version of the same movie from the husband's point of view and call it *Diary of a Mad Housewife's Husband.* I loved playing Tina, although she was nothing at all like me, but let's face it, she's not the greatest treat around. People keep saying the Richard Benjamin character was a drag and why would a girl with Tina's education and intelligence stick around so long with someone who kept asking for damson plum preserves on his English muffins. Well, it's a movie about two people trapped in the dilemma of letting too much time go by before they realize it's not working anymore. They are in this rut and they don't know how to walk out. We've all had relationships like that. You should see my father when *he's* sick! Of course I don't know if I could survive

a marriage like that in New York, with all the other things
you have to put up with here. After I tested for Frank
Perry, he and Eleanor said 'We're going to help you with
your homework' so I went out every Friday and Saturday
night with them to these incredible New York parties and
every few minutes I'd hear something or see something
right out of the script and I'd go running over to them and
say 'Hey, remember that scene where so-and-so said
... well, it just *happened!*' and they'd say 'Yeah, you forget
we wrote it because we've been through it' and I am here
to tell you there isn't one phony scene in that movie. And
now people are all asking the most incredible things, like
this one girl came to interview me and kept asking 'What
are the Perrys really like?' and I said 'They're super people' and she said 'But they're really very *bitchy*, aren't
they?' I mean, everyone is so jealous of everyone else in
New York they spend all their time learning how to be
put-down artists. People hate success in this town. Another girl came to interview me and spent the whole time
trying to pump me about some old boyfriend of mine she's
been dating. She didn't take one note. People are crazy
here."

Since she admits she has never been part of the New
York social jungle, I asked about the hardest adjustment
she had to make in getting the part of Tina down straight.
"The nude scenes," she said instantly and casually, as
though she had just said "Ginger snaps." "When I went to
Hollywood I said 'Well, that's one thing I'll never be asked
to do' because I really have nothing to show. I was determined never to take my clothes off. Well, there I am in the
first scene and I'm all there, folks. I guess the shower
scene was the worst, though. We were supposed to be
wet, so this prop man with a spray machine sprayed us
and there we were, Frank Langella and me, stark naked,
standing in this dry shower like fools and there was no
reality to relate to. We weren't wet and we hadn't taken
a shower together and we weren't sleeping together and
I hardly even *knew* him. It was really weird. Finally, I
turned to him and said 'Look, man, we've got to do it, let's

just *do* it' and we did the scene. I guess it was all worth
it, because the film is a big hit. But anytime my head gets
too big I can just look back at my first film, *Rabbit, Run,*
which has never been released. If we're all lucky, it never
will be. That was a good example of the other side of the
business, where everything turns out rotten. Jack Smight
was the director, but after we were into the film the old
regime had left Warner Brothers and the new rent-a-car
regime was in power, so they let the man who wrote the
screenplay, who was in real estate until a year ago, cut the
film himself because he had friends in high places. Now
I've been practically cut out of it and Jack Smight is suing
to get his name off the picture and it's a big mess. So it
hasn't all been perfect, man."

Still, her batting average isn't bad for a twenty-four-
year-old rookie fresh out of Park Ridge, Illinois, who has
been a professional actress less than the amount of time
it takes some people to find a two-and-a-half-room apartment. "My mother was an actress. She was in a production
of *Little Women* in Chicago, but I can't remember what
part she played. We can ask her. She's in the next room.
I didn't know that until recently. She never told me. My
father leases cars. Neither one of them tried to lay a whole
trip on my head about being an actress. They let me work
through my whole thing myself. I have three brothers and
that gave me a lot of physical energy, which I still have,
just keeping up with them. When I got into high school,
they were like heroes and I got into acting because I had
to compete with their popularity in some way. My entire
motivation throughout school was how to get into the
school paper and the only way I knew how was to act in
something, then maybe they'd do an article on me. So in
my senior year I was cast as Puck in *Midsummer Night's
Dream* and everyone was superimpressed, except that
three days into rehearsal I fell off a platform and broke my
leg and never got to do the play.

"My drama teacher liked me enough to suggest that I
become an acting teacher, so I went to Northern Illinois
University but I liked the idea of acting more than teach-

ing it, so after a year I left and enrolled at the Goodman
School of Drama in Chicago and that's where it all
started." In 1967 she won the Sarah Siddons Award playing Doreen in *Tartuffe*. Shortly before she got her degree
the following year, an associate of Alan Pakula's saw her
in *Caesar and Cleopatra* and gave her a script of *The
Sterile Cuckoo* to read. "I never gave any fantasy thoughts
to movies or even Broadway. At that point, my ultimate
goal was to find some way to get into the Tyrone Guthrie
Theater in Minneapolis. But Alan Pakula flew to Chicago
to see me, and asked me to come to California to do a
screen test. I didn't believe any of these people, mind you,
but during the two-week semester break I got some
money from my dad and just went out there on a lark and
called Alan Pakula. I had never heard anything else from
him, but I called him anyway and said 'Hi! I'm here!' and
he said 'Oh, I was just writing you a letter' and I said
'Yeah, sure.' He never tested me, but I did meet an agent
at a party who was so fascinated with my name that he
flew to Chicago and talked my folks into letting me sign
a contract. I kept saying 'But I've got to audition for the
Tyrone Guthrie,' but I went out there to give it a try on
June 1, 1968, and for eleven days nothing happened. Then
on June 11 I was offered the lead in a series at CBS and
three weeks later I tested for another one and in September I got my first lead in a *Judd for the Defense* and I had
never even seen a camera in my life. There I was on this
incredible set and my mother was Margaret Leighton, my
brother was Brian Bedford and my sister was Penny
Fuller. I nearly fainted. I thought 'What am I *doing* in this
town?' Like a big Know Nothing, I walked into my first
scene and with all my college training started hollering
my lines so loud I nearly knocked the boom man off his
stool. I had a big brown glop of a wig on my head and I
didn't know how to hit marks or talk into a mike—I just
didn't know what the hell I was doing. But people really
talk in that town and mostly they were talking about my
name being so crazy. They might forget my face, but they
couldn't believe the name, man, so I got this offer for a

Universal contract and everybody started warning me
they'd give me crummy parts and make me do dumb TV
series and pay me nothing and then sell me down the
river. Everybody said don't, but I signed it. Five hundred
dollars a week! More money than I ever dreamed of! So
I said great, terrific, and the day after I signed the contract
I had my second job. Now I'm up to $750 a week."

You can't live much like a star on that, but she is wise
enough not to even try. She rents a two-bedroom house
on three-quarters of an acre of land for $300 a month in
a very un-chic section of North Hollywood where she lives
with an English springer spaniel she calls Timer (named
after a song by Laura Nyro). "I'm not interested in
material things or having babies to prove my womanhood
or living up to any kind of image. I want this business—
I want to be part of it—but I just won't pay anybody's
price, that's all. When I came to New York, they warned
me 'Don't talk about politics, don't talk about James Earl
Jones' . . . I used to go with him, but that was over five
months ago and they're still uptight about it. They don't
want me to criticize these creeps in the White House or
support Jane Fonda or anything. Well, if being in this
business depends on playing games, I'll get out of it. My
folks and my twenty-eight-year-old brother Mel are here
with me and I think it's freaking Universal out. My
brother is a sort of hippie who lives in Spain, but he paid
his dues. He made electric Sunbeam mixmasters for five
years before that. Now he's doing his own thing. He
brought me my room key into the dining room of the
Drake last night in his tie-dyed shirt and jeans and they
threw him out. I think Universal will be glad to get rid of
me."

Another Universal press agent entered the suite and
announced the lady with the food column was downstairs
in the bar waiting for *her* interview. "I'll give her my
recipe for red snapper—oh no, I can't remember it and I
can't cook it anyway. What am I going to do?" In his hurry
to leave, the press agent walked into a closet.

"We still have time to meet my folks before he gets

back." She led the way out of the suite and down the corridor to a single room and knocked on the door. Mrs. Snodgress, who has an even huskier voice than her daughter, opened the door in a leopard bathrobe and smiled warmly. Mr. Snodgress shook hands. Just home folks. "Mom, I've got this lady coming up who wants a recipe —what can I tell her?"

"Tell her I cook everything with scotch, gin and whiskey. Oh and by the way, since we're going to dinner tonight with that magazine editor, I bought a copy of his magazine and read an article in it so I'd have something to contribute to the conversation."

The lady with the food column was coming down the hall with her tape recorder. "C'mon, Mom, think of something *quick*. I gotta have a recipe for that lady! Oh my *Godddd* . . ."

The last thing I saw she had one hand on her head, rubbing her bangs, and the other hand across her stomach as she bent over like a pliable willow in a corridor of the Drake. The original kandy-kolored, tangerine-flake, streamlined baby, making it on one hand, fighting it on the other, and determined not to disappoint anyone in between.

Miss Snodgress, with the impossible name, you'll do just fine.

Sylvia Miles

A NEW PHENOMENON has arrived. It stands 5 feet 5½ inches in stocking feet, measures in at 38–24–35 ("I'm narrow in back, but big in the front where it counts"), weighs 121 pounds ("Be sure to give the right weight, because everybody thinks I weigh the same thing as Shelley Winters and I lost thirty pounds on the Stillman diet"), and goes by the name of Sylvia Miles. Sylvia and Shelley used to be girl friends. "I like her," says Sylvia in a husky voice so low it would make a dulcimer jealous. She's not smiling. Says Shelley: "When she lost the Academy Award for *Midnight Cowboy* I sent her a miniature Oscar for her charm bracelet. I don't think she liked it." Says Sylvia: "People think I was mad when I didn't win, but they're wrong. It's not that I minded losing, but losing to Goldie Hawn? That was the insult." She's not smiling.

Now it is no easy job being a phenomenon. These are
hard times for actresses. It's not enough just to work. You
have to go out and sell yourself like the grocer sells
tomatoes. And Sylvia Miles, while all too willing to sell
herself, is at the same time determined not to end up just
another tomato.

So, at some point in her cluttered life, she must have sat
herself down on one of the zebra rugs in her one-room
apartment nineteen floors above Central Park she calls a
"wardrobe trunk with a view," and held the biggest de-
bate since the Devil talked to Daniel Webster. With the
kind of courage equaled only by Jan Sterling taking off her
makeup in *The High and the Mighty,* Sylvia faced her
drawbacks—a New York accent, a bad peroxide job that
had ruined her hair, three husbands and three analysts
behind her, a future that looked bleakly like it would be
relegated to a series of bit parts filed away in a drawer
marked "Whores with hearts of gold, waitresses, tough
broads, etc." A number of actresses I won't name because
I don't want my face slapped in Sardi's might have looked
into the same mirror, opened Sylvia's nineteenth-floor
window and jumped. Not Sylvia Miles. Survival is her
middle name. She said to herself: "I'd rather be a woman
with a future than a dame with a past."

Then with her other hand, she counted up her assets—
guts, energy, a fierce determination to become a star, an
abundant sense of humor and one other thing not many
ladies in her predicament could claim called talent. She
set to work. She started appearing everywhere. At parties
for princes and dukes, it was Sylvia who got her picture
in the gossip columns. Said one New York hostess: "She'll
do anything for publicity and the awful part of it is that
all she ever talks about is herself." It's not entirely untrue,
but Sylvia is not dumb. She always puts her money where
her mouth is. Shortly after she announced she was designing French provincial furniture, writers started appearing
from Paris to do articles on her furniture. She told everybody she played chess with Bobby Fischer, probably as
good as Bobby Fischer even ("The only difference is I

don't have the temperament for tournament chess"), and by golly, a few days later there she was, listed in *The New York Times* as one of the ten top female chess players in America. At the good-bye birthday party for Mick Jagger at Madison Square Garden, it was Sylvia who ended up in the papers with Bob Dylan on one arm and Dick Cavett on the other. You hardly knew the Rolling Stones had been there. And when her new underground movie *Heat* was shown at the Cannes Film Festival, she caused a sensation when she failed to show up for the press conference because she couldn't read the time in French. When *Heat* later appeared on the program in Venice, Sylvia let the rest of her entourage revel in the marvels of the ancient city while she sat in the lobby of the Danieli Hotel pondering the ad campaign. "How about 'Crawford was *Possessed*, Hayworth was *Gilda*, Harlow was *Reckless*, but you haven't seen anything until you see Sylvia Miles in *Heat*'? Get it? Sylvia Miles in heat?" And when all else failed, she announced to the press she had just proposed marriage to Tennessee Williams.

"Sure, I've got an ego," says Sylvia, who opened a lecture once at the Lee Strasberg Theater Institute by asking a crowd of 800 people: "Is there anyone here who doesn't know me, please raise your hand." "We're all narcissists in this world. I figure you might was well be a healthy narcissist as an unhealthy one." She isn't smiling. "I've always been dedicated, but in the last three years I've become committed. I can no longer make a separation between Sylvia Miles the person and Sylvia Miles the actress. Listen. I've been around. I'm no overnight sensation, y'know. I've done twenty-six off-Broadway plays, one Broadway show and nine movies. I never got anywhere doing art, so let me enjoy this. I'm not hurting anybody."

The thing to remember when Sylvia pulls out the press clippings that she carries everywhere in her purse is that she really is a fantastic actress. *Heat* is an Andy Warhol movie, directed by the talented Paul Morrissey, that knocked a lot of skeptics right out of their jaded seats. Sylvia plays a faded, practically unknown movie star named Sally Todd, saddled with a lesbian daughter and deserted by an ambitious young stud (Joe Dallessandro)— blind to reality and desperate to hold onto her last ounce of dignity. The film is like an open wound and Sylvia is a kind of cross between Lana Turner and Gloria Swanson in *Sunset Boulevard*, eating her way through the movie like an emotional barracuda and leaving everyone around her for fishbait. The film is such a milestone in her career that everything else in her life is now referred to as "B.H." (Before *Heat*). It cost only $50,000 to make—a far cry from all the waste and hoopla of her previous film, Dennis Hopper's *The Last Movie*—but it has finally made Sylvia a star. "People said I was crazy. But for eight months I stood in front of Andy Warhol at parties hoping to get into one of his movies and nothing happened. Then I burned all my hair off with that bad peroxide job in Peru and suddenly he saw me in some horrible gypsy wig and said 'That's it!' It was Andy's idea of a movie star, I guess. I thought of all the obvious things. They'd want me to do nudity and sexy things. And since there was no script, I decided if I went through with it, I'd have to just become the character. So I created the part—a movie star, in her late thirties, sort of a Dorothy Malone type—in such a way that by the time I flew out to Hollywood and got me at the airport by Elvis Presley's limousine, I was already the person I was playing. If I was feeling lousy or good that day I felt lousy or good as that woman. To the extent that I lost thirty pounds during the filming and you won't even notice it on the screen, because you think, 'Well, that lady just got herself together.' We did the whole movie in two weeks in a Hollywood mansion, except for the love scenes, which we couldn't do because there was a hippie love cult living there, so we did them three months later back in New York at Andy Warhol's house in East Hampton on Labor Day weekend.

"Let me tell you. It might have been a cheap film to make, but don't anybody sneer at underground movies. It turned out to be the best move of my career. I'm getting raves from people I haven't seen in years. The first job I had in the theater was an off-Broadway play by Harold Robbins and my boyfriend was played by Sydney Pollack. So the first thing I saw when I arrived in Cannes was a huge billboard announcing a new film directed by Sydney Pollack and one of the first people I saw was Harold Robbins and it was my picture that was getting all the attention. Small world, huh? Harold Robbins saw *Heat* and said 'Sylvia, you're incredible!' You think he meant it as a compliment?"

Heat opened October 5, 1972, at the New York Film Festival, then went into general release the next day at a New York movie house called, ironically, the Festival. It looks like clear sailing for a girl who has known her share of clouds.

"Listen. It's about time I got a break. The first job I got paid for was doing background crowd noises with George Segal for a phonograph record of *A Tale of Two Cities*. For three days, we yelled 'Behead them, behead them!' in French. My only Broadway show opened during a newspaper strike. My Oscar nomination for *Midnight Cowboy* was announced during a mail strike and the ballots never reached the Academy voters who lived in New York. In *The Night They Raided Minsky's* I played Jason Robards' girlfriend and got cut out of the film. In *Going Home* with Robert Mitchum I played a whore who gets eaten by rats, and my scene ended up on the cutting room floor again. Then they had a print of *Heat* flown to California because they thought I was such a brilliant actress. That's really throwing dirt in your face. In *The Last Movie* I went all the way to Peru to play a script girl and it was cut, but they're having a retrospective of the out-takes this fall in Washington that will last a week. When I flew to London in 1963 to make my London debut as a contortion dancer in a Chinese restaurant in a play called *The Magnificent Gourmet*, the producers forgot to get me a work permit and I never went onstage. So don't ask me if I mind doing nude scenes in an Andy Warhol movie. You can learn a lot about people during nude scenes. I was in bed all day with Jon Voight in *Midnight Cowboy* and when I got home that night I was so tired I went to sleep without even taking my makeup off or taking a bath. Then in the middle of the night, I woke up and smelled a strange body aroma in the room. I thought someone had broken in. I turned on the lights and realized it was Jon Voight I still smelled from the day's scene. Well, don't laugh. Everyone has a particular body aroma. Jon Voight smells like peanut butter."

Where does she go from here? "Well, the Swedish people in Cannes said as soon as Ingmar Bergman saw my film, I'd be coming to Sweden shortly. Robert Altman said 'You'll never work for me because what you have to offer is so special there's no need for a director.' Louis Malle has seen *Heat* twice and wants me for a film. I'm doing *Virginia Woolf* at the Pittsburgh Playhouse. There's talk of doing a remake of *Rain* with me as Sadie Thompson and Marjoe as the preacher. But I don't think I'll do another Warhol underground film. I've done that. Now my head's in another place. What I do next is going to be great. To do another underground movie would be like going to a gambling casino after figuring out all the odds and placing only a twenty-dollar bet. I've got a white Harlow dress, a fox stole, a beaded bag and some gold shoes that cost fifty cents at the MGM auction and all that stuff you dream about is happening at last."

But just in case you think she's getting too big for her bra, Sylvia adds: "Last week I read for a TV commercial voice-over. The part of a chicken. I've done twenty-six off-Broadway shows, I was nominated for an Oscar, I'm a major underground cult figure, I'm considered one of the greatest actresses in America and I didn't even get the part of the chicken." Let's face it. Sylvia Miles just isn't ever going to be the girl next door. "Listen. That doesn't bother me, sweetheart. I am very well read in theater lore and I don't remember Tallulah Bankhead playing that many housewives."

She still isn't smiling. Well, maybe just a little.

14

Joan Hackett

I'M IN LOVE. Her name is Joan Hackett, but I'm standing in line. The problem, you see, is that everybody else is standing in line to love her, too. She hypnotized New York with her triumphant performance in Broadway's suspense thriller called *Night Watch*. Onstage, she was a neurotic, marathon-smoking heiress fighting off insomnia and madness, trying vainly to convince everyone around her she'd seen a couple of corpses in the vacant tenement across the street, and suffering so appealingly in the good old Barbara Stanwyck tradition that you were still worrying about her long after you'd forgotten what the play was about. Offstage, she's a nervous, marathon-talking beauty with skin like pink japonica petals, a mind so fascinatingly alive it often plays tennis with ten thoughts at once, and fingernails bitten down to the quick.

But I'm lucky. I get to go to the head of the line. After a month of strenuous rehearsals and previews without a day off, an opening night that sent critics into the kind of ecstasy most girls would give up a corner table at Sardi's for, an attack of flu that left her voice trailing off in tiny, ladylike coughs at the ends of sentences, and a previous twelve-hour day of the kinds of interviews, photograph sessions and ringing phones that accompany stardom, you think she'd be prostrate with her feet in a tub of hot water and an ice pack on her pretty head. Not Joan Hackett. It's 1:30 A.M.—about the time of night she sees those corpses in the script of the play—and she's not even sleepy.

She's on her way from the kitchen of her warm, friendly apartment overlooking Central Park, carrying a coffee-pot, two wineglasses, a bottle of Pouilly Fuissé and two cats named Chips and Pumpernickel. Although her husband Richard Mulligan, the fine young actor who played General Custer in *Little Big Man*, is asleep in the next room, she isn't especially quiet about it. "I don't understand marriage any better than I did six years ago," she begins, pouring wine and talking in that crisp, cool voice that sounds like a poet reading Little Orphan Annie. "He played the man who seduced me in *The Group* and we got married two months later . . . but I'm Pisces and he's Scorpio and he's as spooky as I am . . . . I spent the first year of our marriage sleeping on various couches just to get away from him . . . I mean, he *snored*. . . . It just wasn't like the movies. . . . We had three bathrooms in California and I never met him in the hall before noon. . . . I have to be private. . . . I was like the invisible man as a child . . . . I didn't even speak until I was eight years old. . . . I finally got two separate king-size beds and it's worked out because we understand each other's needs and besides, he just wouldn't go away. . . ."

Why should he? Now that they're back in New York, where they were born, she's made a home of warm brown-velvet chairs the color of hot marzipan, tomato-red lamps, baskets of fire-engine-red flowers, baskets of pine cones, inviting Indian rugs, porcelain oil lamps and her own paintings that line the walls. One depicting the assassination of Martin Luther King hangs just over her head as she talks into the night with equal passion of astrology, Women's Lib, sex, football, the bomb, alchemy, magic, persecution of the Jews, the spaying of her cats, the psychological motivation of Central Park muggers, Adolf Hitler and her favorite new friend, an ex-convict marked for death by the Mafia. I have long since given up getting it all down on paper. I have never heard so many words pour out of one perfectly shaped mouth after midnight. They stream forth like columns of picnic ants, scurrying in every direction, carrying food for thought, coming at me in sections. I just listen:

"The key word is energy. . . . I never think of myself as my own age (thirty-eight) because to me the key to youth-fulness is energy. . . . It's when you're tired, when you don't continue to generate that sort of force and energy —that's when you get old. . . . An actor's job is to get out there onstage and fake a whole new life-force, and it takes energy to do this. . . . I used to sleep all day, miss appoint-ments, see two movies a day. . . . Now I conserve energy, sleep between shows, lock my dressing-room door, not talk to the other actors or let them massage my back so I can build up the nervous energy I need to work for me in this play. . . . I get it from my mother. . . . She was Italian, my father was Irish. . . . I left home when I was seventeen and had to learn how to do everything. . . . I became a landlady and learned how to buy caskets for them when they died. . . . I grew up fast and my mother instilled it all in me. . . . She was incredible. . . . When her father died, she was so melancholy they signed her into Bellevue and she jumped out of the goddam window and swam the East River and I can't look at the East River to this day without smiling. . . . She was the only one of fourteen kids in her family who finished school. . . . She was four feet eleven inches high, wrote and spoke three languages, and when she died she was suing three people and acting as her own lawyer. . . .

". . . I'm a fool about money and so was my father, who

died broke. . . . He did all the cooking and was passionate and colorful, but he was seldom sober. . . . I hated him . . . . He worked for the post office. . . . All the other Hacketts carried guns and were absolutely crazy. . . . He called me 'the rock,' which diminished my older sister and we're not close to this day. . . . She wore platform shoes and looked like the Dragon Lady in *Terry and the Pirates* and was always fainting. . . . She should've been the actress, not me. . . . Anyway, where was I? . . . Oh, yes, my father. . . . He drank and had epileptic fits and used to wake us all up at midnight to discuss politics and religion. . . . One day I played hookey from school and got a modeling job and left home and never went back. . . . Then I won a beauty contest and the prize was two weeks in Miami. . . . Then when I was eighteen, I was assaulted by an attempted rapist in the street and had a nervous breakdown and moved to South Carolina for a year. . . . When I got back to New York, I was on a lot of magazine covers but I hated wearing lipstick, so I took some acting classes with Lee Strasberg and just kind of fell into acting but the trouble was that everybody told me to forget about studying and just act. The two most valuable things I learned were 'Don't cry with your hands in front of your face— not when they're paying nine dollars apiece to see the tears' and 'Even if they crucify you, enjoy it!' and I said I'm not paying thirty dollars a month to hear *that,* so I went out and got my first acting job on my first interview but I couldn't get my voice above a whisper and I couldn't handle props. . . . Got into *Much Ado About Nothing* with John Gielgud and he was a mean bastard, but his acting always surprised me. . . .

". . . And then I was in this tacky movie in Zurich called *The Assignment* after I finished *The Group* and nobody ever saw it but I got a trip to Zurich. . . . I drowned in a bathtub in it and the ads read 'Dominique was always in hot water—but now she was in over her head!' and a friend went all the way to Brooklyn to see it and stole the poster and sent it to me in California and now it's too big to get on this wall. . . . I was in scores of plays that never

got to New York and one called *Peterpat* that did, in
which I was quite terrible but would have been much
better if I hadn't been forced to play opposite a stand-up
comic. . . . I'm a very hard worker because it's the only
thing I do in life. . . . I don't make shoes, I don't have
twelve kids, *I act*. . . . And if you make a mistake, it's there
for a hundred years and every rerun on TV forever, so I'll
work until four A.M. in the rain if necessary, to get it right
. . . . Give me a needle and thread and I'll remake the
drapes on the set. . . . I'll even rewrite the script if you ask,
but I'm a perfectionist and it drives people crazy. . . . But
I'm appalled at the way other actors work. . . . On *Will
Penny* Charlton Heston, every day at five in the afternoon, would say, 'It's cold as hell, let's close this thing
down,' and go off and have a brandy. . . . On *Support Your
Local Sheriff* I was hired without ever meeting the director Burt Kennedy, and when I finally met him I offered
to read through the script, go through costume fittings
early, anything to make the film better and improve my
part, and he took off his dark glasses for the only time
during the entire film and said, 'Listen, Hackett, if you
cross me, I'll hurt you!' . . . I mean, it's incredible, they just
don't *care*. . . .

   ". . . The best thing I've ever done was my first musical,
a thing called *Park* that ran eight performances and was
a big flop but I loved it so much I couldn't wait for the next
curtain to go up. . . . I was so happy I didn't even realize
the audience hated it! . . . But out of it came Harold
Prince's promise to put me into *She Loves Me* and I now
have a clause in my contract for *Night Watch* that frees
me if that movie gets off the ground. . . . Listen, acting is
nothing. . . . Singing and dancing is what it's all about
. . . . I loved doing *Park* because I got to kneel down and
sing like Al Jolson . . . my greatest dream in life was always
to be Al Jolson. . . . I saw *The Jolson Story* twelve times,
which is incredible, because do you know how terrible
The Jolson Story was? . . . What's funny is that *Night
Watch* will be a big hit because it's a thriller play, not
because of me . . . this isn't work. . . . I've played neurotics

hundreds of times . . . they've all seen me do it on *Ben
Casey* . . . acting is as easy as getting up and making toast
in the morning. . . . I don't even know why they pay me
. . . on TV I've had legs amputated and had babies in
surgery at six A.M. before my body was even functioning
. . . acting if you have half a brain is a snow job. . . . I've
never been in analysis because I save up all the things that
trouble me for the stage . . . everyone should go on the
stage to straighten themselves out . . . what amazes me is
when they can't act. . . . Raquel Welch and Candy Bergen
are curiosities to me. . . .

    ". . . For the last six years Richard and I have lived in
California. . . . We had an English cottage with three
fireplaces, a kidney-shaped swimming pool and a lemon
tree and I cried every day for one whole year. Every
morning I woke up praying Bloomingdale's would be
looming outside my window. . . . They don't even have
shopping bags out there and Richard was arrested for
walking in Beverly Hills and I used to talk to people at red
lights to keep from losing my mind. . . . Then we got an
apartment and instead of giving *A* parties and *B* parties,
I think we moved into the *C* category . . . and you cannot
fail there or nobody ever speaks to you again . . . the word
that somebody's TV series is a flop travels faster than the
scent of orange blossoms in the air . . . they don't know
what to make of me out there . . . you can't raise a dime
on my name in movies anyway . . . to raise money for
Night Watch they had to use quotes about me from the
critic of *Women's Wear Daily* on *Park* and if I wrote a
camp review satirizing an actress' greatest dream I
couldn't duplicate the raves I got from that man and I can
honestly say the critic for that paper got me my job in
Night Watch even though I don't even know him . . . now
the irony is that he hates *Night Watch* . . . but you know,
we none of us realize how we affect each other's lives
. . . possibly now from this play my life might be easier,
but now I just want to see if I can run in a hit without
getting bored by it, because you know it's an entertaining
play, but there's no great substance to it . . . and whatever

happens, it has not been an overnight success! As a model, I was being rediscovered every two years by *Harper's Bazaar,* then in movies I was discovered in *The Group* and later rediscovered in *Will Penny* and I don't know where it will end, but I figure I've got about twenty good years left and . . . oh, would you mention I'm nominated for an Emmy Award for playing Isadora Duncan in the TV show, *John Dos Passos' USA?* But check it out first. . . .

". . . I'm a Pisces, so I believe in hereafters, extrasensory perception . . . we're drug-oriented, too, but I never take drugs. . . . I took bennies when I was seventeen because I wanted to die, but now I know I will never live long enough to do all the things I want to do with my life so I savor every day instead of tearing it down and I'm committed to many things besides acting. . . . I hate cars and gasoline and the lead in Central Park and I don't believe women should take alimony. . . . I hated *Clockwork Orange* because the night before I had seen eleven-year-old children raped in the Pakistan War on TV and it was Christmas week . . . there are so many things I don't understand, but the mystery of life fascinates me. . . ."

Suddenly it is 4:30 A.M. "Listen," she yawns, "I watch all the rushes of my films, but hate the actual films because I've already made up my own cut in my head. Same with interviews. I'm always disappointed because I've already written them in my head and they never turn the same on paper. So if you want to just make up the whole thing, I don't mind. Do you want to sleep in the guest room?"

Outside, in the dark before dawn, I seem to be going blind. It's not the night, or the muddle in my head about my notebook of half sentences that, like the rushes of her movies, look good but will never cut together the right way. It's just that when you leave the crackle of electricity surrounding Joan Hackett, it's as though somebody just turned all the lights off.

15

On Location:
Cliff Robertson and
Joel Grey

WE ARE STANDING in front of the Stop and Shop in the parking lot of the Milford (Connecticut) Shopping Center, where Frank Perry is preparing to direct Cliff Robertson and Joel Grey in the most dramatic scene of a tense suspense thriller called *The Man in the Swing*. The heat pounds down, drenching the cast and crew in a lather of sweat. It is so hot you could poach an egg in the palm of your hand. No umbrellas, no Nubian slaves holding these battery-operated portable fans. It's not like Hollywood. "I've done twenty-seven setups in the past two days, who has time for umbrellas?" says Perry, who is rushing to get the movie out before Christmas.

Everything has been very polite so far, but we're coming to the big moment where Joel Grey, who won an

Oscar for singing and dancing in *Cabaret,* tries to strangle Cliff Robertson, who won an Oscar for *Charly.* Rumors are flying that the competition between the two Oscar winners is more tense than the movie itself. They tell a story on the set about the day Joel was talking to the twenty-five-year-old actress who plays the murder victim, and Cliff came up to Joel and asked, "Joel, aren't you going to introduce me to your daughter?"

Frank Perry, himself, describes the set as "Tension City." "Let's just say there's no love lost," he adds. "And frankly," he says impishly, "I've encouraged a bit of competition between the two of them. Cliff plays a chief of police who doesn't believe in mysticism and Joel is a clairvoyant who becomes a suspect while he's helping Cliff solve the case. So the two characters shouldn't be chums. All I can tell you is they are both brilliant."

The boys have just finished a catered lunch of dried-out Swiss steak, and now Perry is waiting for them to come out of their dressing-room trailers. "I delivered a speech this morning about violence," he says, wiping his forehead. "A sacred rule in the theater, I told the boys, is that whenever you have to attack anyone's body or commit any act of physical aggression you must show great respect for the other person." He sighs. "I think it worked, but I've been pretty nervous about today's scene. Joel is inside getting padding, because after he tries to choke Cliff to death, Cliff has to throw him on the ground, and we don't want Joel to get hurt when he hits the concrete. Joel is much smaller than Cliff." Joel is often referred to as "the littlest star," a label that makes him furious. Cliff is wearing elevator heels to make himself even larger.

"I'm glad you use padding," interjects the press agent. "Stanley Kubrick never uses it and in *A Clockwork Orange* when they kicked Malcolm McDowall they broke one of his ribs."

Joel's wife Jo is the first one on the set. She comes out of the Liggett's drugstore with a $10 watch she just found on a bargain counter. "It's a small world," she grins. "Frank Perry and I worked together off-Broadway in

Threepenny Opera when he was an actor. I was Polly
Peachum and he was one of the gangsters. I was dating
Cliff Robertson at the time." The tension builds.

Joel comes out of his trailer in Flagg Brothers shoes, an
out-of-date thrift shop suit, an imitation alligator belt, a
black skinny tie with a fake pearl tiepin, a monogrammed
handkerchief and clock socks. Cliff is wearing a hot cor-
duroy safari jacket. They don't shake hands. Frank Perry
takes them into a huddle like a football coach and takes
his place behind the camera operated by Adam Hol-
lender, who shot *Midnight Cowboy.* "This is a very hard
scene to do," he says, his face assuming the look of secret
prayer. "It's no fun choking somebody or being choked in
the middle of a parking lot with two hundred people
standing around with shopping bags and their mouths
open."

The scene begins. A girl has been murdered and found
in a Volkswagen parked in the shopping center lot. Joel
is using ESP to help the chief of police track down clues.
"Action!" yells Perry, as gently as possible. Joel says:
"Someone hit her near here." Cliff: "What then? What
happened next? Was she killed? Who killed her?" Joel's
eyes are closing as he goes into a trance. "A pair of hands
. . . around a neck . . ." He seems to be having a fit. He
falls to the ground, whimpering, feeling the dead girl's
pain. Cliff bends over him. Joel's hands suddenly go to
Cliff's neck. He squeezes. "Tighter . . ." Cliff, with tremendous force, breaks his grip and shoves him to the ground,
gasping for air. Joel twirls his right arm as if he were
spinning a model airplane and spins his body dizzily, yelling "Zzzzzzzzzz!" as he dashes across the street.

Frank Perry is back on the other side of the highway
shooting them with a 400-mm lens. The scene has to be
repeated. People trying to get their station wagons out of
the parking lot keep getting in the way. Teenagers on
their way to get a lime rickey at Liggett's keep getting in
the way. They take a break while the camera is reloaded.

Cliff takes off the remote mike system taped inside his
sleeve. "I'm so bugged I feel like the Oval Room at the

White House." Everyone laughs. "This scene is the closest
thing to violence you'll see in the film. After all the rodeo
action in *J. W. Coop*, this film is a very quiet experience.
No violence and no sex. I don't think I even kiss my wife."
I gingerly mention the feud rumors. He laughs. "Those
myths usually crop up because, one, they are usually
true." Pause. Everyone waits, breathlessly. "Or, two, because they make good reading. In this case, it's nonsense.
It always happens on pictures with two Oscar winners. In
Poseidon Adventure there were something like six Oscar
winners. . . ."

"And four of them were Shelley Winters," says the
press agent. Everyone laughs. Cliff continues, "That's not
what upsets me. What makes me mad is the *Hollywood
Reporter* erroneously reported Dina Merrill and I were
getting a divorce. We expect this every few months, but
it's getting out of hand. We're more in love now than
we've ever been in our lives. Dina has a cosmetics line
which forces her to travel and I am always on location,
which causes us to be apart a lot, but this time she was in
Las Vegas on a convention and her son just got out of the
Marines and came to visit her. He's a strapping six-footer,
and when they went out, some clown saw them and
thought she was with another guy. They put two and two
together and got sixteen."

Cliff is very cool. Nothing rocks him. "I've had the yoke
of mediocrity hanging around my neck so long I just roll
with the punches. I've been in so many bad movies and
worked with so many bad directors that I go into a film
expecting nothing. That's why I respect and admire
Frank Perry so much. He's a rare man and I've worked
with enough stiffs to know the difference, pal. Now that
I'm a director, I'm in a difficult position. As an actor, you
have to say 'OK, Chief' and do it. As a director, I want to
go over and look through that lens and say 'Let's try it this
way.' But Frank knows the problems of the actor and I
know the problems of the director and we've hit a happy
medium. He's so sweet and sensitive. I want to say 'Don't
worry about me, pal, I've got calluses on my ass from

sitting around on sets all my life,' but I'm just so grateful for his concern that I don't say it. He's as far away from an Otto Preminger as you can get.

"I feel sorry for actors who get these fast breaks with the cream of the crop at the beginning of their careers. When they have to work with hacks they don't know how to take care of themselves. I started out with Kazan. Then I'd work with a guy who didn't say one word to me and I'd worry maybe I had the wrong deodorant or something. Those days are over. It's a long haul between a Kazan and a Frank Perry, and everything is so terrific on this film I'm getting suspicious."

Between takes, Perry sips lemonade from a curb-service cup. Cliff haunches on the concrete pavement like a quarterback on the forty-yard line. Joel paces and asks questions. For him, it's a serious business. Everyone knows he's terrific on a nightclub floor and a dancing doodlebug in musicals. But now the world will see him in a straight dramatic role and he wants it to be good. "When I read this script," says Joel, "I had to make sure the doors were locked. It gave me the willies. There is a lot of mystery about the film because the people are still alive and I guess there's a danger of lawsuits. But it says at the beginning of the film 'This is a true story,' and that the case is still unsolved. So without being able to talk to the clairvoyant I'm playing, I did some research. I never believed in anything but scientific fact, but now I'm not so sure. I've studied thought control and met some spiritualists and clairvoyants and I'm convinced there's a lot of power around in a person's ability to think and transmit thought. When the phone rings, I know exactly who it is before I answer it."

Like Cliff, Joel says he is not ruffled by feud rumors. "I don't know what they're talking about. What bothers me is the two recent stories in that thing they call 'the Gossip Column.' One said as the little man got big, the Waldorf Towers was no longer good enough, he had to bring in his own silver and linens. All I brought was my humidifier. The second story said my ego was so big I added a lot of bravos and applause to my new album on Columbia. The truth is that the audience track broke down on the recording and they had to take applause from other spots in the show so there wouldn't be gaps of silence on the record.

"But as far as feuding with Cliff, I don't work that way or think that way. I want to do it right and all that concerns me is the quality. After the picture finishes, I go to Lake Tahoe for ten days, then a week at the Greek in LA, then the London Palladium, then a vacation in Rome, then a Sonny and Cher show, then a week in Vegas. Just to find the time to do this movie I had to cancel ten weeks of bookings. Who has time for a feud? There aren't that many good musicals around and I want to act. So I'll go anywhere anytime and do anything if it's a good role. Next, I want to tackle Shakespeare."

They hit the hot sun again for a close-up. This time, Joel really chokes Cliff with a force that seems willed from the planet Krypton. His eyes fly back into his head like a maniac. Cliff knocks him to the ground. The crew freezes. Is it all publicity, or is this the moment of truth? The two Oscar winners dust themselves off and start back to their trailers.

"How was it?" asks Joel.

"As a guy who's been strangled a few times, pal, I'd say on a scale of ten, you rank pretty close to the top," says Cliff with his shy, boot-shuffling grin.

Frank Perry wipes his forehead nervously. "From here on in, it's all gravy."

Tennessee Williams PHOTO BY CHRISTOPHER MAKOS

Gregory Peck and
his wife, Veronique
(*Group A*)
WIDE WORLD PHOTOS

Angie Dickinson and Burt Bacharach (*The Fun Group*)
WIDE WORLD PHOTOS

Denise Minnelli Hale, queen of *Group A*

Actress Marlo Thomas (*The Fun Group*) and Henry Kissinger (*Group A*)
WIDE WORLD PHOTOS

Burt Reynolds and Dinah Shore (*The Fun Group*)
WIDE WORLD PHOTOS

Princess Lee Radziwill and Truman Capote (*Group A*) UPI

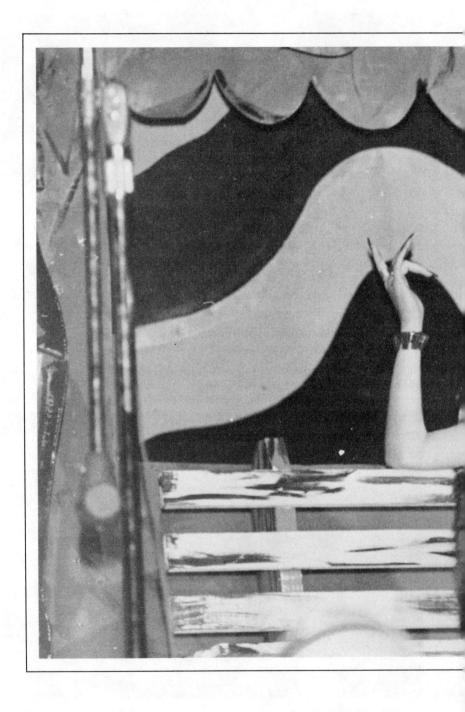

Bobby Venus of the Cockettes LEEE BLACK CHILDERS, MAINMAN, LTD.

Merle Oberon
and her "new man,"
Robert Wolders
WIDE WORLD PHOTOS

Christopher Makos, photographer, and Goldie Glitter of the Cockettes
LEEE BLACK CHILDERS, MAINMAN, LTD.

Marcello Mastroianni and Sophia Loren in *The Priest's Wife*
WIDE WORLD PHOTOS

Sally Kellerman in $M*A*S*H$ WIDE WORLD PHOTOS

Joe Namath
at his bar
in New York
UPI

Grace Slick at home with her baby, China
WIDE WORLD PHOTOS

16

Troy Donahue

TROY DONAHUE IS SLEEPING with Merle Johnson. Don't faint as you reread that sentence for the fortieth time. It's not what you think. Merle Johnson, see, is a perfectly ordinary fellow (well, maybe not so *ordinary!*) from Bayport, Long Island, who, in 1956, went to Hollywood where Henry Wilson, the talent scout who discovered Rock, Tab, Lance and God knows how many other people who sound like carbonated drinks, named him Troy Donahue. You sort of know the rest. Merle, or Troy, became the king of the teenybopper soap operas. When he crawled out of the Malibu surf and pawed all those faceless, now-forgotten girls with bubble-gum names, women everywhere felt the fingernail marks, and no guy was secure on any campus in America without a red Troy Donahue windbreaker. Troy was as big as Pepsi-Cola and Merle got lost in the fizzle.

Then something happened. The world changed its mind. Platinum-blond beachboys with toothpaste grins were out; hippie freaks with unwashed toenails giving the peace sign were in. Troy Donahue faded from sight like a Hula Hoop. But now Troy, or Merle, is back, starring in a new movie called *Sweet Saviour*, about a Jesus freak who leads a hippie cult in a series of savage murders based on the Charles Manson "family." I think it's Merle, because he certainly bears no resemblance to the old Troy.

He rises from the dark recesses of a bar in the Holiday Inn, where he lives. No Waldorf-Astoria for this star. No Beverly Hills threads, either. He wears Lee jeans cut off at the bottom, scuffed fry boots, a wrinkled T-shirt, a white denim overall jacket that has obviously been lived in, an orange smile button and four bracelets. He has long dirty blond Jesus hair down to his shoulders with gray streaks in it, his face has lost its boyish Fifties look, there are tired half-moons under his eyes, the complexion is red and parched from too much sun, and unless I'm wrong, there are crow's feet scampering along his eyes from too much living. Only one trace of the old Hollywood Troy remains: He is accompanied by a press agent who says too little and the director of *Sweet Saviour*, a fast-talker named Bob Roberts, who knows the value of old-fashioned hype, and says too much.

"I play Moon, a religious creep who murders a lot of the Beautiful People," says Troy, "a real heavy trip. But I don't want anyone to think I'm really playing in some phony exploitation flick that takes advantage of the Manson case to make a fast buck. I don't like many things, man, but I dig this picture."

"I had the idea not to make the Manson story per se," interrupts Roberts, "but to inform people the Sharon Tate thing was not just an isolated incident. Many other cults are murdering people. They're just not as publicized. There are a lot of so-called families like Manson's, with one dictatorial leader who controls his group through drugs, pills, LSD, sex and many other ways. These people are a threat to the fabric of society because they commit murder without conscience. The most amazing thing to me is that after the Tate murders, Susan Atkins came back to the ranch and asked for ice cream."

"We're trying to show both sides of the problem," says Troy. "The Hollywood glamour society is as guilty as the depraved hippie cults. They pick up creeps on the Sunset Strip and tease them. When they picked on Manson, they just picked on the wrong guy. I was up at the Tate house. It was a freaky scene. Sure, I met Manson at the beach playing volleyball. After the murders, Hollywood was paralyzed with terror. I left four days later and I've been in New York ever since."

"Troy is a great actor," says Roberts, working up a lather. "I wanted to give him something to do besides boy-meets-girl. He comes off as the most menacing heavy I've ever seen on the screen. . . . *I bet he gets an Academy Award. . . .*"

"I had to kill this girl in the movie who plays the Sharon Tate character. She was really four months pregnant during the scene. It blew my mind. . . ."

"People wonder why I thought of Troy for this part," offers Roberts. "I met him when I had this TV show that was piped into forty thousand hotel rooms on closed circuit. He had long hair and a beard and he came to me on a motorcycle. . . ."

"Everybody changes, man. Even the kids change. One of the extras in the orgy scene in *Myra Breckinridge* was my roommate in military school. I had long hair a long time ago, but Warner Brothers threw a net over my head in *A Summer Place* and never let me out. I was never the boy in the red windbreaker. I wanted to burn the goddamn thing. They had to lock it up. Finally, they made copies of it because they knew I'd destroy it. That image of the all-American boy on the screen had nothing to do with me as a person. In the same day, they had me going from *Surfside 6* on one stage to playing a beachboy in some dumb Connie Stevens movie on another. They set a pattern to make money and wouldn't let me play anything else. So I went to see Jack Warner and told him, "I don't wanna make any more dumb movies," and he said,

"What'll you do?" and I said, "What difference does that make to you, man?"

"Troy was Number One box office at Warners; I think after they see him in this flick playing a hippie freak, he'll be Number One again. . . ."

". . . So I walked out in 1966 and I had to sit out three years of my contract. I couldn't work anywhere. Jack Warner called every studio I tried to work for and used his muscle to keep me busted. I was blackballed and everyone in the business knows it. Please print that. I made one film in Europe playing a Victorian astronaut, but nobody ever saw it. Then by the time I could get work again, it was too late because my type was already out of fashion." He slugs down his vodka.

"He never lost his following, though," chirps Roberts, sounding like the coach on a losing team. "When I took him up to my lawyer's office to sign his contract every girl in the building came in to look at him. They come up to the pool at the Holiday Inn and ask him to sign autographs in the water."

"I'm just lucky I was named Troy Donahue in the movies. I coulda been called Crack Widens . . . hey, how about that? Crack Widens in *Sweet Saviour*. . . ."

"I like it, I like it," says the press agent.

"It took guts to walk out of Hollywood, but it would've been worse to stay. I had a house, seven black Cadillac convertibles and two wrecked marriages. I already had my head turned; turning my back was easy. It doesn't matter if I have a beard or a crew cut. People respond to me because I have a human quality. I know I'll be put down by Hollywood, but I don't speak to anybody out there anyway. If you really want to make a statement, man, you have to be prepared to make enemies. *The Village Voice* said I took acid and made me sound like a drug freak. I smoke grass, ride cycles, my life-style is casual, but I'm not a dope fiend or a hippie freak. I've found strength in Jesus Christ and he's easier to follow than Zen Buddhism. I'm not strung out. I'm a very responsible, professional actor."

"Hey, listen. I heard about how temperamental Troy was at Warners, but he's the most disciplined pro I've ever worked with. If he had to be on the set at six A.M., he was there at five forty-five. This movie was high class. I got a Pulitzer Prize winner to write the script. . . ."

"If the movie is so good," I ask, "why did this Pulitzer Prize winner write it under a pseudonym?"

"I want to stop all this B.S., man," says Troy. "I told him, 'What Goody Two-Shoes' image are you trying to protect by putting a phony name on this picture? So now I think he's gonna come out of the closet and use his real name. It's heavy, man." (I still don't know who it is.)

"Richard Nixon sent me his best wishes on the film," beams Roberts. "I was his biggest campaign supporter in 'Sixty-eight."

"Ah, Nixon'll never see it, man. He doesn't want to learn anything. . . ."

Meanwhile, Troy has signed for three more films with his new friends. He will play a man who gets mugged in New York and goes after his assailants one by one in *The Mugging,* an underground resistance leader fighting the Chinese Communists in *The Lucifer Cell,* and a right-wing hard hat in *The Weathermen.* Nixon may not see those, either. Never mind. His family approves. "My sister is a good example, man, of how they've defended me. You know how they play that game of sitting around guessing which Hollywood stars are homosexuals? Well, my sister, who is married to a disc jockey, was sitting around with her girlfriends and they came to my name. "I'll bet Troy Donahue is gay," one of them said, and she said quietly, "No, he's not." And they said how did she know? And she said, "Because I slept with him." He roars. The press agent roars, too.

Troy Donahue gets up to leave. "I gotta check on my cycle. I like New York and now that I'm into a new life-style and starting over again as the person I always was, I think I'll stay here and settle down. But I had three motorcycles stolen in New York last year. Last time it was an $1,800 750 Honda that I locked to a mailbox with a $60 chain. They sawed the mailbox in half and took it along with the cycle on the back of a truck. I'm getting another cycle, man, but this time I'm gonna sleep with it. The best advice I ever got in life is that "Anything in life worth owning, you gotta sleep with."

Troy Donahue is sleeping much better these days now that he's been reintroduced to Merle Johnson. They're getting along just fine.

17

On Location:
Sir Laurence Olivier and
Michael Caine

I T IS EASIER to get into Buckingham Palace than it is to visit the set of *Sleuth*. As a matter of fact, I know several people who had tea with the Duchess of Windsor at the palace on the day of the Duke's funeral, but I don't know anyone else who has been allowed on the set of *Sleuth*. I'm just lucky, I guess.

"You're going out to see Joseph L. Mankiewicz direct Laurence Olivier and Michael Caine on the *Sleuth* set?" gasped one London reporter. "Could you steal a few photos for my paper? They won't let me within a mile of the place."

"I hear they've got Doberman pinschers guarding the gates," warned a photographer friend.

Why all the mystery? In London, rumors were flying through the air like cinders from a chimney sweep's broom. One wag said it was because Laurence Olivier was blowing his lines and they were too embarrassed for any-one to see the greatest actor in the world doing so many retakes. Somebody else said it was because a lot of famous stars were doing guest "cameos" under phony names and one favorite story had it that Bette Davis was playing Olivier's wife under the name of Margo Channing (the character she played in *All About Eve*). To visit the closed set, I had to promise not to give away any of the secrets. In return, I was promised I would not be forced to have a blood test.

At Pinewood, a movie studio outside London that looks like a prefab Army training camp, I didn't see any Dober-man pinschers, but I did see Morton Gottlieb, the Broad-way producer who made *Sleuth* one of the most success-ful whodunits in the history of the theater, and who is making his film debut as the producer of the movie, stand-ing next to a big red "Keep Out" sign. "I am having a wonderful time," said Morty, who is one of the world's biggest movie buffs. "Producing a movie is a life's dream come true." He means it, too. He drives around the En-glish countryside in a spiffy sports car that plays cassette tapes of Alice Faye, and after showing me the set he warned me he had to dash off to a screening of Clara Bow in *It*. And working with Laurence Olivier? "A genius. He never sees the press when he's working because they make him nervous. He tends to act for the reporter and not the camera. But he's one of the nicest people I have ever worked with. He was sixty-five years old on May 22, 1972, and we had a party for him on the set. We had champagne and birthday cake and he took the rest of it home in a doggie bag."

Just folks. Everybody on the *Sleuth* set calls him Larry. Just then, "Larry" was eating lunch in his dressing room. He eats the same lunch every day—three apples. So we joined Michael Caine, set designer Ken Adam and An-thony Shaffer, who wrote the screen adaptation of *Sleuth* from his fabulously successful play. Commissary food is terrible all over the world, but in England it is even worse

than that. Michael Caine settled for a bowl of rice pudding
and said *Sleuth,* coming on the heels of a string of disastrous movies, was the best thing that ever happened to
him. "We had a bomb scare here on the lot last week. The
word was out that it was Keith Baxter sabotaging the set."
I had already heard that Baxter, the brilliant young actor
who originated the role Caine is playing in the film in
London and on Broadway, was very angry he wasn't re-
peating his role for the movie. "Yes," said Shaffer, "he was
hurt. He didn't speak to any of us for weeks." "Look," said
Caine, doing his best Alfie send-up, "tell him I didn't fancy
not getting his part onstage." "Now, Michael," somebody
reminded him, "you know nobody could afford you onstage." That ended that and lunch was over, most of it
uneaten.

There was still time before the next scene, so I got a tour
of the set. Some set. When *Sleuth* is finished, they should
donate the sound stages to the British Museum. I think it
is the most magnificent set I have ever seen. Since most
of the film occurs in the home of a mystery novelist
(Olivier) invaded by his wife's lover (Caine) the house
becomes the scene of all the charades, masquerades,
games and suspense between the two duelers of wit. The
house is therefore a third star. And I must say they've
given it star treatment. Modeled after an actual thir-
teenth-century manor in Dorset called Athelhampton,
the set is erected to match the actual dimensions of the
original mansion. We ambled along the fake driveway
with chopped cork structured under the massive trees
like gravel, into the living room filled with mechanical
eighteenth-century toys—laughing puppets, Egyptian
block games, elaborate chess sets, and maddening all-
white jigsaw puzzles that would even drive Stephen
Sondheim and the devious inventors of the *New York*
magazine competitions crazy. Through hallways lined
with penny-arcade machines, dice games, picture puzzles
and talking dolls (the cast keeps coppers in their pockets
to play the machines during tea breaks) we came to the
sunken kitchen. This was a museum in its own right, with

antique butter churns, enamel weights, brass milk pitchers, coffee grinders, cider jars and black coal ovens. Back in the main part of the house, we then descended the stairs into the wine cellar with dungeon walls, steamer trunks, skeleton skulls, gaslights from the Jack the Ripper era, Victorian bicycles and an elaborate collection of mechanical theaters showing moving scenes from each of the mystery novels the leading character has written. As elaborate as it all looks, it is constructed and designed so that all of the walls can be whisked away in seconds, allowing scenes to be shot from various angles. The toys alone are so valuable and rare they have been insured for three-quarters of a million dollars!

All this, and a few surprises, too. In one of the rooms, my eyes spotted an oil painting of the woman who is supposed to be Olivier's wife in the film. "Why, that's—"

"Shhhh," whispered Morty Gottlieb. "That's one of your secrets. We call her Margo Channing." (Clue: It's not Bette Davis.) Another star in the film is Alec Cawthorne, who has been shrouded in mystery each time he has appeared in a scene. (Clue: It's not Alec Cawthorne. Look fast. I don't know anyone who has ever actually met Alec Cawthorne. One of the biggest and best-kept secrets on the *Sleuth* set that will have audiences guessing even after the movie comes out, is: Who is Alec Cawthorne?) Michael Caine wears a dress. Laurence Olivier disguises himself as Charles II in a powdered wig. If you look closely, you'll even see Agatha Christie in the film. One thing is certain. *Sleuth* won't be dull.

Back on the set where the day's action takes place, it is time for "Larry" to do his thing. For someone who is called the greatest actor in the world, he is astonishingly warm, witty and down-to-earth. A distinguished ascot is tucked neatly into his tweed jacket, the twinkle in his cool blue eyes has a devilish glint, and although his hair is polished silver around his receding forehead, the profile is still so John Barrymore one senses he could play Heathcliff again tomorrow with no challenge. The scene is brief. Olivier watches from a bedroom window as Michael

Caine erects a ladder outside to break into the house. A smile crosses his lips as he steals across the room, past a fireplace, his face framed by a bookcase of his mystery novels shrieking titles like *The Case of the Crucified Countess* and *The Grisly Affair of the Gloucestershire Graveyards.* The smile deepens into a dark and chilling laugh. Another mystery is about to begin.

Joe Mankiewicz yells "Cut!" and Olivier sees me hiding behind the bed. He laughs and extends a cordial handshake. "That was an easy scene, but you should be here when I have dialogue. We've had two delays on this film. Joe lost two pints of blood when he fell over a cable and punctured his leg. It caused internal hemorrhaging and he had to direct most of the film in a wheelchair. The other delay is me. When you reach my age and become a white-haired old man the brain begins to fail in strange ways. I have great difficulty learning lines. I had to go off the drink for three months to learn *Long Day's Journey into Night* for the Old Vic and now I find myself in another marathon role. Trouble is, I can't ad-lib because there are so many hidden details and clues in every line of Anthony Shaffer's script that I might throw away the whole movie if I say the wrong thing. I find myself at an age when it is insulting to indulge in this childish game of learning little words. It's bloody hard. My wife Joan Plowright has a photographic memory, but not me. Sometimes I can get away with making it all up, but not in this film. This bloody playwright insists every adjective must be in the right place all the time."

Sir Laurence Olivier? Ad-libbing? "Oh, yes. During the run of *Othello* I used to drive poor Iago mad. He used to come out and say 'Does my lord remember a strawberry-stained handkerchief in fair Desdemona's pocket?' and I'd look at him blankly and say 'No!' Of course the poor bastard would almost drop dead then, because the whole play went dead. Once I looked into the wings and saw the entire company standing there with their faces frozen in horror waiting to see what I'd say next. I ad-libbed for twenty minutes in Shakespearean blank verse. Just absolute gibberish, but the audience never knew the difference."

He gestured to the photos of himself on the wall. "That's a shot of me taken in my lawyer's office signing my first movie contract for RKO. This one was on the Marilyn Monroe picture. That's me in Mexico. I can't believe I had so much hair then. Doug Fairbanks and Bob Montgomery and I sailed there on C. B. De Mille's yacht and they had me arrested and thrown in jail as a dangerous criminal arriving illegally. Of course, it was a joke, but I didn't know it and I was scared to death. The funny thing is that if the Mexican authorities had ever actually asked to see my identification, I might still be there. What they didn't know was that my papers weren't in order at all. Ah, yes, and this is me in *Wuthering Heights*. I saw it on TV the other night and you know, it was a bloody awful film. Geraldine Fitzgerald is the only thing that still holds up in that one. My kids saw it and all they said after was 'Daddy, why did you change your hair?' "

He's celebrating his fiftieth anniversary as an actor on the set of *Sleuth*. He made his debut at the age of fifteen playing Katherine in *The Taming of the Shrew* at Stratford-on-Avon and he's played almost everything of any importance since and yet he still has no inflated opinion of his work. "Whether it's Greek tragedy, Shakespeare, Restoration comedy or the kind of part I'm doing in *Sleuth*—acting is all a convention, really. When you get over the sound of your voice (which I've always hated) and the way you look, and accept what you are, one of your biggest problems is solved. But Christ, you never get to the point where you feel secure. There are lots of things I can't do."

As I left the studio, they were putting the "Keep Out" signs up again, making the working conditions absolutely perfect once more for the greatest actor in the world. Maybe there are things he can't do, but the world will never know.

PART

TWO

18

George C. Scott

SOMEBODY ONCE WROTE that it is impossible to sit in the same room with George C. Scott without eventually getting punched in the nose, but you can't prove it by me. Out here on his farm, where folks call him G.C. and there is nothing to punch but a bunch of chickens, he seems more like a friendly fertilizer salesman than a slugger. Dark has fallen early and a raw wind moans up from the birch trees on the farm road below. Beams sigh, floors creak and a warm fire cuts invitingly through the logs he has just brought in from the woodshed. His two sons are doing their homework. G.C. settles down in front of the fire with a bottle of brandy. His straight black hair, which was shaved off every day during the filming of *Patton,* has grown back and he is wearing a wool sweater, baggy pants and black-rimmed history

professor spectacles. Red Van Johnson socks peer over the
tops of his lumber boots and when he looks at you his eyes
are like small cumulus clouds that make tiny swirls of
hypnotic vertigo if you look into their direct focus.

"You should see him on regular days, when we don't
have company," says his son Alexander, nine, who looks
like a young Huck Finn. "I'll leave my *Mad* comics for
you, Dad," says his other son, Campbell, eight, who looks
like a young Alain Delon. Then, after being promised a
ball game at West Point, they both go up to bed. He is left
alone with the fire and his bottle of brandy.

In the corner of the room a white dove of peace given
to him by Joanne Woodward makes a gurgling sound. He
covers the cage with a quilt and the other two doves in the
cage begin to flap their wings noisily. "Those doves of
peace are going to kill each other," he says with a dirty old
man chuckle. He was once quite a hawk himself, but then
he went to Vietnam and wrote a story about it for *Esquire*
and now, since his magnificent performance in *Patton*,
he's pretty much of a dove, too. I don't blame him. He
takes over the film and for three hours, he owns it—with
no love interest, no subplots and no other noteworthy
performances to distract from his own personal fireworks
display. It is one of the most brilliant acting triumphs of
the decade. He has a lot to be peaceful about.

But one thing troubles. Patton was a psychopath, yet
Scott has sometimes been accused of whitewashing the
general in his recent interviews. True? "False," he insists.
"From the beginning, all I asked was that we show him
as multifaceted as he really was. It caused trouble. Con-
flicts grew out of trying to serve too many masters. We
had to serve the Pentagon, we had to serve General Omar
Bradley and his book, we had to serve the Zanucks. If you
ride that many horses at the same time, you're going to
have problems. I simply refused to play George Patton as
the standard cliché you could get from newspaper clips of
the time. I didn't want to play him as a hero just to please
the Pentagon, and I didn't want to play him as an obvious,
gung-ho bully, either. I wanted to play every conceivable

facet of the man. There were three basic scripts and several revisions before I got the character I wanted. Francis Coppola wrote the first one, which was a combination of Bradley's book, *A Soldier's Story*, and Ladislas Farago's *Ordeal and Triumph*. Then there were memory differences—one guy remembers one thing, another guy says 'He wasn't like that at all!' Then Bradley got into the act and we had the problem of pleasing *him*. He got credit for being a technical adviser on the picture, but it was really General Harkins who had the best memory about Patton, who was with us every day in Spain and who did all the work. Then the James Webb script came out and I yelled and just said 'Forget the whole thing' and negotiations came to a screaming halt. It lacked color and imagination and I felt it was just another conventional Hollywood screen biography. Three months later they called back and we kicked around the Coppola script again. Then a third version by Eddie North came out of those talks and became the basis for the shooting script. We reworked it the whole time we were shooting and I kept screaming a lot and now I think it has flaws in it, it has lies in it, it has license in it—but basically, I think the film captures the essence of Patton, which is the point of the whole goddam thing.

"I ran three thousand feet of film here at home and really studied the man. I watched the way he moved and talked. Some of it I absorbed, some I threw out. For instance, he had a high, squeaky voice, like a football coach. The more excited he got, the higher it got. I didn't use that. People are used to my gravel voice and if I tried to use a high little voice it would be silly. I also tried not to editorialize about his beliefs or the things he said. Hell, you get paid for acting, for giving the *illusion* of believing, not for *actually* believing. Shit no, I didn't believe in what he did any more than I'd believe in the Marquis de Sade or Frank Merriwell! This is a schizoid business to start with. The biggest mistake an actor can make is to try to resolve all the differences between himself and the characters he plays. Patton actually believed what he was doing was right. So did Hitler. The face-slapping scene? Hell, he really struck *two* men. We only had time to put *one* in the movie. But he wasn't a hypocrite. Even though war was all he cared about, it was what he did for a living. It was a profession. Patton's war was unavoidable, not like Vietnam, which is an obscenity. At least he had no political ambitions, which is more than you can say for our generals today. I told Frank McCarthy, the producer, 'I don't want to play another *Strangelove*. I already played that fucking part.' But on the other hand, I rejected the glory-hunter cliché. Patton was a mean sonofabitch, but he was also generous to his men. Even making it as fair and objective as we did, his family washed their hands of the project. His wife even had an injunction in court against his biography being published. I guess they've lived with enough black eyes. To my knowledge, none of them have seen the film. But now that it is over, I feel we did right by the man. There are still things about him I hate and things I admire—which makes him a human being, I guess. On the whole, it was one of the best working situations I've ever had and it came wholly from my interest in Patton."

It didn't always seem so rosy. There were reports sifting back through the press of drunken brawls and angry disappearances which held up production in Spain. Scott denies the rumors. "There were times when I got frightened. Things weren't going right, so I just went out and got shit-faced. That's me. Something goes wrong, I find a bottle. I don't like it about myself but I've done it before and I'll do it again. But I never vanished for days or held up shooting or quit the picture. All actors feel insecure at times. Just try doing a play eight times a week and you'll find out how good and how bad you can be. There's no guarantee in this business that things will go right. You're on top one minute and the next minute—*zappo!* It's a cruel and capricious profession and you've got *nothing* to fall back on. So actors find shields to hide from their insecurity and pain. Sometimes mine is a bottle. Once somebody asked Patton why he wore his helmet and swaggered around and carried on all the B.S. and he said, 'Because, if I don't people will think the old man is over the hill.' So in a sense he created his own monster."

And in a sense, so has Scott. Ever since he began his remarkable career, playing the meanest Richard III ever seen by human eyes in Joe Papp's 1957 Shakespeare Festival, people have been calling him "the wild man of Broadway." He has one of the great tempers of the age. His nose has been broken five times in barroom brawls. He once smashed in a Hollywood set because he didn't like the way a scene was going, and when they posted the closing-night notice for his first Broadway play, *Comes a Day,* he went into a drunken rage, threw his fist through a glass window and played the last act bleeding into a rubber glove before being forced into a hospital where he required twenty-two stitches.

Today he is mellower, with the aid of Alcoholics Anonymous and Colleen Dewhurst, who was his third wife, a fine actress and lone pine of a woman whom one friend describes as "able to survive anything—if the day ever comes when there's a problem too big for Colleen to solve, we might as well *all* give up." G.C. is the first one to admit he has changed since the days when his coactors feared he would murder them all onstage. "I think of myself as a fairly decent human being and it gives me great pain to be considered for all the mean SOB's that come along. I've played bird decapitators, puppy stranglers, woman beaters, wife poisoners, child molesters— every goddam thing you can think of. It was quite a scene there for a while. But I think the image is changing. My TV series, *East Side, West Side,* helped, *Plaza Suite* helped, the man I played in *Petulia* helped. I hope to God the old image is fading from people's minds."

His old mama dog is having a bad dream in front of the fire. He scratches her head and the tough-guy logo seems no more real than the drivel you read in gossip columns. He loves animals, especially German shepherds. He has one dog who once had a litter of pups and a simultaneous nervous breakdown and is now the family neurotic; another who was nursed back to health by G.C. and his bodyguard after being poisoned in the Hilton Hotel in Cairo during the filming of *The Bible*. Watching him with his animals, you can see that he is a gentle man. A sour green apple with a soft core, hounded by the furies all his life.

He was born in Wise, Virginia (population 1,200), in 1927. His dad was a surveyor in a coal mine. His grandfather, who is still alive at eighty-nine, spent forty years in the mines. His people were rural mountain folks, hillside farmers and coal miners. ("Your basic Appalachia," grins G.C.) When the stock market crashed, his father went to Michigan, got a job in a tool crib at General Motors for thirty cents an hour, and G.C. grew up in Detroit. He was strong as an ox and full of muscle, but inside, he was a sensitive boy who wrote short stories and dreamed of becoming a writer. After a hitch in the Marine Corps he attended journalism classes at the University of Missouri on the GI Bill, but after three years, he felt he didn't have what it took to be a newspaperman, so he quit and bummed around for a while. In college he had met a campus actress who married him and planted the seeds of his acting career. They were divorced three years later and he drove a car to Hollywood with two friends, trying to find himself. "I got a job as a short-order cook, made some rounds, went to the studios, but mostly sat around in MacArthur Park watching the drunks," he says. Then he lived with his sister in Washington, D.C., for a while. Her husband, who was in the construction business, got him a job puddling concrete and driving a truck. He met his second wife, singer Pat Scott, and they moved to a cold-water flat in New York. He worked in a bank from midnight until 10 A.M., "shoveling checks into a registering machine," and during the day he made the rounds of casting offices. He auditioned for *Richard III* three times and got the job with no reputation or anything, playing the entire run while still working at the bank. ("To this day," confides one of the friends who knew him then, "G.C. despises banks. He probably keeps all of his money from *Patton* in a shoe box guarded by one of his German shepherds.")

In 1958, José Quintero hired him to play a wife poisoner in the third act of *Children of Darkness* down at the old Circle in the Square. J. D. Cannon and an unknown named Colleen Dewhurst had the leads. She was married, Scott was married, and they were off and running. With all the divorces and legalities, it was 1960 before they got married. They've been divorced and remarried three times since, and are currently divorced. "We couldn't live together and we couldn't live apart," says G.C. "That's about the size of it. I guess I'm just the marriageable type." He is now married to actress Trish Van Devere.

As for movie critics, he has no use for them at all. "Over a period of time you learn who is destructive and who isn't. Most critics are necessary, but years ago I gave up being affected by them. They do their thing and I do mine. The only critics you can learn anything from at all are theater critics, because if they give you valuable advice you can still do something about it. In a film, it's too late. Good or bad, your performance is cemented forever. But I have never really learned anything from *any* critic and I don't know any other actor who has, either. They have more value for writers and maybe even for the public, but not for actors. The thing an actor learns from is the audience. I don't know anything about acting teachers, either. I never had a lesson in my life. I don't think it can be taught."

He is violent on the subject of the "method" and his comments on Sandy Dennis, with whom he once appeared in a disastrous London production of *Three Sisters,* are unprintable. "Cagney and Bogart taught me how to act. During the depressing periods of most actors' lives, they sleep a lot. I went to the movies. Movies kept me off the streets and taught me everything I know. I'm probably one of the few actors in the Fifties who never once auditioned for the Actors Studio. It performed one of the greatest disservices to the theater in its entire history and probably ruined the potential of more good actors than any other force. Most method actors work their way out of my heart in no time at all." He also has little in his heart but larceny for British actors.

What he *does* love is the stage and he makes no secret of the fact that "I make movies largely for the money and always have. It's a tedious, deadly, boring way to make a living. I *have* to work in the theater to stay sane. It costs me money to do a play, but I have to do it. You can attack the stage fresh every night, you can say, 'Goddammit, it isn't right yet,' and go on working on it. It's living all the time. What's happening now in both mediums is appalling. This nudity crap. Most of it is trash and in spite of all those naked actors' claims, there is very little freedom in it. I don't think that kind of tastelessness will pay off for long. Dirty jokes are only fun for half an hour. I have not seen *Oh, Calcutta!* or *Che* or any of that garbage. I have no interest in it. I've seen all the stag films I want to see. They're like the old Moon Mullins books we used to hide in our desks at school. It's called turning a fast buck. But it's changing. I'm encouraged to learn that the Swedish film industry has taken a big drop in the last six months. Nobody's going to the movies anymore in Sweden. They've orgied themselves right out of business. It's the same in the theater. How many times can you watch people doing everything in the book to each other before it begins to look like a short-arm inspection and you wanna yell 'Cough'?"

He once directed a play called *General Seegar* which ran for two performances on Broadway ("I lost all my money and several thousand of some other people's money as well") and last year he directed *Dr. Cook's Garden*, from which he withdrew a week before the opening ("I wanted to get rid of Burl Ives and I couldn't get rid of him, so I got rid of myself"). But he still wants to join that growing list of actors-turned-directors. He directed a TV version of *The Andersonville Trial* and a movie called *Rage*. He should be an interesting director. He's certainly had enough experience working *for* them. All kinds:

Richard Lester: "I didn't know what the hell was going

on in *Petulia* and I don't really think he gives a damn about actors as much as he does about camerawork, but I really liked him. He makes it so much fun you don't worry somehow. I can't ever recall having a close-up in *Petulia*. They were all from fifty feet away. None of that B.S. about a master, then a reverse, then a medium shot. If I was going to emulate anyone, it'd be him."

Kubrick: "He has a brilliant eye; he sees more than the camera does. He walks in in the morning and says 'This is awful!' and you get used to changing things around. I used to kid him by saying I should've gotten screen credit for *Dr. Strangelove* because I wrote half the fucking picture. There's no bullshit with him, no pomposity, no vanity. The refreshing thing is he hates *everything*."

Otto Preminger: "He lent me money on *Anatomy of a Murder* when I was broke. So I like him. I was never one of his whipping boys. He's not a great director, but he's a great promoter."

Anthony Asquith: "On *The Yellow Rolls-Royce* I couldn't understand a fucking word he said. He was very fey, very nice, wore a red jump suit and a red bandana and everybody called him Puffin. But I never understood a fucking word he said throughout the entire picture."

Irvin Kershner: "He shot a good picture with *The Flim-Flam Man*, then he went mad in the cutting room and butchered the whole thing. Some of these guys get Jehovah complexes."

Mike Nichols: "He glows. Inside he may be going through the tortures of the damned, but it never shows. He creates an atmosphere for an actor to work in that is so easy you can't believe it. I loved working in *Plaza Suite* and I'd work for him again anytime anywhere—provided I liked the script, of course. He called me up and asked me to do *Catch-22* and after I read the script, I just said, 'No way . . . it's just awful!' "

His greatest ambition for the future is to have a live theater group of his own, like Orson Welles's Mercury group, combining a stage and television situation. "That would be the best of two possible worlds—an ensemble working together with no economic pressures, where you could make money by working out a play on the stage for a live audience until it was perfect, then put it on tape and start all over again with a brand-new project. Richard Boone had a similar situation, but he was under the gun, having to do a new play every six days. I wouldn't want a weekly time slot like I had on *East Side, West Side,* just a guarantee to do things when they were ready. TV has got to realize it can't all stop with *Petticoat Junction.* It is going to either be the savior of the world or send us all to hell fast. It's the most powerful communications device since the discovery of language and it is full of shit. We're still in the horse-and-buggy stage with television. In the next decade, I believe the networks as we know them now will be obsolete just as the Hollywood studios crumbled under the changing of the times. Too many forces are hammering at them now. The marketplace is too competitive for them to stay in control. The Mike Danns of the world will become as archaic as dinosaurs."

He completed the movie, *They Might Be Giants,* with Joanne Woodward and is now planning ideas for two television series. "Writing is still something I'd like desperately to succeed at and my favorite idea now is a historical anthology series using events and people from history in theatrical terms. People get hooked on characters —look at *Peyton Place*—so there's no reason why they couldn't get just as excited about Abraham Lincoln, for chrissakes! History is fascinating, man, yet every time it is shown on TV it is so dry, pompous, lifeless. There's a kind of reverence about historical figures that puts people off, but nobody expected this kind of wild reaction to a man like Patton, so why not tell the truth about Lincoln or somebody like *him*? Granted, *Patton* is a fairly good film, but to me, it's the *man* that grabs people!"

He is excited now. His voice, like Stromboli struggling to life, begins to widen. He grabs his son's *Mad* comics and whacks the sofa hard. Then he settles back again, his rasping Rasputin of a voice chipping away in a series of lecherous heh-heh-hehs. In 1962, he rocked Hollywood by being the first actor in history to refuse an Oscar nomination for *The Hustler*. Before he won one for *Patton,* he claimed, "They won't nominate me anyway. They're not *that* stupid. Besides, I want to get back to the stage. Colleen Dewhurst [his ex-wife] and I are planning a new version of *Macbeth.* She'll be a great Lady Macbeth. We won't do it in the nude! I don't want to subject the audience to that sight." His eyes gleam behind the spectacles. "Unless . . . . How about me as Macbeth, Colleen as Lady Macbeth, and, on the opposite side of the stage, Steve Reeves and Raquel Welch as our alter egos?"

Somewhere in the night, a dog barks at the moon, but it doesn't have a chance. The brandy bottle is empty and all you can hear is that famous dirty old man laugh, rich and healthy, crackling through the dark old house.

19

Elia Kazan

ELIA KAZAN, one of the most famous directors in the world, on a dismal New York afternoon in winter. Outside, it is snowing. Inside the editing room on the basement floor of his house on West-Sixty-eighth Street, he is pacing energetically, getting things off his chest, talking about *The Visitors*. The world has waited three years for a new Elia Kazan film, and now that *The Visitors*—about rape and violence in a peaceful Connecticut neighborhood following the return of two soldiers from Vietnam—is finally here, a lot of people are wondering why it's here at all. This crude, low-budget "home movie" is not what everyone expected from the director of some of the greatest movies ever made, and they want an explanation. It has been scalded by some of the critics, praised by the New Wave of underground filmmakers who want to change the face of cinema history, and hotly discussed by everyone who has seen it. Kazan is aroused by the controversy. He wears a baggy gymnasium sweat shirt, tennis shoes, runs his hands continuously through a mushroom cloud of wild white-cotton hair, and puffs cigars. It's like being in the room with one of the Marx Brothers.

The room is lined with projectors, splicers, cans of film, reels of sound effects, the tools of his trade. His wife Barbara Loden edited her film *Wanda* in this room. *The Visitors*, which Kazan made for only $150,000, was assembled here, too, and one gets the impression that whatever he does from now on will come out of this room. It seems like a good place to question a man who turned his back on his own legend, ignoring fame and money in order to make home movies, and Kazan, on this bleak afternoon, is ready with some answers. "You're right. *The Visitors* is a home movie. My son Chris wrote the script and coproduced it with Nick Proferes, the cameraman on both this one and my wife's film *Wanda*. We literally made it at my home in Connecticut, and put it together right here at my house in New York. We shot in sixteen-millimeter, using only Nick and three friends on the crew. Four of the five cast members had never been in a movie before. I picked up the guys in various acting classes and at the Actors Studio; the girl was a senior at Yale. Everybody lived in my house for eight weeks. We ate all our meals together and discussed everything as a family. If we had a pancake scene, Chris would cook the pancakes and I would carry the tripod. If I saw a hemlock tree with snow on the branches, I'd say, 'Let's go out and shoot that.' There were no pressures. Nobody complained about the cold weather in subzero conditions. We worked around the clock. You cannot shoot that way in Hollywood, where a union crew arrives at a certain hour and leaves at quitting time and the costs are astronomical. Chris and I borrowed the money from the bank and made it ourselves because we believed in it. He got $5,000 for the script and I worked for nothing. If it makes money, I'll get a percentage. If it doesn't, I won't get anything. We knew it would disturb a lot of people. It isn't rosy, or funny or the kind of film you can while away a summer night with. But I've never enjoyed working so much. It was like going back to my starting days as a director, when I was making left-wing documentaries. It's been a wonderful experience. It changed my life."

Kazan is a man going through a lot of changes. His plays (*Death of a Salesman, J.B., A Streetcar Named Desire, Camino Real, Tea and Sympathy, Cat on a Hot Tin Roof, Sweet Bird of Youth, The Dark at the Top of the Stairs, After the Fall*, etc., etc.) and his movies (*A Tree Grows in Brooklyn, Gentleman's Agreement, Pinky, Viva Zapata!, Panic in the Streets, A Streetcar Named Desire, On the Waterfront, East of Eden, Baby Doll, A Face in the Crowd, Splendor in the Grass*, etc., etc.) qualify him for sainthood. Most people believe the reason he doesn't direct much anymore is because his last two films—*America, America* and *The Arrangement*—were such financial disasters that he doesn't get many offers. That's not true. (Scripts still flood his desk; only last year he turned down *The Godfather*.) He simply prefers to make movies his own way. For *The Visitors*, he got no salary, no fee and no expenses. By donating his services on a nonunion film, he violated the rules of his own union, the Screen Directors Guild. Kazan says he doesn't care. "I'll go and talk to them. But they're all in trouble out in Hollywood, and if I can't make them see the way I've been doing things, then I'll resign."

He lights a fresh cigar and narrows his eyes. "I have a feeling I will never make another picture that will be universally popular, but now I must make films that I can control and edit and release myself—films that cost very little money and say something about how I feel about the world. If they don't make money, the financial risk will not be so great, because I know how to make them cheap. *The Arrangement* ended up costing $7,000,000 and you don't see the money on the screen. That's Hollywood filmmaking, and I'm sick of the waste. One day Deborah

Kerr had to have a bathrobe for a scene. I said wear your own bathrobe. But we had to pay two union wardrobe ladies, so in order to justify all that money we were spending, they couldn't let her wear her own clothes. They had to design something. By the time that scene got on the screen, that bathrobe ended up costing $1200 and it's only on the screen one minute! For $1200, I paid everyone's salary on *The Visitors*. In fact, the entire movie cost less than what Faye Dunaway paid her agent on *The Arrangement*. I was very wounded by that whole experience and I will never make another film like that again."

OK, but would he have made *The Visitors* if it hadn't been written by his son? "Yes, because it's the only script I've been offered in three years that dealt with something real and vital—in this case, the aftermath of Vietnam. But I'm glad Chris is the one who did write it, because it brought us closer together. He saw his old man not as some odd figure, but as someone he could talk to and work with as an equal. But I also wanted to say something about the violence in peaceful, everyday men. I didn't like *Straw Dogs* because it made it easy for people to reject their own violent natures by saying, 'Those people on the screen are brutes, but they are not like us!' Violence has always been accepted on the screen if it happens in the Old West, or in foreign countries or in the past. But people refuse to recognize it in themselves, their kids, their friends. We don't deal with it until something shakes us up. It's beneath the surface in each of us and when we're frightened or threatened, it's amazing how we react.

"Look at Calley. You see him in newsreels, or on TV, and he doesn't look remote or villainous. He looks like someone you'd like to watch the Super Bowl with. Yet he committed all those violent atrocities. My wife Barbara was mugged in front of our house, not ten feet from all the doormen on Central Park West, and dragged halfway down the block by a man aiming a gun at her head in broad daylight and nobody came to her defense. Violence is all around us. I wanted to make a movie about that, but I would never have gotten the money if I'd gone to the

Hollywood studios. Good or bad, it's the movie I wanted to make, and that's all I care about at this stage of my life."

In answer to all queries about why he deserted the theater, Kazan (or Gadge, as he's known in show-biz circles) says he never wants to direct another play. "Why? Because when I turned fiftyish, I began to realize the problems of all the playwrights I adored and was associated with—Tennessee Williams, Robert Anderson, William Inge, Arthur Miller, etc.—were not *my* problems. I don't see life the way they do. I wanted to write books that told my point of view. So I wrote *America, America* and *The Arrangement,* and I found it more fulfilling than directing the work of others with whom I sympathized spiritually but not personally." (His third novel, *The Assassins,* has just been published by Stein and Day.) "Also, I'm not catholic in my tastes. I'll admit that. The plays I liked and had a success with are not in favor now. What else can I do? Shakespeare? I'm not interested in reviving old classics. Barbara getting mugged in front of my house is twenty times more interesting to me than *Hamlet.* There is no goddam theater anymore, anyway. It's boring and archaic and I never go to the theater. Playwrights aren't writing what they feel inside; they're writing plays to fill seats. I hate the theater. Movies is where all the action is. Film uses all the arts combined—it is the only art form that moves as fast as we do, that speaks the way we do in sounds and images and pictures. I feel more alive today than I did when I was directing plays.

"The problem is to make the kinds of films I want. To do that, I've had to hold out. A lot of Hollywood directors in my age range are facing the same problems—guys like Fred Zinnemann, William Wyler, Billy Wilder—but the difference is that they've gotten themselves into an expensive life-style that has them by the throat and I don't need as much money to live. My books have made a lot of money and that tides me over between films. The way I filmed *The Visitors* will affect everything I do from now on. I'm just as enthusiastic about filmmaking today as when I started, but I think my films will be better in the future. Knowing what I've learned about saving on the costs, I could go back and remake all of my old films right now, and they'd be better. When I made *Pinky* it stirred up all kinds of hell, but it was a phony picture. If I made it now, I'd never try to make the Fox back lot look like the South, or use Jeanne Crain, the blandest person I ever worked with, as a black girl trying to pass herself off as white. I made all kinds of compromises in those days, but never again.

"Even if I did *The Arrangement* now, with people I know, using real elevators and my own house instead of Hollywood sets, it would be a simpler and truer film. The only film I ever made, however, that I'm truly ashamed of was a western called *Sea of Grass* that keeps turning up on the *Late Show*. I was completely intimidated by Spencer Tracy and Katharine Hepburn, and it showed. Every time she went to the toilet she came back in a new gown and he was supposed to be a cowboy born to the saddle, but he took one look at the horse and he hated the horse and the horse hated him and the whole thing was a disaster."

No matter what the fate of *The Visitors* will be at the box office, he's not ashamed of his home movie. Unions or no unions. Hollywood or no Hollywood. Critics or no critics. Meanwhile, there's more writing and thinking and self-analysis in the house on Sixty-eighth Street to digest. He's not down for the count, even though all of his Academy Awards are hidden in a closet covered with New York soot and fallout. "I feel in control of my own destiny as a creative man," he says. "The more I read and write, without the former pressures of doing things for money I didn't believe in, the more I reflect on life around me. I was fifty-five when I started writing and making movies my own way. I'm sixty-two years old now, and I'm just beginning."

20

Richard Chamberlain

HEN THE BRITISH press saw *Lady Caroline Lamb*, the violins-and-valentines romantic saga, they were startled to see America's own Ivy League Dr. Kildare, Richard Chamberlain, peacock-strutting across the screen as the poet Lord Byron. Lipsticked, silk-ruffled—this couldn't be that mild-mannered TV intern with the basketball player casualness who had half the women in America making up fake diseases just to get to Blair General Hospital! The physical appearance was so shocking, one critic wrote: "It's as if Aubrey Beardsley had supervised his dress, diet and decadence."

Richard Chamberlain has come a long way, baby. It's not a career; it's a reincarnation. He went out Dr. Kildare and came back an actor.

When you meet the real Richard Chamberlain, it's ee-rie. Like seeing an old college friend you haven't seen since the old frat-house panty raids. He's been living in England, and there's something out of step about his man-ner. The voice is soft, the style is polite to a fault, the delivery is hesitant. He's wearing Edwardian hair and a coachman's suit that went out of style when the Beatles retired, but never mind that. It's as though the college yearbook editor went away and got possessed by Dorian Gray.

Politely and meticulously sipping alternate glasses of red and white wine with his fettucine at Orsini's, Richard Chamberlain laughs at the suggestion, but even the laugh has a slightly affected edge. "There is no question that my life has changed," he says. "I haven't played a contempo-rary American person since *Petulia*, and I'd like to see if I can do it again."

He was an impotent sadist in that one. Since then, he's played Tchaikovsky in Ken Russell's *The Music Lovers*, the Duke of Windsor on TV, Hamlet at the Birmingham (England) Repertory Company, Richard II in Seattle, Oc-tavius in a movie version of *Julius Caesar* and a lot of other weird things no American actor ever tried. He just re-turned from playing *The Fantasticks* in Chicago, and his next role will be Cyrano de Bergerac at the Ahmanson in Los Angeles. The man knows no fear.

It has been a gingham-checked career, undoubtedly fired by an indescribable ambition, and Richard Cham-berlain doesn't deny it. But where is the real Richard Chamberlain? One of his friends from the old Dr. Kildare days says: "Richard has no private life. He has never loved anyone but himself. His entire life has been dedicated to proving to everybody he can act with the best of them, and everything that interferes with that goal is elimi-nated. He started out like a million other pretty faces in TV, and he achieved the unobtainable. He played Ham-let. Now he doesn't know where he's going as an actor, but he's just beginning to blossom as a man."

"It's been a long haul since Pomona College," he sighs.

"I majored in philosophy, ran for the track team, and did five lines in *King Lear*. After college, I was drafted and went to Korea, where I nearly died of boredom. I thought of being a painter, but it was too lonely. So I worked as a box boy at Ralph's Market on Wilshire Boulevard, waited on tables, worked as a chauffeur, collected unemployment checks. I didn't have much money. My mother owned a small percentage in an oil well that only produced enough oil to send me through college before it ran dry. I started doing bits on television. Then I sort of fell into the Kildare series. That's when I really started thinking seriously about acting."

At the height of his popularity, he was receiving 12,000 fan letters a week—more than the king of the MGM lot, Clark Gable, received in his salad days. But it wasn't enough. Sir Cedric Hardwicke told him: "You're doing it all backwards. You're a star, and you don't know how to act." So the star took singing lessons, acting lessons, fencing lessons, and the ambition grew.

"I feel like Dr. Kildare is dead and buried now, but at the end of the five years, everybody treated me like Kildare. My first reaction was total freedom. My second reaction was incredible insecurity because I didn't realize how much I had come to depend on the steady income. I found I wasn't welcomed with open arms in the movies, and I didn't want to do another TV series. I had to do something challenging, but I had no real experience except what I had learned on the show.

"I hated any reference to Kildare then, but I'm mellower now. There were things about the series I liked— the money, the steady employment, the recognition. It wasn't all taking pulses and reading thermometers. I got to play angry scenes, happy scenes, the committed rebel scenes. That's all the training I had as an actor. Then I did *Petulia*, and working for Richard Lester made me want to work more for the British.

"So there was this talk show in London that offered to pay my way over. It was fate. The second day I was there I got the lead in the Henry James *Portrait of a Lady* series on the BBC, and that was the turning point in my career.

Hamlet came out of that, the role of the French lover in *Madwoman of Chaillot* came out of that, the Ken Russell film came out of that. I just sort of turned into a British actor."

But surely it was not as easy as falling out of bed. Not just every run-of-the-contract TV actor gets to play Hamlet with the Birmingham Rep. "No, and let me tell you I was accepted only after all the young British actors turned it down. British Equity didn't want me to do it. I still don't have a work permit in England. But the director had faith in me. I was terrified. The British are very snobbish and protective about Shakespeare.

"I was surrounded by twenty-year-olds who came in and read like John Gielgud on the first day. On the second day, they had learned the entire play. I was still stumbling around onstage, not knowing where I was. I'm a slow worker. I can't give a performance until I know exactly what I'm doing and understand the part completely. But it had taken me three months to get up the courage to do Hamlet, and I was determined to go through with it.

"I was in a state of shock. But amazingly enough, the company did not resent me. There was none of that 'We're better than you' or 'We're doing you a favor letting you work here' stuff. In America, they would have eaten me alive. If I had suggested playing Hamlet in Hollywood, they'd have said 'Who the hell do you think you are? Get back into your white doctor's coat.' But the British were helpful and kind, and the project was a matter of personal discovery for my own growth as an actor."

The critics were in shock, too. The reviews glowed. Richard Chamberlain was off and running.

There have been low periods. After the Broadway-bound musical, *Breakfast at Tiffany's*, closed in previews, he went into analysis for four years. "I have never felt such hostility from an audience. They wanted to kill us. When the closing was announced, Mary Tyler Moore gave a wake and I got very manic and uptight. I walked past the marquee to see my name in lights for one last time, and then I cried all night."

After Ken Russell's *The Music Lovers* was over, he "was

determined to give up acting. I've never been so depressed, and it took me weeks and weeks to get over it. I love Ken and would do anything for him, but on a movie set he's so serious and demanding that he made Glenda Jackson and me do those scenes over and over, sometimes twenty times, until we couldn't move. It was no fun. That picture nearly put me in a loony bin. But I loved the film."

He just finished a run in *The Lady's Not for Burning* at the Chichester Festival in England. "I'm the first American who was ever invited to play there," he said proudly. I reminded him that Irene Worth, that "great British actress from the London stage" had made it before him. She's from Nebraska. He looked crestfallen. "Well, don't tell anyone. I'm passing it around that I'm the first."

Still that need to impress, to prove. Why? "I guess I just don't revere my own personality that much. I don't have much skill or technique, but I have learned about myself through acting. When I'm not doing a role, I cease to interest myself. During my four years in analysis, I worked through my uptightness. I felt barren, inhibited, unhappy—nothing was happening to fulfill me. I always took myself seriously, but I was afraid people would laugh at me.

"These last few years have been an intensely personal period in which I've tried to find new things to do, to find out what I could do, and now nobody's laughing. They really are forgetting all about Dr. Kildare. A few years ago, I would have been afraid to wear so much eye makeup in *Lady Caroline Lamb*, but Robert Bolt, who wrote it and directed it, convinced me it would be all right. Lord Byron was amazingly vain. He wore his hair in curlers, went on reducing kicks, ate potatoes and vinegar to whiten his complexion. I played him as a kind of mad genius, but with a kind of cheapness.

"I could only do that because I felt more secure as an actor. And now I'm feeling more secure as a person. I went back and did *The Fantasticks* just to see if I could do a musical, and now I don't think that's what I want to do. It was frivolous and not very rewarding, like eating too much dessert. I wasn't tired enough when it was all over. I like to be tired. Everything has built up to such a momentum, and I don't want to drop the ball. The next thing I do has to make me tired again. I'm still trying to prove something to myself, but I'm enjoying myself more and bringing people into my life now. It's been a long and painful odyssey."

Like Lord Byron, Richard Chamberlain, still neurotically attracted to the excitement of conquest, but allergic to commitment. Later he phoned to make sure he hadn't said anything unkind about Robert Bolt making him wear eye makeup in *Lady Caroline Lamb*. I assured him he hadn't. "I guess I'm being silly," he laughed.

Not silly. Just unnecessarily insecure. Still trying to prove when there's no need. Richard Chamberlain is a very nice man and a very fine actor. When other actors push and shove, he gently begs for approval. He's diplomatically getting on with his reincarnation. Then he'll work on his life. It may be the hardest role he has ever been asked to play.

21

Alice Faye

SHE WAS BEFORE MY TIME, but I remember Alice Faye. Last week, she was back and you know something funny? I've grown up, but Alice Faye hasn't changed at all. At the age of fifty-six, she doesn't look like Tuesday Weld, but then who does? Tuesday Weld doesn't even look like Tuesday Weld. And Alice Faye sings better. She still has those big navy-blue moo-cow eyes, the same soft blond hair gently coiffed back from the neck and tied with a girlish scarf, the same husky, moonstruck voice, the same warm, easy laugh full of nice-girl surprise. Remarkable.

She sat on the edge of the sofa in her hotel suite at the St. Regis, the same petite 120-pound dish she was when she walked off the 20th Century-Fox lot at the height of her fame and told Darryl F. Zanuck where to stuff it. She wore a chic black turtle-neck sweater and a red plaid skirt that showed two of the prettiest legs this side of *Playboy*, sipped a scotch and water, played with a magnifying glass that hung from her neck on a gold chain and chatted amiably about a comeback. "It's all coming back and I think it's wonderful. The songs, the old clothes. If you wait around long enough, it all comes back. A girl from *Women's Wear Daily* came to interview me yesterday and she said, 'I'm so sad the glamour passed my generation by, will I ever live to see pink dressing gowns and maribou feathers again?' and I said, 'It's all up to you, honey.' I'm holding on to my old Irene suits."

She was in New York for two reasons. The newly revived *Liberty* magazine threw a big party in the Rainbow Room on top of Rockefeller Center and gave her a plaque as the "Film Star to Remember" and Benny Goodman was there. And Lillian Roth and Hildegarde and Ruby Keeler and all kinds of Nostalgia Queens. "And last night I went to see Ruby in *No, No, Nanette* and cried my eyes out. It's just wonderful what's happened to Ruby. Now I'd like my chance. Not a comeback; I don't have to work and I wouldn't do just anything. But I'm in great shape. My voice is a heckuva lot lower than it used to be, but I swim every day, play golf and go to Elizabeth Arden's twice a year for massages and exercises. I don't go to lunches or play cards with the ladies and I never smoke until after six P.M. And I can still kick. For a long time, I didn't want to work. I've been married to Phil [Harris] for thirty years and we have a beautiful ranch house in Palm Springs. But now our two girls are married with homes of their own, I've got four grandchildren, and Phil's away in Vegas doing his act a lot, so I'd like to get back into the swing. There comes a time in every actress' life when she feels like making herself useful again. Loretta Young is selling her jewels to run some kind of Boys Town in Arizona, Janet Gaynor sells squabs in Palm Springs and makes her deliveries in her own truck, now it's my turn.

"I don't go to movies much anymore. I don't understand the Jane Fondas, I don't understand the *I Am Curi-*

ous—Yellow's. I went to see that thing with a girl friend
in San Francisco and we had to have three double martinis afterwards. I don't live in the past, but the old movies
are still the ones people remember. I watch them on TV
and cry like a slob. I don't think Rita Hayworth or any of
those stars are shown as often on TV as my old films. There
is always someone around ready to knock you, to call the
whole nostalgia bit corny, always somebody who will ridi-
cule you and say, 'Why didn't Ruby Keeler and Alice Faye
stay home and play golf ?' But I sat in *No, No, Nanette* and
it was nothing but bravo, bravo, bravo! Where else can
you go today where people stand on the tops of their seats
screaming their heads off ? I'm all for it."

And why not? Veterans of the silver screen no longer
fade away; they return to thunderous glory, carried aloft
on waves of nostalgia that mean big money at the box
office. Ruby Keeler and Patsy Kelly are hoofing it up on
the Great White Way. Poor clutzy Yvonne DeCarlo, elegant as a giraffe, can't sing *or* dance, but she's a hit doing
both in *Follies*, surrounded by other old-time favorites
Alexis Smith, Gene Nelson and Dorothy Collins (who, according to Miss Faye, is "that girl who sold Lucky
Strikes"). Ann Miller is machine-gun tapping her way to
the bank in the TV soup commercials, Jane Russell is doing *Company* and Rita Hayworth and Arlene Dahl auditioned to replace Lauren Bacall in *Applause*. So why not
Alice Faye?

In a sense, she was never away. Her movies play constantly on TV. Her fan clubs are still active all over the
world. In London, there is even an "Alice Faye Cinema
Club" that shows an Alice Faye movie twice a week to
members ranging in age from their early twenties to
midfifties. And what movies! *In Old Chicago, Hello Frisco
Hello, Alexander's Ragtime Band, That Night in Rio, Rose
of Washington Square, Tin Pan Alley, Weekend in
Havana* . . . the list goes on and on. She had come out of
Hell's Kitchen, little Alice Leppert, whose father was a
cop. When she was fifteen, she was dancing in the chorus
of *George White's Scandals,* and later she toured with

Rudy Vallee's band. The band hit Hollywood and Alice became America's singing sweetheart. "I was living with my mother in Mae West's apartment building and Rudy took me to meet Sidney Kent, the banker who financed a lot of the movies, and I sang 'Oh, You Nasty Man' with Vaseline on my eyelids to look sexy and the next thing I knew I was replacing the star of the movie *George White's Scandals* over the objections of George White himself!" In 1934 Rudy Vallee's wife named Alice in an ugly divorce case, but to this day she claims she "was never part of any wild Hollywood scene. My best friends were my stand-in and my movie crews. I never had a man drink champagne out of my shoes or anything like that. That all happened during the Gloria Swanson era. When I got there, it was all over."

She married Tony Martin in September, 1936, but broke up three years later because in order to talk to him she had to send him telegrams. She married Phil Harris twice in 1941—once in Mexico, later in Galveston, Texas, to make it legal—and after that she began putting the skids on her own career. Darryl F. Zanuck, the head of Fox, had been feuding with her for years. He banned her from the radio and harassed her further by bringing in Betty Grable, but the two stars honeyed and darlinged each other all over the lot to his dismay. Finally, the dam burst in 1945 when she made her last picture, a dud called *Fallen Angel.* "I had fallen in love with a movie called *Laura,* and begged the studio to find me a drama. So they got Otto Preminger, who directed *Laura,* and Dana Andrews, who starred in it, and found a property for us all to do. I had some wonderful scenes in it, but Zanuck cut them all out and behind my back he built up a new girl named Linda Darnell, bless her soul. She's dead now. I had nothing against her, but I thought Zanuck played a dirty trick. I drove right through the gate and left the key to my dressing room with the guard, along with a note for Mr. Zanuck." She rolled her Lillian Russell eyes and I could only guess what the contents were. Unprintable. "I never went back. Zanuck begged me to do *The Dolly*

Sisters with Grable, but I never answered his calls. I didn't want any part of that place again. I walked out and stayed out. Never even cleaned out my dressing room. I just left everything hanging right where it was."

Sixteen years later, she did go back to do a remake of *State Fair.* It was a disaster. When she talks about it, her face turns white. "Everything had changed. In the old days, the studio was like home. All the actors like Ty Power and Don Ameche and John Payne—they were like a family to me. On picture after picture I had the same hairdresser, the same lighting man, the same wardrobe girls. The street they now call Avenue of Stars was just a dirt road and in the background you could see oil wells pumping. I couldn't wait to get to work in the morning. Going back crushed me. The studio was in such chaos you couldn't even tell who was running it anymore. I think they hated me, because I was too young to play Pat Boone's mother, I had absolutely no direction from José Ferrer, I was lit wrong, photographed badly . . . and they made me play opposite Tom Ewell!! Do you *know* Tom Ewell??" She just stared, those CinemaScope eyes growing large as targets, refusing to say anything more about Tom Ewell, but you know she *could.* "The whole thing was a nightmare. I never even saw it until it played on TV. It was awful. I don't know what happened to the picture business, but I'm sorry I went back to find out.

"I don't want to say anything bad about anybody, but the only thing I hope is that I live to see Darryl F. Zanuck washed up in this business. . . . The stories I could tell you if this wasn't for publication! And another thing that bothers me. All those musicals we did never won an Academy Award. We gave so much of ourselves, but we were taken for granted. Then millions and millions of dollars were made when the old musicals were sold off in chunks to TV, yet I don't get a penny. For all that work, you'd think they'd at least give me a pickle dish!"

22

Dorothy Malone

*S*o you think you got it made, my friend . . . but
oh, the kick is brief. . . .

The lyrics from that song by Alec Wilder could
easily have been written for Dorothy Malone. In 1956, she
won an Academy Award as best supporting actress of the
year for playing a memorable tramp in a mediocre movie
called *Written on the Wind*. Today she is back in her
hometown of Dallas, where her unlisted phone seldom
rings and she talks vaguely of selling real estate. It's a nice
lemon-yellow house with grass-green carpets on a quiet,
tree-lined street a few blocks from Southern Methodist
University, where she was once the prettiest girl on campus. She still looks like a movie star. During a visit, she sat
in her living room sipping a Dr. Pepper in orange sunglasses, white slacks and a white sweater, her lustrous

yellow hair catching glints of the Texas sun. A Doberman pinscher named Gretchen ate the oatmeal cookies off the coffee table and her soft, slightly nervous conversation was occasionally interrupted by the laughter of her two daughters, Mimi, eleven, and Diane, nine, splashing loudly in the backyard swimming pool. None of it ruffled her. She's had all that. Now she's settling for the life of the prettiest girl at the PTA.

"I'm a very peaceful person now," she said bravely. "People think if you win an Oscar you're set for life on Easy Street. Forget it. After *Written on the Wind* I did scads of pictures. Sometimes I was working on two at the same time. I'd report to MGM at six o'clock in the morning, then drive all the way out to the San Fernando Valley when I got off at five to do night work on another picture at another studio. I was overworked, exhausted and anemic, and the pictures were all terrible. I remember one called *Quantez* with Fred MacMurray that I did because we were old friends and I thought it would be nice for auld lang syne. I hated the script, but I knew he wanted me to do it, so I said OK. The night we previewed it, he said to me, 'Why did you want to do a dog like this?' So I confessed. I told him I did it just because he had been keen on it. He roared. 'I hated it!' he said, 'I did it just because I thought *you* wanted to do it!' And that's what happens to you out there. You get into a work habit and after a while you can't tell a good movie from a bad one."

But why so many bad ones after winning an Oscar? "It's funny. Winning an Oscar can be a jinx. After I won it, I could sense it in people's faces. It was a look that said, 'Why did I vote for her?' There aren't many plum juicy roles in the first place, but after you win an Oscar you have a choice. You can either sit back and wait until the good roles come along or you can work constantly so people won't think you were a one-time joke. Instead of sitting around waiting, I tried to keep working, but instead of the good scripts I got nothing but second-rate bombs. People who weren't aware of my existence before I won the Oscar suddenly began offering me everything under the sun just because I had this award. But instead of better

roles, they got worse and worse. The same thing has happened to others. Look at Lila Kedrova, Mercedes McCam-
bridge, Maximilian Schell, Ernest Borgnine, Red Buttons,
Shirley Jones, Gloria Grahame . . . the popular misconcep-
tion that an Oscar guarantees fame and genius forever is
a myth!

"Then although I had fought against doing TV for a long
time, I decided to do the *Peyton Place* series just to get
my teeth into a good part again. I hated it. I worked like
a dog and the hours were very long. Then my marriage
to Jacques Bergerac broke up and it was a very nasty mess.
He wasn't very nice about it and every two weeks I'd get
a court summons. It got so bad that every time someone
walked up to me with a piece of paper it was either an
autograph book or a subpoena. The idea of a courtroom
hearing terrified me and the work and the fear, combined
with my delicate physical condition, took its toll on me
finally. I got blood clots in my lungs and nearly died.
While I was flat on my back in the hospital recovering
from major surgery, I got another subpoena. I finally collapsed."

Shades of Carroll Baker, where the husband tries to sue
the movie-star wife for *his* support instead of the other
way around. It is clear, listening to the emotion in her
voice, that she is a woman who has been wounded in the
school of hard knocks. But there must be something to the
old wives' tale about the indestructibility of Texas Long-
horns. She survived. "I finally got myself together long
enough to spend fifteen days going over all the accounts
check by check to prove what was mine. Between the
doctors and the attorneys, I've paid almost everything I'm
worth as an actress just trying to buy peace and quiet. I
was finally told by the court I could leave California on a
Friday, so I packed up the kids, the dogs, the cats, my
mother, and we rented a trailer and drove to Dallas. This
has always been my home and my family encouraged me
to come back to Texas and try to get back in touch with
my own sanity again. I stayed with them for a while until
I could find a house all my stuff would fit into."

It still doesn't fit. The paintings from her beach house

in Malibu are stacked all over the house because there
isn't enough wall space to hang them, and the rooms are
too small to contain all the French provincial furniture,
the venetian glass mirrors, the chintz-covered sofas and
the elegant Queen Anne chairs that clutter the place and
make it look like a furniture store. But the inconvenience
of being a displaced person seems to be compensated for
by the new luxury of freedom and independence. "I'm a
very peaceful person, really. I love people and I'm never
bored. I never was very good at living like a movie star
and I always knew I'd come back home someday. I was a
languages major in college when I did a screen test in my
living room with a boy I knew. It was his test, but RKO
sent for me instead. It was one of those fluke accidents,
really. Even after I arrived in Hollywood, I attended
classes at the University of Southern California at night.
I was working in a movie with Dennis Morgan called *One
Sunday Afternoon* at the time. I got off at six-thirty and
classes began at seven. I got over one hundred speeding
tickets, so I finally gave it up. But I never gave up my need
to get back to real people again. My father does my income tax and my mother is in California selling off my
property. I may get into the real estate business here in
Dallas. I used to go out and look at property investments
between scenes when I was working in pictures. I'm very
good at it. It'd be nice to never have to work again, but
I'm not financially secure enough to stop working
forever."

She may not have to worry. Last year she costarred with
Harvey Korman in *Little Me* at the Dallas State Fair Musicals, followed by a movie in Rome, several TV guest shots,
and now there's talk of doing *Cactus Flower* on the stage
this summer. She doesn't go to many movies and some of
her ideas are surprisingly radical for a girl who once
played the classiest whores in Hollywood. "I took the children to see *Thoroughly Modern Millie* and it was dis-
graceful! It was murky and depressing and what they
were *really* talking about was white slavery! Walt Disney
movies promote cruelty to animals and that terrible *Oli-*

ver! was about thievery, crime and prostitution! I can't stand nudity, either. All the wrong people are doing it. I suppose if we remade *Written on the Wind* today, we'd be naked as jaybirds. I simply do not want to clutter my mind with such garbage."

Instead, she occupies her time in Dallas swimming, flying kites and riding bikes. Her girls go to school only one mile away from her front door, she attends every school function and writes skits for the PTA programs. (She also took time out from all the vitamin D to marry again recently, but a few days later she told a Dallas judge her new husband tried to swindle her savings and the marriage was annulled.) One makes do.

"I'm not running away. Today you can't run away from anything, because you're always only a phone call away from Hollywood if a job offer comes through. I've lived in Oregon, New York, Rome . . . and I loved them all. It only takes me a few weeks to settle in. I love it here in Dallas. It's impossible to be unhappy in so much sunshine." Hot rays of Texas sun filtered through the magnolia tree in her front yard, ricocheted off the top of her station wagon and caught a brief glint in the center of a bookcase where a lonely gold-plated Academy Award stood half hidden behind two porcelain nuns. At that moment, Dallas didn't seem so far from Hollywood after all.

23

Doris Day

DORIS DAY SPRANG into the Brown Derby for breakfast like a lost daisy looking for a spring bouquet to get lost in. Although her car was parked outside, she looked dressed for a bike ride. Her sunny blond hair bobbed under a perky tam-o'-shanter, her babbling brook of a voice gurgled from behind a wad of sugarless gum, and her white, regular teeth gleamed behind that dazzling smile that has been an American trademark ever since she walked across the screen for the first time in *Romance on the High Seas* in 1948 and became a motion picture institution. But something was wrong. Her vivacious eyes were puffy from crying. Even her famous freckles seemed troubled. Doris Day, who practically never gives interviews, was anxious to talk about something.

"No matter what you expect her to be like, she'll be different," I had been told by her son, Terry Melcher.

"The thing about Doris," said one of her closest friends, "is that she's been treated so badly by the press because of her genuine honesty and niceness in a town that considers these qualities eccentric, that she's stopped seeing the press. That gave her the reputation for being a recluse. But it's not true. She's totally involved with life and very dedicated to what she believes. Meet her and you'll see. She's not a phony."

I did. And she wasn't. The first thing she did was present me with a button from her purse that said "Dogs Are Human Too." I thanked her. "It costs a buck," she winked. I paid her the dollar and we were off. During a week in which people were proclaiming gloom and doom from every Hollywood phone booth, Doris had jolted the city of Los Angeles by leading a raid on a slum shack in the San Fernando Valley and rescuing more than 100 diseased and dying dogs from a "tiny Dachau for animals" in which they were being tortured and neglected to death. Saving the animals is the only thing Doris Day cares about these days. Other stars have pet charities because they get to wear new gowns and be photographed in the society pages, but Doris couldn't care less about publicity. She's saving the animals so she can sleep nights. She likes animals better than most people and is devoting her life to their cause. Go ahead and smile. The girl really means it.

"I don't want to talk about me, for criminy sakes! I'd do anything for CBS. They pay me well, and if I want to pay for all the new kennels I plan to build, they better pick up my option, but I've talked about my broken leg and how I got started in the business and how I traveled with Les Brown's band for twenty years now and I'm beginning to hear myself in my sleep! This is the first time I've been to the Brown Derby in years. I haven't been to Wilshire Boulevard but once in the past year and that was to pick some clothes for my show off the rack. I haven't been to a Bel-Air screening since the night a group of famous people started attacking *The Roots of Heaven* and I got mad because it was all about saving the elephants. I used to worry about what people thought of me, but every time I tried to explain myself to people I got hatcheted in the press for having a soda fountain in my home or riding a bike to work and I finally just gave up. Whatever I am is what I came in with. I've had no acting or singing lessons, no training. What you see on the screen is me. I'm not a business. I don't want to sit around and be a big movie star and eat chocolates while fourteen servants clean the house. I don't know where the Goody Two-Shoes image got started. I'm the image created by my parents and whatever people think is their problem. So I like ice cream better than scotch. Sue me. But since my husband died, I've had to do a lot of thinking about myself and, if people think I'm square, then terrific! I do like old-fashioned values in a world that looks pretty much to me as though it's falling apart and as long as I stick up for my own little corner of that world, I know God will protect me. Tomorrow will take care of itself. Meanwhile, I have to do something about this lousy world today."

What she's doing is starting out small, with the little fellows who can't look out for themselves. In Hollywood, she's known as the Joan of Arc of the Four-Legged Set, leading the crusade for an organization called Actors and Others for Animals. "We're small, with only $11,000 in our fund, but we're making tremendous progress. The reason I look like I have the flu today is because I've been crying for three days after that raid. Let me tell you about it, because I'm sure there are people out there who have no idea about the deplorable conditions that exist in this country for animals. We got a report on this place in Burbank owned by some woman.

"It was just a shack with no windows and no ventilation and no heat, filled with animal droppings and she actually slept there, although there wasn't even a bed in the place. She had this board fence eight feet high and behind that was a mudhole filled with more than 100 dogs. They were blind and sick. Many of them had to be put to sleep. She was feeding them with old wet bread which she kept in a hearse in the front yard. I stood there, covered in dirt and blood, while they handed each dog to me in a towel, and the tears just started streaming down my face. I'm telling you, I wanted to flatten that lady. Meanwhile, the dogs are all in the city pound until we can have this woman prosecuted. And the humane officers do nothing. She was brought up on charges before, but they were dropped by a lady judge! I'm having her investigated, too.

"And the city pounds, even the boarding kennels, are like concentration camps. Do you know that to put an animal to sleep costs only six cents a shot, yet they refuse to do it, claiming they would need more manpower and that is too expensive for the taxpayer? So they put animals into decompression chambers that explode their lungs and when they take them out the next day, there are some dogs and cats still crawling around alive because these inhumane, so-called euthanasia methods do not work. These little creatures have no protection against society. We need legislation, we need new laws, we need to get rid of the do-nothings who have been appointed to the Animal Regulation Boards, and I'm going into politics. I called Ronald Reagan on the phone and, of course, they said it was impossible to speak to the governor and I said, 'You tell him it's his costar from *The Winning Team*. I was married to him when he was only Grover Cleveland Alexander the baseball player, and he'd better call me back if he knows what's good for him.' Well, he was on the phone in four minutes flat. I said, 'Ronnie, this is Doris, and we're in big trouble down here in LA,' and he said, 'It's a city problem.' He hates Mayor Yorty, and all these politicians do is shift the blame. But the animals suffer. Animals don't vote."

But Doris does, and her voice is being heard loud and clear throughout the country. She has so many people in a tizzy that the animal regulation officers in Los Angeles are making speeches on television announcing plans for increased revenue for the city pounds. "It's just lip service," says Doris. "I'm out to get rid of the animal regulation officers and replace them with people who care about their jobs. My goals are to get more heat into the city pounds, get the dogs off the cold cement floors. When we took the dogs from that woman's house back to the pound, they wouldn't even let me put newspapers down on the floor of the cages because it was against regulations. I want more women working in the pounds, I want the personnel trained. You can imagine some of the people who work there, the kind you find in mental institutions. Nobody else could put dogs and cats into decompression chambers with a clear conscience. And we want to cut down on the population explosion by having free mobile units to spay them. This takes time and money, but anybody who wants to make a contribution can write to me in care of Actors and Others for Animals, P.O. Box 67601, Los Angeles 90067. I want to hear from every person who knows of one cat or dog in pain. We'll get all the animals out of these shelters, pay their vet bills and place them in good homes, and eventually, I hope to open my own kennel where animals will really be cared for properly. But it will take time.

"I have already auctioned off all my old fur coats and even the bicycle from my TV special. To raise money, I set up a shop on the set of *The Doris Day Show* over at CBS and went around with one of those cigarette trays girls wear in nightclubs, selling nuts, popcorn balls, fruit cakes, pie by the slice. Jeff Donnell baked cranberry bread —she gets two bucks a loaf but she gave it to me for the fund—Barbara Hale made candy, the guys in the CBS paint shop made a sign that said 'Dodo's Gift Shop and Kennel,' everybody pitched in. I made $2,000 and there's more where that came from. In May, I'm planning a huge charity bazaar. Kaye Ballard has a friend in Texas who is getting celebrities to do drawings on beer mugs, and we'll sell hot dogs and I'm getting together hairdressers and makeup artists to sell their services and I'm trying to get Chrysler to raffle off a new car and we'll give away tickets to Hawaii, and all kinds of things. I'm selling every gown I ever wore in my old movies. I don't need them. I never go anywhere."

Until then, Doris has all the actors in Hollywood saving the aluminum cartons from TV dinners to feed stray cats and dogs throughout Los Angeles. At 7:30 A.M. she goes around ringing doorbells with cats in her arms, lecturing her neighbors who have left their gates open all night. "You're Doris Day!" screamed one hysterical housewife in curlers recently. "That has nothing to do with this!" screamed Doris right back.

One day she saw a collie on a curb near Santa Monica Boulevard without a leash, tracked down the owner in a local bank, and waited with the dog for twenty minutes until the man cashed a check to reclaim the untended dog. At 5 A.M. a few mornings ago, she called some reactionary bigot on a local telephone radio show because he would not give out the box number of the "Actors and Others for Animals" fund and read him the riot act. "This is Doris Day, and I'm furious," she announced over the air to sleepy early-morning risers on their way to Lockheed and cruising taxi drivers. "What are you doing up at this hour?" asked the announcer, who is still in shock. "I was going to the bathroom and I heard your lousy attitude and I just had to get my two cents in," said Doris, who then did half an hour on saving the animals, giving the box number and soliciting money all over town. They can't get her on the *Dick Cavett Show*, but there she was guest-starring at 5 A.M. on some local radio show. Don't tell me she's a phony.

At home, Doris has ten dogs. You saw them all on her fantastically successful *Doris Mary Anne Kappelhoff Special*, first broadcast in March, 1971. All of them were saved from ghastly fates in various kennels, pounds and rainstorms. "Some of them were in such bad shape I had to tranquilize them just to get the mange solution on them, but they are all beautiful and healthy now. I carry blankets in the trunk of my car and I'm always picking up dogs all over town and finding homes for them. I think they've got a club. They say listen, there's this blond lady in a green car, so go and lie down on Ventura Boulevard outside the gates of CBS and when she comes out, play dead and she'll wrap you up and take you home and when you wake up you'll be in this fan-*tast*-ic place! I have a picket fence with a gate and a park on the set of my show and nobody works on the show unless he likes dogs. They go to the studio every day and sit on my stand-in's lap and they are very quiet, but when the director says, 'Cut, print!' their tails start wagging. We have no arguments at home. I say, 'Look, fellas, you're all in the same boat. You're all adopted and I knew you when.' We have a house of harmony."

All that work requires more than goodwill, of course. To keep in shape, Doris swims, rides her bike, drinks protein drinks, and eats eight leaves a day from something called a godakola plant. She never goes to fancy restaurants, hangs out at Nate and Al's delicatessen, where most of her mail arrives and gets dropped off at her house later in the day by a waitress named Helen. "I have no ego. I'm not selfish. I live just as I would in Vermont. Most of my furniture is from the old farmhouse set on the show. I have a sweet house, but it's not fabulous or anything. I was born in 1924 and I've been in the business a long time, but being a name doesn't mean anything to me except being able to use it in some way to help others. The cancer funds and the leukemia foundations and the Salvation Army have hundreds of people already, but the animals have nobody. Now that I've discovered how useful I can be in that direction, I'm going in one direction only, with no detours, and I'm as sane as any person you've ever met and getting saner every day."

I left, feeling as though I was having a milkshake hangover.

24

Carroll Baker

HI!"

There was a lilting sweetness in the voice that *sounded* like Carroll Baker, and although she was dressed in a simple blue T-shirt and slacks instead of the shimmering moonlight-on-waves Harlow dresses that made her famous, she *looked* like Carroll Baker. But what was she doing in the lobby of the Castellana Hilton hotel in Madrid? Five years ago, she was an all-American girl who couldn't order an ice cream soda in Spanish. Today she's an exiled American, living in Rome and working mostly in Italy and Spain—speaking all the languages fluently, living a new life, away from the insanity and the neurosis of Hollywood. "I'm not unique—many, many Americans are moving to Europe. We all talk about going home, but I can't bring myself to leave the gaiety and the security here. Hollywood kicked me out and although I was suicidal at the time, it was the best thing that ever happened to me. I've never been happier. Frankly, I don't know how I survived the Hollywood rat race as long as I did without going completely nuts."

One minute she was making a sensational movie debut in Elia Kazan's *Baby Doll* complete with Academy Award nomination and all the trimmings, the next minute she was a big movie star and by the third round she was down for the count. Carroll Baker is living proof of the dangers of too much celebrity too soon. They made her into a sex symbol, a new Jean Harlow they said in the press releases, and when it didn't work, they wrote her off and canceled her klieg light. And it never did work, because all the time she was grinding out flicks like *The Carpetbaggers* and *Harlow* and *Sylvia* she knew the scripts were lousy, she knew she was still an uncluttered girl who looked like she wore too much lipstick in her mommy's high heels. They laughed, but they forgot her brilliant comic timing when she stole scenes from Clark Gable in *But Not for Me,* they forgot her sensitivity playing opposite James Dean in *Giant,* they forgot that between *The Carpetbaggers* and *Harlow* she also played a Quaker girl for John Ford in *Cheyenne Autumn.* But that's what it's all about in the movies—easy money, quick publicity and short memories.

Where did it all go wrong? "Oh God," she sighed. "What happened to me was a combination of so many things. Suddenly I was living in Harold Hecht's house in Beverly Hills—white furs, white rugs, white walls, white floors, white furniture—I said, 'This is great for cocktail parties, but not for real life!' But my husband, Jack Garfein, wanted to maintain a certain kind of life-style. We'd been very poor when we started out at the Actors Studio in New York, and we had sort of built everything together and I was making a lot of money, but there was never anything left because when you make that much all you can do is live well and the rest goes to taxes. I wasn't getting any compensation in my professional life. I was

under contract to Joe Levine, who was going around giving me diamonds and behaving like he owned me. I never
slept with him or anything, but everyone thought I was
his mistress. It started as a joke and suddenly it was all out
of hand and I had nobody to turn to, nobody to advise me,
and my husband thought it was all terrific as long as I kept
bringing in the money. I started objecting to everything,
but it was too late. The sex symbol image had already
started. I turned down parts and they blacklisted me. It
works in an odd way in Hollywood. Joe Schmoe would
have lunch with his cronies and say, 'That bitch—she's
nothing but trouble—don't hire her!' and pretty soon I
couldn't get work. Then Paramount tried to squeeze me
out of my contract and take me for everything I was worth
financially and my marriage was breaking up. Add to this
the fact that for three years I never had one good word
of encouragement from anyone—the press attacked me
viciously at every opportunity—I came very close to suicide.

"I came to Italy in 1967. Cary Grant and I were invited
to represent America at the Venice Film Festival. I was
alone, I hadn't worked in two years, I couldn't speak one
word of Italian, but this producer named Michael Ferrari
came up to me at the swimming pool and offered me an
Italian film. Somebody wanted me! It was called *The
Harem*. It only cost $250,000 to make and it grossed $2,-
000,000. I have now sold my property in California, I've
moved my children to Rome and put them in school, I've
won my divorce case, and now, four years later, I've survived and it looks like Paramount and Joe Levine who are
going down the drain. My pictures in Italy have grossed
so much money that I don't have to search the rest of the
world for work. They build movies around me and the
percentages are sensational. Of course the movies are
never very good—things like *Orgasmo, So Sweet, So Per-
verse*, and so on. But *Orgasmo*, which was called *Paranoia*
in America, grossed $8,000,000 there alone! The money is
great, so what if I have to wait a while for the artistic
successes to come along? I wasn't turning out too many

artistic triumphs in Hollywood, either. Here they like me, they know me, I work well and Italian audiences respond to me. I have more acceptance than I ever had in Hollywood. And the movies are getting better. I'm in Madrid doing *The Fourth Mrs. Anderson* with Michael Craig, and I did *Rain* on British television not long ago and I've been offered a lot of plays on the London stage. But London is too much like Hollywood. My children are in a wonderful school, they speak three languages and we love Rome. We don't feel alone.

"Italians are not screwed up like Americans. They look at you with horror if you have a whiskey before dinner. The values in the community are stronger. Somebody bumped my car the other day and in no time there was a crowd of 150 on the street. Everybody gets involved. There are robberies, but never an armed robbery. They never carry a knife or a gun. I can walk down the lowest street in Rome at four in the morning looking for a taxi, and it never occurs to me to be afraid. They might take my purse, but as a woman I can ask them to give me 5,000 lire back to get home and they would. The dope problem is something new. I attend meetings with other parents at my children's school to discuss problems universal to the world and there are no words in Italian for drugs. The Americans have introduced that problem and it only exists in the American schools, not the Italian schools. There's more time for family life here, too. The work day is constructed from nine to one. From one to four, you have lunch and a siesta. Then from four to eight you are refreshed and ready to begin again. In Hollywood, everyone is so frantic and keyed up they have to start drinking at five o'clock just to relax. I never go into a shop here that I'm not asked to sit down and have a capuccino. People do not suddenly throw white cloths over the counters, whisk away dishes or dim the lights on you. It's a better life here and you have more time to enjoy it.

"That doesn't mean there aren't things I miss. I go potty over American TV. I was in New York recently and I canceled my theater tickets and dinner engagements, ordered a corned beef sandwich up from Reuben's, and watched TV all night. In Rome, we have only two and a half hours a night that includes a sports hour, news and an old movie. Once in a while I get *Variety,* and the international edition of the *Herald Tribune* is my main source of information. I bought a Sony radio and we listen to the American broadcasts for servicemen overseas and the Voice of America. But you lose interest in a lot of it. It's like New Yorkers who are concerned about the garbage strike or what Mayor Lindsay had for dinner. Go to California, and they couldn't care less. It's the same here. I miss hot dogs and ice cream sodas and delicatessens. And I miss my friends. My mother lives in California, my father died last year, and she's sixty-two and she feels she's going to die, too, so I worry about her. I hear from Debbie Reynolds and John Ford and a few others. But when you're gone, they forget about you and you get used to that.

"I have no bitterness. I'm the most fortunate person in the world to survive. I went through agony when I read about Inger Stevens' suicide. I knew her so well. Others go on to drugs, liquor. I was at the point of destruction. It took guts to leave everything behind and start all over again, but I'm happy now and alive. If you can just hold on to life, sometimes what you have ahead of you is more fantastic than the things you thought you couldn't live without. I was interviewed recently in America and they've already forgotten the good things I did in my career. It's not even what you did last year, it's what you did six months ago. America is a fast-moving society. They walk over their past, tear down their old buildings, ruin their parks and destroy their charming streets. They look at people not for what they've done in a lifetime, but for what they did a month ago. Then you're a bum overnight if one thing doesn't work out. Well, I refuse to be brutalized any longer. And by the most incredible people! I read a quote from Raquel Welch that 'Carroll Baker wouldn't be sexy if she was spread-eagled naked on the cover of *Life* magazine!' What does she want from me? I don't even know this girl, I've never done anything to her. But it upset me because it didn't sound like a statement from a real woman at all. It would never occur to *me* to think of another woman spread-eagled naked. It was cruel, but it was also very perverted."

At thirty-eight, sticks and stones are not going to break any bones. She's beautiful. Soft, and warm and funny, with teeth white as meringue and a carbonated laugh that starts down in her throat and gurgles out in captivating hee-haws. "I could go on the way I'm going and at the age of sixty be recognized as a fine character actress. So what? I've only now discovered that it's every day that counts. It's how you survive and how you make your time pay off in happiness. It's been worth all the pain to find myself again."

She didn't say good-bye. She said "Courage!" It means the same in every language and Carroll Baker knows how to say it in all of them.

25

Tuesday Weld

IF YOUR NAME IS Tuesday Weld, you learn to put up your dukes at the age of three. Today, at the age of twenty-eight, it's not so bad. Tuesday is bloody but unbowed. In fact, the bruises don't show at all. They only turn up in her voice—a freckled whisper of a gurgle, lonely and little girlish and faraway. When she talks, candles flicker in her eyes and she gives the impression of not actually being in the same room at all. Somebody is phoning it in.

But she is there, part sex kitten, part Duse. For eight years, she didn't see or talk to anyone. If the press came snooping around her Malibu beach house, she threw whiskey bottles at them—bottles she usually had just emptied herself. Then her house burned down and her marriage broke up and Tuesday Weld had to come out into the sunshine and learn how to talk to people again. And now that she's talking, some of the pieces of a bizarre and often puzzling career begin to take shape. People don't laugh much at the name Tuesday Weld anymore. The critics have helped. Some of us have praised her work in films like *Pretty Poison*, although the sum total of her career represents some of the silliest and most forgettable movies ever made. There are Tuesday Weld cults, though nobody is quite sure what they're made up of. New York recently had its own Tuesday Weld Film Festival, an honor usually reserved for Garbo or Bogart. So the child-woman did not suffocate away in a lost world of aging Mouseketeers. Tuesday Weld lives.

She lives this week in a small suite in an out-of-the-way New York hotel where movie stars never stay. There is a "Do Not Disturb" sign on her door, which is propped open with a cardboard Sylvania light-bulb box because she is always locking herself out in the hall and having to go all the way down to the desk in her bare feet.

She is wearing a long skirt that looks like a patchwork quilt from Grandma Moses' steamer trunk and a long-sleeved red sweat shirt with a Superman star on it. There are notebooks crammed with jottings in soft lead pencil on the floor, a portable radio, vitamin pills, bottled water, ashtrays filled with unsmoked cigarettes. She sits cross-legged on the floor, picking at her toes and playing with her long, dazzling corn-silk hair. She doesn't seem shy, although she insists she is. "Oh yes, at one point in my life, I was so painfully shy that I did not speak for years. When I was nine, I was modeling a slip for a mail-order catalogue and they wanted more flare in the skirt, so they cut it with a razor blade and slashed right through my leg and I was so introverted I could not tell them I was in pain. That's how closed off I was. I retired many times in my eighteen-year acting career and I haven't really done interviews since I was seventeen. It has been very bad for me. I got tunnel vision. I'm trying to change. I even talk to complete strangers in the street, trying to get readjusted to life and new opinions. I'm even learning to treat interviews like they were analysis."

In her movie, *A Safe Place*, she played a disturbed character based on Tuesday Weld, a girl all mixed up in the past, present and future. The movie takes place in her own mind. It is two-thirds fascinating and one-third baloney. She doesn't care. She liked it enough to come to New York and see anyone who would talk to her. She even showed up for the film's unveiling at the New York Film Festival, where the reaction was so hostile she sounded off from the audience and some jerk yelled, "Shut up, Tuesday; you're pretty, but you're stupid!" She threw something at him and chaos broke out. It was one of the few highlights in a festival so dreary the members of the audience were interviewing each other just to stay awake.

Chaos breaks out in her conversation, too. You just have to stay in there: "I thought if I could just go on *Dick Cavett* without having to get drunk first, I could get through anything. I locked myself in my hotel room for two days and wouldn't talk to anyone. I wouldn't even let them interview me ahead of time. I just wanted to walk on the show cold and let it all come out. And that's the way I have to be in all of my interviews. I've lived inside myself too long. It's coming out now. For years, I resented any invasion of my privacy. Acting wasn't fulfilling me, so as rebellious as I always was towards every kind of conditioned thought, I still had the same old ideal dream that marriage and a family was the answer to everything. So I married Claude Harz, a writer, in 1965. For a while it was great, but then it started driving me nuts. The amount of energy it takes for me just to make a bed or do the dishes sends me into a deep depression. But I retired again from the screen and tried to make it work. We lived out at the beach in a shack where I could retreat from the world and look at the water. The marriage was disastrous. It was my house, my friends, my position, my world, but nothing was happening for him. I felt so guilty I smoked three packs of cigarettes a day, took pills and drank so steadily for ten years that people who know me well don't know how I came out of it alive. I would drink anything, everything, it didn't matter. I drank morning, noon and night."

I look at her, not sure if she's putting me on. The rose-bud mouth on her gentle, uncharted face looks like it should be erupting into a graceful discourse on the delights of jellybeans and gumdrops, yet out comes this confession of an aging diseuse. "You don't believe me? It's true. I stopped drinking while I was pregnant with Natasha, but after she was born, I went back to the bottle. Then I went into analysis for a year when I couldn't cope with anything anymore, and my shrink taught me how to stop being self-indulgent. If your thing is to be a doughnut, he said, go ahead and dip into the chocolate sauce and be a *great* doughnut. Natasha was two and a half and I just moved to London for a year. I didn't want to inflict any more pain on myself. I didn't know anyone there. I have never been ambitious, so I don't know how to go out and look for acting jobs and everyone in Hollywood thought I was crazy, so they weren't beating down my door with job offers anyway. I didn't want to work. I just wanted to be totally anonymous and somehow I was able to pull myself out of the depression I was in. So many things have happened to me in the last few years, but I've been able to survive without cracking up. Now I know I can survive anything."

Some of the things are: "My divorce. Then my house burned down. I was in Catalina and my child was in the house with the housekeeper. All the lines were down, so I couldn't even telephone. No boat would take me back to the mainland because the winds were so high. For four hours I didn't even know if she was alive or dead, because nobody had seen them leave the house. I called the Red Cross, I called the lost and found, I called the relief hospitals. It was a long time before I discovered my housekeeper had taken her to her house in Santa Monica and it had an unlisted phone number. It was very close. All the housekeeper's hair was burned off. But later I went to look at the ashes and I didn't cry. I had been through that before, when another house of mine washed away in a flood. Aside from five years of journals I was keeping for a book and fifteen paintings, none of it mattered. I always thought if I had a home made up of things I selected to represent myself, it would be a kind of shorthand and I wouldn't have to explain about myself because it was all around me. Suddenly I was naked and I had to say, 'This is me; it's all *here.*'" She touched her breast. "It's all inside. Since the fire, I have not bought one thing. Tasha and I have one suitcase apiece and that's it.

"Then my 'sixty-two Porsche broke down and will never work again. All my roots exploded at once. I have no pets, just Tasha. She's my only pet. And I will never own anything again. I don't know where I want to live, who I want to be, or what I want to do. So I just walk. I walk about ten miles a day. I know something's wrong. I'm a displaced person. But I know I'll get it all together in my own way. I really feel like I'm starting everything all over again. I know now it's not important to be happy all the time, as long as I keep moving, keep progressing. This trouble was the best way for me to come out of my shell."

She picks up a cigarette and refuses a light. "Oh no, I never smoke them. I just hold them in my mouth." You can't try to analyze her, or she'll do numbers on your head and vanish into the street. A radiant smile covers up an imbalanced jumble of pain and illogic. It's always been that way. "I was born in a Salvation Army hospital where they had to get you in and out fast, so my mother named me Susan, the first thing that popped into her head. But my sister's name was Sally, so she got all the *s*'s mixed up and started calling me Too-Too. Then that developed into Tuesday. I was working since the age of three, and never learned anything. I never went to school on any regular basis, just slipped by cheating. I never read anything but Nietzsche and stuff like that. So my whole frame of reference is mixed up. My mother moved me to Florida, but that didn't work. I felt like a citrus fruit. I just didn't fit in anywhere. I had already retired at nine. Between the ages of fourteen and seventeen, I studied for ten minutes at a time in a cardboard box on studio sets and made about 150 TV shows and between geography and arithmetic, they'd stick me in front of the lights and say 'OK, ready, shoot!' Every studio had a different teacher in a different cardboard box. One week I had ten teachers.

"But the one thing that kept me going was the knowledge that so many people wanted to save me. Critics liked me, even though I was in horrible things like *Rock, Rock, Rock,* made in nine days in the Bronx with thirty musical numbers and Connie Francis dubbing my voice. I only read good reviews. I'm too easily influenced by negative things. If I'm with a bunch of dopers, I'll follow them right into the opium den. So I never read negative reviews. I had enough of defending the name Tuesday Weld as a child. They can't hurt me now. I've outgrown that insecurity. I've outgrown the jokes about my name. Critics can't change or rectify anything. All you can learn from them is a few new words. I select all my movies out of instinct, not because of what critics will think."

Her most highly praised movie, *Pretty Poison,* is her least favorite. "The least creative experience I ever had. Constant hate, turmoil and dissonance. Not a day went by without a fight. Noel Black, the director, would come up to me before a scene and say, 'Think about Coca-Cola.' I finally said, 'Look, just give the directions to Tony Perkins and he'll interpret for me.' I don't care if critics like it; I hated it. I can't like or be objective about films I had a terrible time doing." Her two favorites are *Lord Love a Duck* and *A Safe Place* because they represent "my decisions, my mistakes, my *me.* I don't care if nobody else likes them. I learned more from the old Dobie Gillis shows on TV than from *Pretty Poison.* However, I'm an extremist and I contradict myself constantly."

Where does that leave her future? "I'm restless. It's gonna take time before I really know where I'm at. Frank Perry is trying to talk me into doing *Play It as It Lays.* I could do that neurotic girl, alienated in the Hollywood snake pit. I've been there. But I can take it or leave it. The secret is not success, but knowing when to get out. I do not plan to be an actress the rest of my life or do a bad TV series when I'm thirty-five just because I'm restless for the camera. By that time, I'll be out of this business and doing something else. I've got some money. Not much. Enough for the next year, maybe. The most important thing right now is my friends. I spend a lot of time hitchhiking. As a consequence I find my friends are now people who don't own anything. They're not in show business and they all hate each other. Not five of them can stand to be in the same room with each other. So I'm lucky. I can have five different kinds of evenings in one week. I'm also into writing—sometimes it's poetry, sometimes I just write about myself." Women's Lib? "I'm in and out. I don't like groups. I represent me." Marriage? "I'm soured on the idea. If I ever marry again, it would have to be for money. I mean a lot of money. Enough so I never have to worry about providing for somebody else. I've always supported everybody. It's time somebody supported me."

26

Gloria Grahame

F RALPH EDWARDS ever introduces a honey blond with a novocained upper lip by announcing, "This Is Your Life—Gloria Grahame," the show would be one censored bleep. It would be mostly Gloria herself doing the cutting and editing. The former Academy Award winner (for MGM's aptly titled *The Bad and the Beautiful*) is still very much alive and well and making movies, but she doesn't really want the world to know what happened to her. Because if Gloria ever tells it like it is, Jacqueline Susann will have enough intrigue to fill two more 400-page novels.

She does have a shyness that often retreats into suspicion, only to return either as wit or evasiveness. But then Gloria Grahame's personal life is so confusing, it's no wonder she avoids interviews. The family tree she has cultivated in her exotic life has more intertwining branches than a thatched roof.

First, she married actor Stanley Clements (he played the bad boy in *Going My Way*, if your memory reaches back that far) and divorced him three years later, charging his undue jealousy had caused her to lose her appetite and become dangerously thin. She then married director Nicholas Ray *(Rebel Without a Cause)* and divorced him four years later, charging *him* with such sullen and morose behavior that she couldn't eat properly and was again dangerously thin.

Then she tried a four-year hitch to gag-writer Cy Howard, but divorced him, saying, "Well, at least he made me laugh." In 1964, she married Tony Ray, her second husband, Nick's, son by a previous (to Gloria, that is) marriage. Now you know why Ralph Edwards and Gloria Grahame most likely will never meet on the tube. Can you see Ralph introduce Gloria's son (by Nick Ray), whose current stepfather was once his half-brother and who is now both uncle and brother to the rest of the kids? Nick is both father and stepgrandfather to his own son, Gloria is both stepmother and wife to Nick's son, Tony, Gloria's own husband. And don't forget that in her spare time she was a raging movie star. No wonder the girl dropped out. She must have been exhausted.

Right from the first, Gloria Grahame's life has read more like fiction than fact. Back in the Fifties, when movies were magnificently melodramatic, passionate and full-throated, there was nobody like her. She was sultry, sexy, beautiful and very, very bad. She was so good at being bad that with little previous experience, she walked onto the set of *Crossfire*, a tough one with Robert Ryan, Robert Young and Robert Mitchum, worked for only two days, and walked away with an Oscar nomination. When she was good she was great, but when she was bad she was even better.

Offscreen and on, Gloria had the pizazz and the personality. Her trip to the podium that infamous night in 1952 when she picked up her Oscar remains vivid to movie buffs. A friend, who doesn't want to be identified, says: "Gloria sashayed down the aisle in a very—shall we say—indirect line, reached the stage, tripped and muttered, 'Oh, shit.' Then, too embarrassed to speak, she just smiled through her famous pout, and left in the same tipsy-doodle way she had arrived. The applause was deafening."

That same year Cecil B. De Mille's *The Greatest Show on Earth* won an Oscar as Best Picture, and Gloria's petulant naughtiness was very much noticed even in the cast of thousands, including a sassy elephant that stepped on her face.

"I was petrified. You know, there was one retake on the scene. The elephant came so close he left a smudge on my nose. Even Betty Hutton shuddered. I think it was probably the only time in life when I was more frightened than I am right now. I've always been petrified of interviews. I'm really shy."

Today, the first impression of Gloria Grahame is not one of shopworn world-weariness, but nervous enthusiasm and innocence. She's a harebrained, absentminded shadow of her former self. She wears glasses, lives in a small house in Van Nuys (when I asked where her Oscar was, she said, "Oh, I dunno—it's around the house somewhere"), and dresses like some matron working sparetime behind the Kleenex counter at Woolworth. The face is still perfection and the posture finishing-school correct, but the zipper on her casually worn pantsuit remains only half-closed through an entire day of shopping for her four kids.

She waves the answers to direct questions under a rug of confusion with charm while she foxily directs the conversation to her latest movie—the one she made in Spain last winter with Sue *(Lolita)* Lyon.

"It's called *Tarot* and I'm mad about Sue. She's just the most wonderful person. I think the director, José María Forque, is a big talent, and you should be interviewing him, not me. Oh yes, I still play 'the other woman, the bad one.' I had never been to Spain before and I loved it. I took a bus tour to Toledo, which wasn't much fun because of the narrow roads.

"Everyone was shocked that I would take a tour on a bus. But last year I played with Henry Fonda in *The Time of Your Life* across the U.S. I took a bus tour around Washington and that was delightful. I loved acting with Hank. He's very impressive."

It's difficult to imagine Gloria Grahame on a bus tour anywhere. Or that "Little Green Eyes," as one of her ex-husbands calls her, could elicit this from Fonda: "The highlight of my recent tour, at least for me, was the ten-minute scene I played with Gloria Grahame. She's a most riveting actress." Well, thanks, Hank, but we already knew that.

What we want to know is where has she been between the time she sang her way through the role of Ado Annie in the movie *Oklahoma* and her recent bus tours. Pruning and grafting onto that family tree, that's where. Although she'd like us to think she was doing what so many other women do—being wives and mothers—in her case, it was wives and stepmothers.

If you ask whatever happened to Gloria Grahame around Hollywood, you get a hatful of hyperbole. One rumor has it that she had a nervous breakdown and spent years in a sanatorium. Another one circulates about a drinking problem. A third has her smashed in an auto wreck which permanently scarred that provocative face. One person said she had moved to an upstairs room over a meat market on New York's Ninth Avenue, and one famous director even told me she had committed suicide.

Gloria denies any truth to the rumors, especially the suicide. "How silly, how utterly ridiculous. Are that many people still interested in me? Yes, there was an accident, but I just threw my arms like this [she takes a ballet pose like a white swan turning discreetly away from her odious black sister] and only got cut a little.

"I'm happily married, a devoted daughter to my remarkable eighty-four-year-old mother, and my husband is an associate film producer who just did *Blume in Love* in Venice. Someone named Kris Kristofferson did the music for it. I hope he's a good musician. He's what? Country and western? Oh God, and I did want that music to be good."

Kris Kristofferson knows who Gloria Grahame is. Recently, he told me: "She's sexy in a strange way. Like a woman who's begging you to wallop her in the mouth, 'cause she'd just love it. I used to see her in movies and escape into a world of freaky fantasies."

But Gloria doesn't think movies are an escape. "Maybe because Mother was an actress, and she made me aware that movies were more than just something to do on a Saturday afternoon. I went to them searching, observing and learning. There were performances I will never forget. Olivier in *Wuthering Heights*. God, the way he moved, spoke . . . you could learn so much from that man. Where else did you see people who spoke better than you did, dressed better, thought better? You listened and learned in the movies.

"I could have played Anne Boleyn to Charles Laughton's Henry the Eighth on Broadway, but Louis B. Mayer had seen me in something or other and asked me to come to Hollywood for $250 a week, and that was an extraordinary amount of money in those days, so I did. I just got on a train and never even asked if I could do the play first.

"I was there for years under contract to MGM, RKO and Paramount . . . I don't know how many others. Actually, I do, but who cares? I remember everything, even the dates. But I don't want others to remember the details, just the image."

It was the image that got her her first major job in Frank Capra's *It's a Wonderful Life* in 1946. She had been hanging around MGM for two years when Capra was told by MGM casting director Billy Grady: "Two years she's been hanging around here snapping her garters. You can hire her for a cuppa coffee. But you think I can get these jerk directors to listen? She's got real star quality, but nobody will listen." Capra listened.

Her "bit" as the sexpot who lured Jimmy Stewart away from his thoughts of apple pie in his first film after a six-year absence in the Air Force laid Hollywood on its ears. It captured the sultry look her cult has been addicted to ever since. "It wasn't the way I looked at a man," says Gloria, "but the thought behind it."

It's only fitting that bad and beautiful Gloria Grahame should have been the first actress to strike a blow for realism in movies. She made headlines opposite Humphrey Bogart in *In a Lonely Place* because her lovely bones were obviously starkers under the sheets. It was a movie first.

"Silly, that's the way I was born, and that's the way I sleep." Then she threw me the look. Evidently she still has provocative thoughts in that beautiful noodle. If I tried to explain my thoughts when she looked at me the way she looked at Bogart, they, too, would be censored.

Oh, Gloria, do you really sleep in the nude?

27

Joanne Woodward

I N A STARK and terrifying period in movie history, when practically everybody I meet seems to be feuding with somebody else, suing somebody else, or being just plain neurotic and confused, it is a genuine pleasure to take Joanne Woodward to lunch. Of all the movie stars I know, she is one of the least affected, least paranoid, and easiest to take. God knows, she's easy to please.

"Just let me finish screaming, and we'll grab some fish and chips at O'Neals' Baloon," she says, screwing up her nose for a dramatic take. Then she gives a one-take performance that makes your hair stand up and your stomach turn to buttermilk.

We're standing in an empty apartment for rent in a building on West End Avenue, where Joanne's new movie for Columbia and Ray Stark is being filmed. Here's a new switch for film companies tired of using the same old expensive Hollywood sound stages. Find an empty apartment in the want-ads, move in for a month's rent and use each room for a different scene. One room is an optometrist's office on Tuesday, a bedroom on Thursday. It does keep the cost down.

The movie was called *Death of a Snow Queen*. Then they changed the title to *Souvenir*. It will probably change again before it is finally released, because nobody likes any of the titles, and Joanne is conducting a contest on the set to think up interesting new ones.

The only thing that will not change is the quality of her performance, because, from rehearsal to answer print, there is no finer actress on the screen today, and no better proof than the way she's currently burning a hole through the screen in *The Effect of Gamma Rays on Man-in-the-Moon Marigolds*. If there's any justice left in such matters, it should win her another Oscar nomination.

Joanne Woodward is famous for the tired, bedraggled, forlorn and, almost always, deeply disturbed women she plays in movies. It has always been that way. When anybody writes a script about a nut case, it usually gets offered to her because she plays them better than anybody else.

For seventeen years, she has been going through agony on the screen, and now, in *Gamma Rays*, she's doing it again, this time as a wounded mother, insensitive to the frustrations of her two tragic children—giving one daughter an epileptic fit and killing the other daughter's pet rabbit.

In *Souvenir*, she plays a cold, isolated woman whose marriage has soured into incommunicable silence, whose mother dies of a heart attack while she looks on helplessly, whose daughter has grown apart from her, and whose son turns out to be homosexual.

"Stewart Stern, who wrote one of my favorite films, *Rachel, Rachel*, for me, is also the author of this one," she says, "and it really is a beautiful script. It's about a woman who makes the awful discovery of how brief life really is, too brief even to correct one's worst mistakes, and even worse, too brief really to ever change. It's very depressing, and just between you and me, I've just about had it with being depressed."

She slips into a dressing gown, the camera turns, and Joanne walks through a hall as though in a daze, turns the doorknob to her son's room, fixes her gaze just below a Rudolph Nureyev poster, and sees her naked son in the arms of a man. Her face goes white with nausea as she lets out a blood-boiling scream. Everyone applauds.

"That's my Joan Bennett scream," she giggles. "I suddenly realized while I was doing it that I was imitating Joan Bennett in *Dark Shadows*."

We go up to her dressing room, another empty apartment on the floor above, where she spends her time between scenes reading Bobby Fischer's chess book. Posted over the mirror—photos of Paul Newman, Nureyev and Christopher Lee sinking his bloody fangs into the neck of a nubile virgin. She loves horror movies, trash food and a lot of other things great dramatic actresses are not supposed to publicize.

She's a Southerner straight through, so much so that when the Newmans bought their mansion in Beverly Hills, she had all the palm trees uprooted and Louisiana magnolias replanted on the front lawn. She never spends any time in Hollywood. In fact, she doesn't do much of anything like a movie star.

Both of the Newmans are obvious threats to the press agents who are hired to make them look glamorous: "You know what I got Paul for Christmas? An old-fashioned lorgnette he can wear around his neck because he's always losing his glasses. He can hardly see to read the paper without his glasses." Paul Newman's multibillion-dollar blue eyes? Glasses? See what I mean?

She avoids the fashionable restaurants, settles on O'Neals' Baloon near Philharmonic Hall because it's close to the ballet, where she spends every free moment, and because they serve the best southern pecan pie in New York.

"I had to straighten them out—they were serving phony whipped cream," she adds. She pours ketchup on her fish and chips (well, it's better than Paul Newman, who sprays ketchup over his eggs every breakfast) and talks about that missing image.

"Are you kidding? I'm afraid, as Hollywood movie stars, we're both terrible flops. I never could stand Hollywood. I loathe palm trees, and I also dug up the cactus garden. Paul's whole life is beer and motorcycles, and mine is going to the ballet. We spend all of our time in Connecticut, in an old house in Westport. It is a far cry from that social scene in Beverly Hills. Bette Davis lives nearby, but we've never seen her. She phoned one day to thank Paul for something she read in the local paper, and he said, 'Come over and see us sometime,' and she said, 'Why?' I've loved her for that ever since.

"The only thing I miss about Hollywood is not having a screening room where we can show movies at home. But we're such slobs we always slept through everything anyway. I slept through *Claire's Knee*. I never saw the last half of *Five Easy Pieces*. We started to build a screening room in Westport, but the only place we had any room was in the middle of my organic garden."

The house in Westport is overrun with five kids and Joanne's mother and half the wildlife of the state of Connecticut. The zoo is managed by the Newmans' thirteen-year-old, Nell, who also moonlights as Joanne's costar in *Marigolds*. When she was a baby, they called her Nell-potts, a family nickname. So when she got the lead in her father's movie, she chose Nell Potts as a professional name. When she was two, her parents threw sheets over their heads and played ghosts with her. She wasn't frightened then, and she wasn't frightened by her mother's cruelty toward her as her movie mother, either.

"Nell won't ever need a psychiatrist," sighs Joanne. "She's not an actress in the first place and couldn't care less about it in the second place. She loves the camaraderie of being part of a movie, and she loves the money because she has a whole menagerie to support and it was like getting an allowance. The only similarities between her and that child in the movie are her interests in science and her poetic outlook on life.

"She'd like to be an ornithologist. Her library is a huge compendium of books on hawks and eagles. She owns every book ever written about pigeons. We gave her an electric handsaw for Christmas so she can build pigeon houses. I think she only acted in the film because Paul told her he refused to pay for her pigeon food anymore. Now the other kids want to know when they will get to be actors, too. I think they think it's always fun to go to work if Daddy is directing or Mommy is starring, but if they ever have to face the reality and toughness of the business, they'll change their minds."

Joanne's face also stars in *Sleuth*. She's Laurence Olivier's wife in the painting. Another photo of her gets riddled with bullets.

"They sent me the painting of myself, and there was no place to put it, so my mother has it hanging out in the barn. The other photo of me with Olivier is a fake. The man in the picture was really Gore Vidal. They pasted Olivier's face over the body. It's all a fake, don't you know that? In *Marigolds*, I was supposed to be one of the frowziest hags in town. All the clothes were my mother's because she's a pack rat and never throws anything away, so I went through her closet and dragged out a lot of old junk and dyed it an icky color and wore it. I was so depressed and suicidal during that film, I couldn't stand it.

"Being directed by my husband is not a problem. Paul is the easiest person in the world. We had big fights, but we have big fights at home, too. I never have to explain myself to him like I do with directors I don't know. But I hated that gooky rinse they put on my hair that got all over the pillowcase at night. I hated the way I looked, and I hated that character and what she did to those children. I don't look or act like that. But let's face it—nobody is going to hire me for a comedy. The only part I ever really fought for was *Forty Carats*, but nobody is going to cast me as a forty-year-old sex symbol.

"To tell you the truth, I'm sick of all of it. I am seriously planning to give up acting for a while. I've enrolled in Sarah Lawrence beginning January 15, 1973. I'm studying philosophy."

She shrieks her Academy Award winning *Three Faces of Eve* cackle.

"Doesn't this sound like an old Marilyn Monroe interview? But I'm not putting you on. I'm serious. I never graduated from Louisiana State University. When I was there, I majored in parties, I think. Anyway, I want to go back to school, so I'm just going to drop out for a while."

We rise to go, and she looks so attractive and crisp in the afternoon light that I see her point. The movies missed a big chance not showing her off in lighter roles with dazzling wardrobes. (She did play a fashion plate once in a comedy called *A New Kind of Love*, but, as she freely suggests, "Nobody ever saw it, but you and my mother.") So the movies may lose their best soap-opera sufferer.

"I'm tired of playing worn-out, depressing ladies in frayed bathrobes," says Joanne Woodward with the verbena-accented determination of Scarlett O'Hara. "I'm going to get a new hairdo and look terrific and go back to school and even if nobody else notices, I'm going to be the most self-fulfilled lady on the block. What do you think Sarah Lawrence will think of that?"

She'll love it.

28

Maggie Smith

AGGIE SMITH STANDS in the middle of a grave-
yard, dressed for a funeral. Storm clouds
hover in the bleak sky, threatening rain. She
has just attended the cremation of her sister. Everything
about the scene is gloomy. But Maggie Smith—usually
shy, introverted and painfully serious—seems giddy as a
lark. "You're in the movie," she grins, ushering me out of
camera range like a kindly aunt.

The movie is MGM's *Travels with My Aunt,* which
George Cukor is directing from the best-selling novel by
Graham Greene, and although the entire company has
spent the past four months hiking through Istanbul,
France and Spain, they are ending up in typical movie
fashion on the final day of the film, shooting the first scene
in the movie last. The location is a quiet country church

in north London where a timid bank manager meets his
unconventional aunt for the first time and discovers she
has stashed a fortune in marijuana in the urn meant for his
mother's ashes. From there, it's uphill all the way in a wild
and zany series of adventures that may turn out to be one
of the year's happiest movies. But whatever it turns out
to be, it will no doubt be enriched by the presence of
Maggie Smith.

Safely ensconced behind a tombstone, I'm told by
George Cukor: "We did a scene in the Madrid airport and
Maggie pushed one woman out of the way saying, 'You're
all wrong—you've got too much makeup on!' and the poor
thing turned out to be just a tourist who had arrived at the
wrong gate and had to be carried away in a state of col-
lapse. Maggie is a perfectionist. She spends two hours
each morning just to get her makeup right." In the film,
she ages from a seventeen-year-old virgin to a seventy-
five-year-old crone. Today, on the last day, she wears a
flaming red wig, her face shriveled like a dried persim-
mon with purple rings painted around her eyes, swaddled
in black mourning—black hat, black furs, black parasol,
black knee-high boots—rather like a cross between the
Madwoman of Chaillot and Auntie Mame.

George Cukor, who has directed every great star from
Greta Garbo to Marilyn Monroe, says: "She's very daring.
At the height of her career, she doesn't mind hiding her
own loveliness behind a hideous mask. I've worked with
fine actresses who were difficult. Claudette Colbert would
only show one side of her face. She was a good actress, but
she concerned herself too much with how she looked and
whether the camera angles were flattering or not. Judy
Garland caused a nightmare of delays and we went over
the budget on A Star Is Born because she wouldn't come
to work. Her face would swell up when she was unhappy
and she would refuse to be photographed. But when she
did get to the set, she worked like an angel. Marilyn
Monroe? She was shy and frightened and very intelligent
all at the same time, which made her dangerous. She
would take on anybody! But Maggie Smith does not play

it safe and never once shows fear that the way she looks might not be becoming. She is also one of the most astonishing actresses I have ever worked with. All of which probably sounds like Mary Baker Eddy, but believe me, it helps to have a great actress who is also nice."

The scene goes so well that the director calls it a day. In her dressing room, Maggie Smith looks out over the ancient tombstones that surround her trailer and smiles. "The people on every film are like a family. The last day is always sad. I will be glad to get out of this makeup for the very last time. I still don't feel secure in films. It's a medium I don't know much about. You have to make courageous decisions and stick with them. I am a nervous wreck, but the moment you stop and realize what you are doing is cemented forever on film and you can never change it, you're lost. If the audience knew how nervous I was, they'd stop believing in me. You can't let an audience see nerves. I don't care what I look like. Bette Davis would have done what I'm doing when she was my age. I'm never recognized in the street anyway, except by Americans. I'm sort of a nothing, I think. I don't make any impression at all, really."

She sits in a barber's chair, clad in a white terry-cloth bathrobe, while the makeup man bends over her, beginning the backbreaking job of taking off her hag face. She reaches for a bottle of Haig in her purse and pours into paper cups. "Happy funeral!" she announces wryly in that voice like cracked crystal. "I feel like I'm being peeled, like an old onion." The makeup man describes the aging process. Every morning at dawn, he smears her face with latex rubber applied with spirit gum and cotton wool. The skin is stretched, then flapped back into place as it dries, leaving wrinkles. It looks dead like a corpse, but it can spring back and move naturally so Maggie doesn't crack when she speaks. Then it is removed with castor oil, applied with a watercolor brush, and peeled off.

"How sorry I feel for girls who think acting is glamorous," sighs Maggie. "If this muck stays on longer than eight hours the skin stops breathing. There were days in

Spain that were so hot my skin dried up and I thought I
was dying. There is nothing glamorous about the sheer
physical agony of acting. Oh how I remember freezing
mornings at dawn on location, dragging myself out of bed
when I didn't feel well. In any other job you could just ask
for the day off. The easiest thing about this role is that it
doesn't matter if my eyes are bloodshot or I have bags
around my ankles. The constant worry of what you look
like is removed when you play an old woman. George has
directed so many of those elderly film stars who were like
the crazy aunt I play that his stories helped. Everything
fell into place. Besides, I didn't have time to work on a
characterization or a voice. I only had ten days to think
about it."

Travels with My Aunt was created for Katharine Hepburn, who demanded so many script changes that Maggie
got the part at the last minute. But nobody was surprised,
since the producer is Robert Fryer, another outspoken,
peppery redhead who produced *The Prime of Miss Jean
Brodie*, the film that won Maggie an Academy Award in
1969 and established her as an international screen star.
She is not impressed. She has no illusions about her profession and uses the Oscar statuette as a doorstop in her
split-level house in Chelsea.

She can't remember when she started acting, but she
was born in Ilford, near the home of Lynn Fontanne,
where she was considered "too cretinous" to appear in
school plays. She carried tea and swept the floor at the
Oxford Rep. when she was eighteen, and made her first
splash not in the Shakespeare classics for which she later
became famous, but in *New Faces of 1956* on Broadway.
"I couldn't sing very well and I wasn't funny. Actually, I
couldn't do much of anything, so I ended up introducing
the acts."

Now she can do just about everything, but she avoids
the spotlight and shuns publicity. "I think it's terrible
what publicity can do. It builds you up into something so
big that you have nothing to rise to. You can only fall. I
get very nervous and just cool it. And I don't do many

interviews. Most of them are so dumb. My favorite question, which I get all the time, is: 'Don't you find working in the theater cuts into your evenings?' " She breaks up and the makeup man almost spills the castor oil down her neck. "When American actors become stars, they're stuck. They can't say, Well I'll just go and have a little practice down at such-and-such, because *where*? There's no place they can go. In England, you can always get back to the juices of acting. After I won the Oscar for *Brodie* I went out to Chichester and worked for scale. I am not interested in being a star."

She is not besieged in airports by autograph seekers. She rarely goes to the theater. At the height of her success, she walked across the screen in *Oh What a Lovely War!* and sang a recruiting song because it was a challenge. Few people know what the real Maggie Smith looks like. She will show up as a wise Portia on TV, an iceberg of a Hedda Gabler under Ingmar Bergman's direction at the Old Vic, or a dizzy Noel Coward heroine in *Design for Living* in Los Angeles. She smokes too much; adores her husband Robert Stephens, one of England's most versatile actors (who also appears in *Travels with My Aunt*), and her two sons; prefers the company of children and nannies to actors; hates pretentious talk about the aesthetics and techniques of acting; thinks there is no difference between playing Desdemona opposite Laurence Olivier (which she did) or *Mary Mary* (which she also did, with equal panache); and couldn't care less about critics' pans.

"Christ yes, I read them intensely, and I've even changed performances because of them. But I don't become hysterical if they don't like my work. I got appalling notices in *The Master Builder* and *Miss Julie* at the National Theater, but I actually learned something about my weaknesses from them. You can do that in theater, but you can't learn anything from your mistakes in films. I like to work in big, solid chunks. I don't like standing around, and breaking for tea. When I work in small spurts, on a film, I dissipate too much energy and lose too much time."

She is shockingly frail, seldom eats anything, and when she works all she takes for lunch is a cup of diet broth. But never underestimate her intelligence, wit or red-haired temper. As the makeup man rubs the finishing cream into her raw face, Robert Fryer comes in and kisses her good-bye. Somebody suggests an excellent spinster role in a new film for her next assignment.

"Forget it," says Fryer, "Katharine Hepburn already has it."

"She can't play everything," somebody grumbles.

"Well," snaps the most talented replacement in the world, "obviously she *doesn't*, does she?" And with that, Maggie Smith peels away one last piece of latex from her pretty ear, walks through the deserted cemetery, and heads for home.

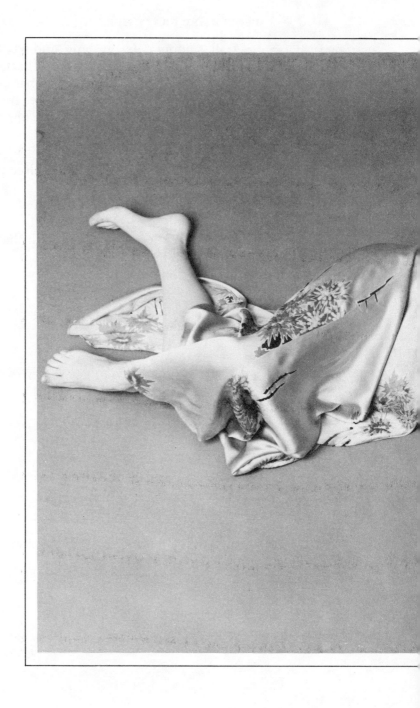

Bette Midler PHOTO BY KENN DUNCAN

Troy Donahue before and after—as the TV hero of *Surfside 6* (LEFT)
and as "Moon," a character inspired by Charles Manson (RIGHT)
WIDE WORLD PHOTOS

Dorothy Malone
retiring from
"the crazy life"
in 1968
WIDE WORLD PHOTOS

Richard Chamberlain before and after—as Dr. Kildare (LEFT) and in rehearsal for *Hamlet* (RIGHT) WIDE WORLD PHOTOS

Alice Cooper WIDE WORLD PHOTOS

Gloria Grahame WIDE WORLD PHOTOS

Maggie Smith WIDE WORLD PHOTOS

Ann-Margret in her Las Vegas nightclub debut
WIDE WORLD PHOTOS

Glenda Jackson in *Mary, Queen of Scots* (ABOVE) UPI
and in *A Touch of Class* (BELOW) WIDE WORLD PHOTOS

Adolf Zukor (CENTER) at his 100th birthday party,
flanked by Dorothy Lamour (LEFT) and Bob Hope (RIGHT)
WIDE WORLD PHOTOS

29

On Location: Glenda Jackson

THE ENGLISH LOVE their bloody history so much that they turn it into movies every chance they get. Hal Wallis, the king of the Hollywood producers, loves it even more. Also, he has more money. So all things considered, his technical savoir faire and the best talent England has to offer should combine to make quite a spectacular movie out of the turbulent and romantic life of *Mary, Queen of Scots*, now shooting in the castles and country houses of England and Scotland where the saga took place.

Wallis is banking on another box-office success to follow in the well-heeled footsteps of his *Becket* and *Anne of the Thousand Days*. For a director, he's rehired Charles Jarrott, who did *Anne*. The cameraman is Christopher Challis, who made movie history with *The Red Shoes*, and the

impressive cast includes Vanessa Redgrave as the tragic
Mary, Oscar winner Glenda Jackson as her archenemy,
Queen Elizabeth, and a supporting roster of British digni-
taries such as Trevor Howard, Timothy Dalton, Ian Holm,
Daniel Massey, Patrick McGoohan and Nigel Davenport.
It's the biggest movie shooting now in England, and on
the day I visited the lavish castle of Queen Elizabeth
spread over five sound stages at Shepperton Studios, it
also looked like the most expensive.

"Only four and a half million," purred Wallis, an energetic, distinguished and totally unflappable Palm Springs
millionaire who has guided more than 400 movies to
glory. "We're not leaving one stone unturned. I'm spending $300,000 on the costumes alone."

But why not make it on the Universal lot in Hollywood?
"Because for many years I made movies on studio lots and
had to be satisfied with an imitation of reality. Movies
have changed. Today you go anywhere in the world
where the story actually took place and you get total reality. We have built twenty-five sets for interiors because
many of the actual Elizabethan castles have been destroyed, but for the Scottish backgrounds we actually shot
in Norman castles in Northumberland, in sixteenth-
century French merchant frigates with seventy-foot
masts like the one that brought Mary to Scotland, and in
the actual Hermitage Castle where she once visited the
Earl of Bothwell before he was tried for the murder of her
husband. You could never duplicate these locales in Hollywood. Also, it would cost a fortune to transport so much
talent to California. I want total realism and I'm getting
it."

In a career spanning forty years in the picture business,
Hal Wallis' films have won 132 Academy Award nomina-
tions and thirty Oscars. He has been the guiding Big
Daddy behind every kind of movie from *Little Caesar* to
Casablanca to *Dark Victory* to *The Maltese Falcon* to
Come Back, Little Sheba to *True Grit*. He must be doing
something right. Yet when *Mary, Queen of Scots* opens,
he will undoubtedly be attacked by historians. According

to strict academicians who have made a study of Elizabethan history, the two cousins Mary and Elizabeth never
met with or without their crowns on, but they will in
Wallis' movie. "Can you imagine the chance we'd miss?
Onstage, it's OK if Mary never meets the queen who
imprisons her for eighteen years because you can see the
two of them on opposite sides of the stage at the same
time, but in the movies you've got to have a confronta-
tion. Especially when you go to all the trouble of hiring
Glenda Jackson and Vanessa Redgrave! Audiences would
feel cheated if they never had a scene together. I'd rather
face the wrath of a few stuffy historians and get my big
dramatic scene."

The big reunion was obviously not scheduled for the
day I visited the set. Vanessa Redgrave was nowhere to be
seen. She flees when the American press is around. A
reporter and a photographer from *Life* magazine buzzed
angrily in one corner of the set, complaining that they had
been assigned to cover both queens for a major story, but
they were so annoyed by Miss Redgrave's refusal to let
them inside her house in the London suburbs that they
thought they might just ignore her completely and devote
the entire story to Glenda Jackson instead. Good idea. But
one can hardly blame Miss Redgrave for hiding from reporters. Accept all that American money for a big-budget
American film while publicly burning the American flag
on the steps of the American embassy, promote the ship-
ping of guns to Fidel Castro, support communism in
Russia with money from American movies—then ask the
American press into her house with walls full of auto-
graphed photos of Mao Tse-tung to take publicity photos
to plug another movie made by the capitalist Hollywood
system she professes to despise? Somebody might call the
lady a hypocrite.

No such problem from Glenda Jackson, as honest, lika-
ble and straight-talking a queen as ever stepped in front
of a camera—or guillotine. When I got to her, she was
reclining in a position of royal repose, her head bald as a
cueball. "My head is shaved from the center of my head

forward, and what's left of my hair, which isn't much, is tied in a stocking cap for the heavy wigs to be fitted over," she groaned, looking like a Chinese coolie. "I seem to always end up with my head shaved. I cut it all off for the madhouse scenes in *The Music Lovers* and it was just growing back when I got into the BBC television series on Queen Elizabeth. I did six ninety-minute shows playing every age of Her Highness, and now as a result of that, I guess, I'm playing her again. I prefer Vanessa's part. Mary was a tart—three marriages, once to a man with syphilis, murders, prisons, intrigue, violence—the whole lot. But I'm doing my best with Elizabeth. She was called the Virgin Queen because she never got married, but she's no virgin the way I'm playing her, my dear."

She laughed that metallic shriek like Brillo on aluminum that has made her the screen's new Bette Davis. "Actually, it's great fun doing a big, expensive movie like this. It has nothing to do with history, you understand. This is Hollywood history. Elizabeth tormented Mary all her life, but they never met face to face except in this movie. But the money is good. I've never made any money before. For *Women in Love* I only made 3,000 pounds, which is about $7,200 in American money, and all of that went out into taxes, so I never saw any of it." But she did win an Oscar, which she found out about when Bette Davis called her up long distance from her TV set in Connecticut to tell her she won. Now the coveted bronze Oscar adorns a shelf in the home of her mother, a supermarket cashier. "It means more to her than it does to me." And what will she do next? "The scripts are not exactly flying through the window just because I won the Oscar, you know. I was going to do a movie about the Brontës with Mia Farrow, but they couldn't get the money together. Nobody has any money these days. So I'm going to play Queen Isabella of Spain. Yes, I know, another bloody queen. Don't frown. I know it could be a disaster. But for that one, they're paying *real* money, although I can't take a penny of it out of Spain and into England. Oh, well. A vacation for six months in Spain won't be so bad, and think what I can do with all those pesetas!"

She changed into her orange wig while workmen put the finishing touches on prison walls, brushing concrete textures on a papier-mâché dungeon, building vaults and dropping cobwebs from the walls of an evil torture chamber. When she returned, her velvet gown was so heavy it took three wardrobe girls to carry the skirt so she could walk. Hal Wallis and his beautiful wife, actress Martha Hyer, looked on merrily like two bolts of California sun invading the gloomy English cold, as Raymond Massey's son, Daniel, played a lute and sang a love song to his queen. The voice came out of a nearby tape recorder. "Who wrote it?" asked Queen Elizabeth. "It is said your father composed it for your blessed mother Anne Boleyn before they were married." Glenda collapsed with giggles at the thought. The rehearsal went well, so the cameras turned for a real take. The tape recorder started and as Massey opened his mouth to fake the lyrics, the lute fell out of his hand, breaking up Glenda, who had just hidden the mint Life Saver she was sucking behind a brocade Elizabethan pillow. (Makes the breath just right for those intimate love scenes.) "Everything happens to poor Massey," said a technician, rolling his eyes toward heaven. "He got his pants caught in the door, then his sword fell off his hip."

In Elizabethan days, you could get your head chopped off for such insolence. But in *Mary, Queen of Scots*, not to worry. Goofs are polished and refilmed until it all comes out right. They broke for tea and went back to work, hiding hot pants under miles of satin. When I left, Hal Wallis was still smiling like Santa Claus in his red Palm Springs golf sweater.

30

On Location:
Liv Ullmann and
Edward Albert

T'S THREE O' CLOCK on a Saturday afternoon. Outside, the rain floods the New York streets like Hurricane Audrey, making the sky black and the atmosphere bleak, but inside the Plaza Hotel it's brighter than ever. Klieg lights bathe the lobby in artificial California neon. Even the potted palms seem to have a suntan. A Hollywood camera moves in to record the gaiety, as though if it isn't captured on film immediately, nobody will believe it. The lobby is crowded with curious observers—desk clerks, bellhops, aging extras tripping over cables, cab drivers, and just plain tourists trying to get through the confusion and into the elevators with their luggage.

Standing shyly in a corner of the crowd a lady with a radiant smile and a charming Scandinavian accent is approached by two lady shoppers from Bergdorf's. "Excuse me," blasts one of the shoppers, tugging at the lady's sleeve, "but what are they doing here?"

"A movie," answers the lady with the accent.

"Oh yeah? What's the name of it?"

"Forty Carats."

"Hey, Sadie, they're making *Forty Carats*. And are there any movie stars?"

"Well," says the lady with the accent, "I'm the star of the movie."

"Oh," says the shopper, narrowing her eyes. "And what's your name, if I may ask?"

"Liv Ullmann."

"Oh. Well, it was nice talking to you."

"Who was it?" pleads her friend, pulling her away.

"Search me. Liz somebody. Never heard of her."

You can't blame them. Nobody seems to know who Liv Ullmann is unless they've seen a lot of Ingmar Bergman movies. Even the autograph hounds in the Plaza lobby seem disappointed. They don't recognize a single face worth asking for an autograph. "Liv who?" they ask, crestfallen. "Who's she?" Chances are, they won't be asking for long. The only member of Ingmar Bergman's repertory company to make it to super-stardom in American films, Miss Ullmann made one disaster in English called *Pope Joan* and survived the ordeal when most actresses would be down for the count. She has just finished the extravaganza *Lost Horizon* in which her name appears with such formidable competition as John Gielgud, Peter Finch, Michael York and Charles Boyer. She won the starring role in *Forty Carats* after just about everybody had been turned down. And now she has three more Hollywood movies lined up to do when *Forty Carats* is completed. Not bad for a girl who never had much more to work with than a shawl in Sweden. But will moviegoers plunk down their cash to see an unknown?

"Listen," says Leonard Gershe, who wrote the screenplay for *Forty Carats*. "Everybody wanted to do this film. Audrey Hepburn, Joanne Woodward, Doris Day, Elizabeth Taylor. It's a great role. A forty-year-old woman in love with her daughter's twenty-one-year-old boyfriend. I had never seen her on the screen. I've only seen two Ingmar Bergman movies in my life and she wasn't in either one of them. Then one day I was talking to Richard Avedon, the photographer, and he went on about how exciting she was and his passion rubbed off. She is an incredible actress! Wait until you see her in this picture. She is sensational. And Mike Frankovich likes unknowns. Look what he did for Goldie Hawn. Of course, I had to change some of the elements of the original French farce for the film. We won't see them in bed. They do it on the beach, in a sleeping bag. It won't be a picture for the children. Yes, she gets the younger man in the end; the daughter gets an older man. Just like in real life."

Forty Carats is being made by the same team who made *Butterflies Are Free*—producer Frankovich, writer Gershe, director Milton Katselas, cinematographer Charles Lang and costar Edward Albert. All of them say Liv Ullmann is a delicious person. A happy Swede? Whoever heard of such a thing? "She's not Swedish, she's from Norway," says the wardrobe lady. "She's like Ingrid Bergman—very jolly, very together. But when she acts, there isn't a dry eye on the set."

They clear the lobby for a scene. She has agreed to marry the boy. His parents have come to New York to meet her. She arrives early and they break her down. Now she's running out, destroyed. The boy chases her through the lobby, pleading: "We can make it, wait, I've never been so sure of anything in my life!" Her face is lined with despair, streaked with tears. But when the director yells "Cut!" all traces of sadness disappear. She is once more a healthy, bubbling Scandinavian, chattering with her daughter about the Lassie movie she's just seen. She stops for a Coke and her candor is refreshing. "Why do Americans think I should be depressing because I was in a lot of Bergman films? I was always the girl who got killed or the woman whose husband left her. I've always wanted to play comedy. Bergman always said I should play comedy, but he never gave me anything to play. It is ironic that it should be American films that finally gave me the chance, but don't get me wrong. I am not moving here. I never wanted to act in America. I came here to do publicity for *The Emigrants*, which was nominated for an Oscar last year. I arrived in Hollywood with one small suitcase, and I planned to leave in ten days. Then somebody suggested I see Ross Hunter about the part in *Lost Horizon*. He thought I was probably very neurotic, so he didn't want me for the part. But the director, Charles Jarrott, who directed *Mary, Queen of Scots*, talked him into seeing me and I guess he liked me. I don't know why. I didn't tell him jokes or anything.

"But I did not like Hollywood. There is so much luxury there, the kind of riches and beauty we never dreamed of back home. It is so sad to be that fortunate and have so little communication, though. I found it frightening. I saw no people walking, no children playing. I never even saw any people in the windows of those beautiful houses. Hollywood seems to have just a lot of cars living there. I did *Lost Horizon* and they gave me a fantastic house to live in, but you couldn't even see the toilets because they were discreetly disguised as chairs. As soon as the film was over, I went back to Sweden to make another film for Bergman on a deserted island with no drinking water where you had to walk almost a mile to an outside toilet. It was more fulfilling than doing *Lost Horizon*. And after *Forty Carats*, I will go home again. I could 'go Hollywood,' as they say, but I don't like it there. I still don't know how to get anywhere on the freeways."

Edward Albert, the blind boy in *Butterflies Are Free* and the twenty-one-year-old son of actor Eddie Albert, chimes in: "I've lived there, off and on, all my life, and I still don't know how to get to the San Fernando Valley." Suddenly the lobby fills with people. Max Von Sydow appears from nowhere to kiss Liv Ullmann. Some lady who says she's Phyllis Newman's aunt. Eddie Albert, pretending to read a magazine so as not to make his son nervous. "He doesn't make me nervous," says the boy, leading the way to his hotel suite for a private chat. "I rather like it. He doesn't coach me or anything. I think he just feels good being around. There's no generation gap problem. My only problem is not letting any of this go to my head."

He seems to worry a lot about that. Although he exerts the eagerness of a kid under the tree on Christmas morning, wondering what the next moment will bring, Edward Albert counters his open-faced freshness with a quiet sensitivity and a determination to please everyone around him. He says the overnight success of *Butterflies Are Free* doesn't faze him, but you can see the bafflement in his blackboard-gray eyes. "I made a movie called *The Fool Killer* when I was eleven years old. I remember twenty-eight weeks in Tennessee, catfish three times a day, a Holiday Inn with slimy floors and everybody sucking on ice all the time. To fight off nausea, I guess. And I did not want to be a child star. So I didn't work again for ten years. I went to school, majored in psychology, played my guitar, and then *Butterflies* came along. Even that came about through a friend of the family. So I haven't done anything that challenged me. I still haven't settled into acting for the rest of my life. It's exciting, fun and also hard work, but I am trying to keep my feet on whatever foundation I've built in twenty-one years so I won't lose my balance from all this."

He almost loses his balance when he enters his suite. His stand-in has been sleeping in the next room. Two girls are in the bedroom, giggling. Room-service trays are stacked everywhere. The place is littered with oyster crackers, Tabasco bottles, half-empty beer bottles, coffee cups with scum on top, cashews, guitars. He sweeps aside a place to sit and orders a whiskey sour. "I worked on *Patton* as a translator and general apprentice in Spain. And I haven't had to work for anything, so people say I haven't paid my dues, I haven't suffered. But you know something? I haven't changed. It's all the people around me who are changing. All the actors I used to know have stopped calling me. Most of my friends are artists or musicians.

And my family. They have been terrific. But I'm still not secure."

He still works on his guitar, plays everything from flamenco to twelve-string acoustic. Totally self-taught. But now it seems like the movies are forcing him into a commitment he didn't have to make on his own. "I've never studied acting. I'm totally intuitive. I don't have the self-confidence to try the things I'd really like to do because I don't have any technique. All I can do is find things in myself that correspond to the characters I play and work them out naturally rather than imitate a character. I don't have the experience. And I'm not kidding myself one bit."

Downstairs in the lobby, they're ready for the next scene. The star nobody knows and the boy without the self-confidence take their places at the elevator once more. "Who else is in the movie?" asks a Michigan housewife in town for the weekend. "Any stars?" Somebody tells her Gene Kelly is playing a small part. "Now there's a real star; is he here?" Somebody says no, just the leads.

"What's the name of the picture?"

"Forty Carats."

"I'll catch it on TV."

And the beat goes on.

PART

Digging the Crazy Life

THREE

31

Jacqueline Susann

HER FRIENDS call her Jackie. Her enemies call her lots of other things. Jacqueline Susann used to worry about it. But now she's mellowed toward her critics. She knows that writers are the bitchiest people in the world, and since she has sold more books than any female writer in the history of literature, she is going to turn some people green with jealousy and that's all there is to it. When Truman Capote called her a "truck driver in drag" on the Johnny Carson show, she slapped him with a lawsuit. Now she's mellowed. Looking about as much like a truck driver as Raquel Welch, now she just laughs at her assailants. Especially Truman Capote. "Poor thing. You realize, don't you, that he has never written a full-length novel in his life. There has to be something wrong with a man who, in *In Cold Blood*, had more empathy for the two killers than he had for the murdered Clutter family because to his way of thinking the Clutters were middle-class. And you have to be slightly off-balance to say that Laurence Olivier, Alec Guinness and Marlon Brando have no intelligence or that Sammy Davis, one of the world's greatest entertainers, has 'no talent, only energy.' He hasn't written a book since 1965."

So Jacqueline Susann is crying all the way to the bank, and after this week she'll be making several more trips. This week is D-Day in the publishing world because it marks the publication of Jacqueline Susann's newest novel, *Once Is Not Enough,* and there is no reason to suspect history won't repeat itself. *Valley of the Dolls* sold 25,000,000 copies and stayed on the best-seller list for sixty-five weeks. *The Love Machine,* on the list for thirty-seven weeks, sold 10,000,000 and is still climbing. The new one is expected to break all previous records. Forty-eight hours after her photo appeared on the cover of the February 5, 1973, *Publishers Weekly,* 56,000 orders had been taken. The book isn't even in the stores yet and it already has a guaranteed first printing of 150,000 copies. So say anything you like about Jacqueline Susann, but spell the name right.

I'll tell you something. I've read *Once Is Not Enough* and all I can say is fasten your seat belts. Not only is it the best book Jacqueline Susann has ever written, it's like a pot of fudge. You can't put it down. It has warmth, humor, wit, sharply defined characters, complex relationships, startling plot twists, a hypnotic story and enough thinly disguised public figures to keep cocktail parties guessing and every movie star in Hollywood fighting duels to get into the movie version for months to come. Nineteen seventy-three won't be dull. There's a Mike Todd type of figure whose daughter is in love with him, a legendary Greta Garbo recluse, an Ernest Hemingway figure. Look closely and you'll find Truman Capote and John Simon, too. There are no plain folks. Everybody is somebody—astronauts, millionaires, Palm Beach hostesses, stars of

nude rock musicals, speed-injecting Dr. Feelgoods. Like
I said. It isn't dull.

I'll tell you something else. I like Jacqueline Susann, too.
She's generous and kind and candid and enormously intelligent. The door opens to her lemony-chiffon penthouse
twenty-five floors above Central Park and the first thing
I see is a giant pop-art book cover that says *Once Is Not
Enough* in bright red neon lights. All the salesmen for her
new book chipped in and bought it. She's talking to Doris
Day on the phone about animal shelters, so I settle down
with a Dr. Pepper in a Tiffany glass served on napkins
advertising *The Love Machine.* Then she flows in like
somebody in a Noel Coward play, and we're off. "Don't
say I'm 'a fortyish novelist,' for God's sake. Just say I was
born in November, 1963, because that's when my first
book, *Every Night, Josephine,* came out. It was about my
poodle, who was a bigger celebrity than I am, and it's still
my favorite of all my books. It took nine years to get two
hundred forty good pages and it sold thirty-five thousand
copies. The new book took three and a half years to write,
and I edited it in five days. I'm a natural-born editor. I
know instinctively when something's wrong. When I
write a book, it's bought sight unseen. I don't audition. I
write by myself and nobody sees it until I'm ready. Then
I sit down and tell Irving, 'Welcome to the Monday-night
fights!' and he reads it. If he objects to something, we talk
about it, but I don't always change it. He hated the name
Neely O'Hara in *Valley of the Dolls* and it stayed in. But
Irving is the only one who reads it before the final draft."

Besides being a great businessman, her husband Irving
Mansfield is also the best press agent an author could
have. Each of Jackie's books is treated like a production
and together they have revolutionized the promotion and
publicity of publishing. She married him when he made
$250 a week producing Fred Allen's radio show and
they've been a team ever since. Now he has edged out of
a successful career as a TV producer and devotes full time
to Jackie. Together, they've made millions, but Jackie insists she does not write for money. "All I care about is my

husband, my friends and my work—in that order. I like pretty clothes, but I hate shopping. I once had a lot of jewelry and everything was stolen. I never replaced it. I had a watch from Eddie Cantor that said 'To my sixth daughter, Jackie' and I was so upset about losing it that I developed a philosophy right then that I would never care that much about possessions again. If I die, my royalties will take care of Irving for the rest of his life. That's all money means. My work is much more important than the money it brings in. I am tired of people saying, 'She's a born storyteller, it pours right out of her.' It's ground out of me. There are moments of such anguish and desperation, when nothing works, that I sit here and watch the sun rise over Central Park many days.

"There are no simple folks in my books because I don't know any simple folks. I write about people I know. This book is about spiritual and mental incest. It's about a girl who loved her father but only saw the glamorous side of his life—the black limousine, the corner suite at the Plaza, dinner at '21.' Then after a motorcycle accident that keeps her in a hospital for three years, she returns to New York all grown up to discover the whole world has changed. It is not a frivolous book. I did tremendous research on the evacuation of Poland. I went to twenty different places to learn about how they ravaged nuns in Siberian labor camps. I knew all the people who took speed shots years ago and started to write about that in *Valley* but Irving said stick to pills. Now people think I'm cashing in on the publicity of the speed-doctor craze. I'm just writing what I know about. And the process is lonely and torturous."

She begins a book with yellow scratch paper in her typewriter, sitting on an orange leather chair covered with a white towel because the upholstery makes her fanny perspire. Then she types on the backs of press releases. ("The only thing I'm chintzy about is paper.") Thousands of pages come out of her typewriter without the aid of a secretary. She has never hired a professional typist. Every word of her books is typed with two fingers. She corrects the yellow pages by hand. Then as the book progresses, it travels through various drafts on blue, pink and finally white paper. Then Irving reads it and Jackie xeroxes it herself for the publisher. "I don't trust one page out of my sight, even as far as the Xerox machine."

This book has taken a lot out of her. She worked night and day for three and a half years to meet her deadline, and has been ill ever since with eye infections, double pneumonia and bronchial asthma. But she did it all without a cigarette. "I stopped smoking in January, 1968, and I've had a cough ever since," she laughs. "I'm always making bargains with God. I gave up drinking for Lent. One year I gave up hash-brown potatoes for twelve months. I promised God if I made the best-seller list on *Valley* I'd give up smoking. Then I got so nervous going on talk shows I had a cigarette in both hands. So then I promised I'd give God a month for every week I stayed on the list. Well, who would have thought I'd be on it for sixty-five weeks? I was picking up butts out of other people's ashtrays. It was disgusting. Then Irving had a polyp removed from his intestines and I promised God if it wasn't malignant I'd give up smoking for good. I finally made it."

Two things she didn't make were good movies from either of her previous novels. In fact, they were lousy and she's the first to admit it. "They kept *Valley of the Dolls* a secret from me and I was too stupid to know I had the right to see my own film. The first time I saw it was on a press junket aboard a cruise ship. There was supposed to be a party after the film. I went back to my cabin, took two Seconals and a slug of scotch with tears running down my face, and the hostess came in and said something about my 'moment of triumph' and I yelled 'Get the hell out of here.' It was a very embarrassing thing. They cut important scenes and it made no sense, but it made money because the book was so popular.

"Then on *Love Machine* they didn't even make the book and the word-of-mouth killed it. It was even worse than the first movie. It was totally miscast. I hated it, but I made a million and a half on it, the highest price ever paid for a book, so I never knocked it. But I never promoted it, either. I'll never make that mistake again. On the next one, I'll have more control. I am going to write the screenplay myself."

Jackie's father, Robert Susann, was a famous portrait painter who lamented the fact that he had no sons to carry the family name. Her new novel about incest has a dedication: "To Robert Susann, who would understand." Raised eyebrows? "I loved him. He taught me a lot about people and everything he taught me has stayed in my mind. It comes out in my books like litmus paper. There's a sculpture of him that dominates my living room and I often talk to him. I say, 'Don't go away, I'm getting a drink, be right back.' I guess I wanted to make it as an actress to carry on the Susann name, but I was always the girl who got murdered, stabbed or shot on *Studio One.* Then one day George Abbott turned me down for a part and I said, 'I hope he dies, I hope he gets leprosy!' Silly kid stuff like that. And Eddie Cantor said, 'Kid, if you'd just take that energy and turn it into being a success, George Abbott will say, 'I could have had her and I blew it!' That's always been my philosophy, and now the Susann name is still alive through my writing."

That's the understatement of the year. She's got everything now. Except for one remaining fantasy. "My secret wish is to spend one night with George C. Scott and one night with Mick Jagger. It doesn't have to be sex, but if we end up in bed Irving gives me his permission." Like she says, once is not enough. And Jacqueline Susann is just the girl to prove it.

32

On Location:
Ken Russell

L IKE AN UTRILLO WATERCOLOR, the sleepy seaport
town of Portsmouth, England, looked peaceful.
A few weeks after I left, it probably *was* peaceful. But when I was there, Ken Russell was in town. He
was storming up and down the lazy cobblestone streets in
knickers, boots, outsize tinted granny glasses, a black
Dracula cape and a stone crucifix, brandishing an evil
cane with an ivory dog's head handle, and frightening the
horses.

Small wonder. He's England's resident mad genius, the
director of *Women in Love, The Music Lovers* and *The
Devils.* Everything he touches is surrounded by controversy. He is respected by studio heads, who spell his name
RU$$ELL, and savagely mauled by critics, who call him a
maniac because his films are filled to capacity with exces-

sive sex and perversion. Recently he did some mauling himself when he showed up on British television and physically assaulted Alexander Walker, London's leading film reviewer, for his acid dismissal of *The Devils,* and according to Russell, "also because he deserved a good thrashing." He's not dull.

And now a soothing about-face with a musical family picture, *The Boy Friend,* which MGM is rushing into Christmas release before the color is dry. Is this cherubic monster turning soft? "Don't be insulting," he said, glaring. "I haven't begun to shock people yet. I'm just doing this for therapy." Russell had agreed to let me visit his closed set without a blood test despite the secrecy surrounding the project because I was one of the few American critics who liked *The Music Lovers.* He likes the people who like his movies and hates the ones who don't. (He hadn't yet read my review of *The Devils,* which made me throw up.) But like most egomaniacs, he didn't surprise me when, after a brandy and a sour English lunch that tasted like boiled socks, he asked me point-blank about *The Devils before* I visited the set. "You give critics ammunition. You must've known you were setting yourself up when you showed Louis XIII shooting French Huguenots dressed like blackbirds dropping dead in the water while the sound track played 'Bye Bye Blackbird'! Not to mention the masturbating nuns, people being burned alive and close-ups of torture. You gave the Catholics alone enough ammunition to gun you down for the rest of your life."

He blanched and grabbed a steak knife. I waited for him to stab me to death. His eyes rolled back and his breathing stopped. "The church has always been appalling. I'm an ordinary, run-of-the-mill sinner who only pays lip service to the church, but I was trying to tell the truth about how it uses totally illiterate people to seduce everyone through terror. It has always been like that and it's like that now and the masses have always gone along with it. America is full of narrow-minded bigots who are terrified of any criticism of the church. They forced me to make twenty-three cuts before it could be released in America and the ones who made the biggest fuss were atheists—movie moguls at Warner Brothers who give some of the wildest orgies in Hollywood. Hypocrites! Some of my best scenes had to be cut. I had a great scene in which the nuns tore down the cross of Christ and stuffed his toes into their orifices. It was glorious stuff!" He cackled with glee.

I asked him about the reports in the British press about the nuns actually getting raped on the set. "It was pretty gory, but they knew what they were getting into. I never force my actors to do anything they don't want to do, but English extras are the lowest form of animal, the dregs of the underworld, and they manhandled two of the girls a bit harshly and the whole orgy scene got out of hand. Some of the electricians were running off the set from nausea. Then Actors Equity got into it and there was a fracas in the papers. But actors love me."

Glenda Jackson tells it differently. She turned down the lead in *The Devils* because she claimed she had foamed at the mouth enough for Ken Russell in *Women in Love* and *The Music Lovers* and this time he had gone over the boundaries of sanity and good taste. "Utter nonsense," he balked. "I'm glad she wasn't in it. She's not a very good actress, she's very cold and intellectual. No emotion. She says she doesn't want to play the same parts, yet she did Queen Elizabeth on TV like a boring schoolmistress, and followed it up in a movie playing the same part. Giving a ghastly performance, from what I hear." Graciousness and charity are not his strong points.

Nor is humility. "I make great pictures," he would say. "I want to shock people until they turn blue. I want to kick them in the crotch." Or "My film on photographers for TV probably influenced *Blow-Up*. People steal from me constantly." Or "I know *The Boy Friend* will be one of the greatest musicals of all time."

Whatever *The Boy Friend* will be, it will not be erotic and it won't go unnoticed. On the way back to the set, he said he decided to make it "to prove to people I'm not

totally depraved. I love the innocence and charm of musicals. When I was in military school, I led all the cadets in
a Carmen Miranda number in drag. I made all the cadets
dress up like Carmen Miranda in drag. I often dance
around naked to phonograph records. I was a dancer once
in a stock company of *Annie Get Your Gun.* I could jump
enormously high, but I came down like a ton of bricks.
Then I became a director and devised a new way to make
dreary biographies of dead people. I did thirty-five films
for TV for very tiny budgets. I couldn't afford period costumes for more than six extras. I had no way to build Paris
in my film on Debussy. In the one on Delius, I only had
three people in a room. In the one on Isadora Duncan, I
couldn't afford musicians, so I used an old Betty Hutton
record. Those films inspired my imagination and now I
know how to make a small budget look like twenty million
dollars on the screen. For *The Boy Friend,* I only have
twenty-four girls instead of three hundred, but the Busby
Berkeley musical numbers and dream sequences in the
movie will knock you out. I'm directing it like a tacky
stageplay in the provinces that is being visited by a big
Hollywood director. You see the big fantasies as he visual-
izes them in his head. It will be fantastic!"

We arrived at the Theater Royal, a condemned music
hall marked for demolition where Edmund Kean used to
play Othello at the seashore. "They're going to tear it
down when the movie is finished and turn it into a super-
market." It wasn't much different from most sets, except
the actors were dirtier, with Band-Aids on their knees. Up
on the stage I saw the executioner, the evil torturers, King
Charles and a couple of demented monks from *The Devils*
in tights and Esther Williams bathing caps, dressed like
starfish. (Russell uses the same actors over and over because they know him well enough to do anything he asks
no matter how outrageous, and the costumes for all of his
films are designed by his wife Shirley.) Two flappers covered in green, blue and silver spangles were decked out
like tap-dancing Christmas trees, and tinsel waves moved
onstage in rhythm before a gigantic papier-mâché sun-

burst. "Everybody onstage for the beach number!" yelled
Russell, like Mickey Rooney in *Babes in Arms.*

There were grinning jellyfish, plum-colored palm trees
and terpsichorean doll babies in straw hats encrusted with
jeweled seashells, stomping and hoofing, rocking and
swaying, like inmates of an asylum putting on a benefit to
buy new shock-treatment equipment. "Show your teeth,
boys—jellyfish have teeth!" shouted Russell. Out beyond
the opera boxes and gold-leaf statues like pornographic
madonnas, under an electric cable strung from an oil
lamp chandelier, sat Twiggy. An emaciated rag doll with
a face painted on like a candy box. The all-singing, all-
dancing star of all this pandemonium, she seemed un-
ruffled.

"I met her three years ago," said Russell, "and she said,
'I'm sick of modeling, I want to do a film.' So one night I
was at a party and some bloody journalist came up and
said, 'What's all this about you doing *The Boy Friend* with
Twiggy? Is it true?' I was so drunk on champagne I just
said yes to get rid of him, and the next day MGM rang up
and said, 'What the hell are you doing? We've owned the
rights to that for fifteen years!' and when we stopped
yelling at each other, they said would I really like to do
it and I said yes before I knew what I was getting into.
Honestly, that's how it all came about."

In the five months it took Ken Russell to make *The Boy
Friend,* I am told it was not Twiggy who nearly caused
everyone involved to have seventeen nervous break-
downs, but her Svengali-like manager-cum-boyfriend,
Justin de Villeneuve, who discovered her washing hair in
a beauty parlor at the age of fourteen and created, pack-
aged, promoted, publicized and exploited her into a pop
phenomenon. It was Justin who teased and rudely antago-
nized the world press into a state bordering on hysteria by
protecting Twiggy as though she was Elizabeth Taylor's
wedding ring, and it was Justin who, at one point, even
threatened to withdraw her from the film halfway
through completion unless Russell promised to pay him
more money and guaranteed to star him in a movie ver-

sion of Thomas Hardy's *Tess of the D'Urbervilles.* Russell
turns purple with rage at the mention of Justin, who was
banned from the set the day I was there, but he was very
complimentary about all ninety-two pounds of Twiggy.
"I'm going to make her the greatest thing since Marilyn
Monroe," he said modestly.

Since that famous interview in which she said she
thought Hiroshima was a Japanese boutique on Madison
Avenue, some folks have come to think of Twiggy as frivolous. But she was working hard. She chewed the ends of
her hair, her feet red and swollen. "It's been risky, but she
danced eight hours a day for eight months and she hits all
the notes and makes me cry," said Russell. "She'll be a
bloody star."

"Oy don't know wot oy'm doin' 'alf the time," said the
bloody star.

Panavision cameras moved in. Christopher Gable, who
played Tchaikovsky's boyfriend in *The Music Lovers,*
chewed bubble gum in blue jeans and an Edwardian coat,
doubling as choreographer and Twiggy's costar: "All
right, girls," he said, addressing the clumsy jellyfish, "keep
in step. Ready now—one, two, three . . ."

I headed out of town, the jazz of the Twenties swing
band fading in the distance. The last I saw of Ken Russell,
he was sitting in a velvet chair, knitting a sweater.

33

Alfred Hitchcock

GEORGE BERNARD SHAW ONCE SAID, "Messages are for Western Union," and Alfred Hitchcock parlayed his advice into one of the most fabulous careers in the motion picture industry. Except for one brief try at directing a musical and a silent film of Sean O'Casey's *Juno and the Paycock* in 1930, all of Alfred Hitchcock's films have been thrillers. So international is his fame that when his latest blood-curdling horror was premiered at the recent Cannes Film Festival, all they did was post signs showing the famous Hitchcock face and everyone got the message.

Frenzy is his fifty-third motion picture and just in case anyone thinks the master of the macabre has lost his touch, the long lines in London, where the film is playing to standing room only, dispel doubt. It's a variation on the

Jack-the-Ripper theme about a sex maniac in Covent Garden who strangles women with neckties and contains
such glorious Hitchcock touches as slow strangulation,
dilated eyes, hand clutching in vain for the telephone,
corpses hidden in potato sacks, soups with eyes in them,
breadsticks that crunch just like dead fingers as they
break and a marvelous opening shot: A politician is giving
a speech about pollution on the banks of the Thames. "It
will be free of filth and foreign bodies," he promises if he's
elected. A cry interrupts the rally. The body of a woman,
strangled by a necktie, floats to the shore. The crowd
(including a rotund, poker-faced onlooker named Alfred
Hitchcock) drags the corpse from the murky water, and
the speaker after a horrified glance exclaims: "My God,
my club tie!"

Hitchcock was seventy-four years old on August 13,
1972, but the years haven't dimmed the mischievous twinkle in his eye. He is alert, crisp, intelligent, and full of
enthusiasm for anything that reeks of murder and may-
hem. In London for the opening of *Frenzy,* his comfortable Queen Anne chair creaks with misery as all 300
pounds of the famous director settles down to discuss the
tantalizing tastiness of terror. His face doesn't move, the
jowls of S. Z. Sakall don't move, the voice is clearly
the low hum of a phantom at a séance. The effect is eerie
enough to keep me glancing at the window below, grateful for a glimpse of sunshine.

"I have always been fascinated by crime," says the man
who is often credited with originating the word. "It's a
particularly English problem, I think. The British take a
peculiar interest in the literature of crime. It goes back to
reading Conan Doyle. Every time you read about a particularly grisly trial at Old Bailey you also read that some
famous actor or director or writer is present. In America
that is considered second-class literature, like Dashiell
Hammett. There is even a club here that meets after
every trial just so both attorneys for the defense and the
prosecution can have lunch in a private dining room and
discuss the case all over again. I have been to these meet-

ings, and they are much more interesting than the actual trials. Of course, it's not as exciting now because you can't hang anybody anymore. I loved the tapes I heard made by the moors murderers. They made tape recordings of children screaming as they were buried alive. That was jolly good stuff. But today killers go into prison at twenty and they're out again at thirty-five."

Hitchcock does not approve of abolishing capital punishment, and when he's in London the first thing he does is head for the black museum at Scotland Yard, a private chamber of horrors which is to nostalgia crime buffs what *No, No, Nanette* is to Broadway. "They've got all the shoes of prostitutes from the gaslight era. Did you know that the color of every scarlet woman's shoe determined what her specialty was? If a man saw a prostitute walking alone on Waterloo Bridge at night he knew she did one thing in red heels, another thing in blue heels. I find that a fascinating bit of information." He is also partial to the vice museum in Paris, where he has actually fingered the knife that cut Marie Antoinette's head off. But his real favorite hangout is Madame Tussaud's waxworks in London, where all the superstars of evil are preserved (including one tourist favorite, Alfred Hitchcock).

"I don't know why parents worry about what their children see in movies when any child can walk into a tiny kitchen there and see the notorious Christie ready to chop up another victim with a butcher knife. 'Who is that, Mommy?' they ask. 'Oh, that's Mr. Christie, darling, he murdered eight women and buried them in his cellar.' They really do an elaborate job to make everything real there. I posed for them and first they made a mask of my face by making me stand for hours of photography, shooting me from every angle. Then a woman came in with an enormous tray full of eyes and held each one up to my face to match the perfect color. It was delicious."

His favorite people in history are Lizzie Borden, Jack the Ripper and a man who murdered his wife and buried her under the San Diego Freeway. "I never drive over that freeway without thinking about that woman lying underneath. She's still there, you know. During my television series, we buried at least two hundred women in the cellar over a ten-year period. There are no new plots anymore. Everything has been done. Now it all depends on how well you do it. When I made *The Lodger* as a silent film back in 1926 I had a continuing mahogany rail rising up through a four-story house with the camera on the roof. All you could see through the house was a white hand moving down the staircase. Then I had the mother, father and daughter looking up and watching the chandelier shaking. The floor dissolved and you could see the soles of Jack the Ripper's shoes walking above. It's a pretty crude film today, but it shows my original preoccupation with horror. I was only twenty-six years old at the time, working as an art director in Berlin, and heavily influenced by the German films of Emil Jannings. But I knew I wanted to frighten people."

He's been scaring the living daylights out of everybody ever since and, although he considers some of his films "awfully corny," his favorite is *Shadow of a Doubt*, written by Thornton Wilder in 1943, about an all-American family that discovers a favorite uncle is a mass murderer hiding out in a room upstairs. "The problem with thrillers is that they always deal with movement and action, with no time to develop character. In that one, I was able to do both."

He heartily agrees with today's trend to make directors the stars of the movie world, instead of actors, and accepts his own legend as though it were a weather report. "When David Selznick brought me to America to do *Rebecca* in 1940, the producer was king. I remember Selznick firing the great cameraman Harry Stradling from *Intermezzo* because he 'wasn't getting Ingrid Bergman.' Stradling was so upset he disappeared for three days and they found him drunk on a gambling ship, convinced his career was finished. Before it was over, *Gone With the Wind* had gone through three directors. But I was lucky, because I was always being loaned out to studios and I was always my own boss. I always develop my films so thoroughly that it is very difficult for me to find writers who are willing to work themselves into my style. Everything is planned except dialogue, so I have the whole movie on paper before we shoot. Then I call in the writer. The film is precut. Every shot is dictated and described on paper, so I know exactly what the film will look like before it ever gets to the editing room. In *Frenzy,* for example, the scene on the truck where the killer must take the corpse out of the potato sack to reclaim an important clue to his identity is composed of 118 shots. Each shot is listed on a numbered yellow file card. All the cutter has to do is refer to the number of each cut and splice it all together. I never improvise on the set, only in the office. As for actors, I used to say all actors were cattle. But that's a lie. I really meant all actors should be treated like cattle."

Frenzy has fallen into bad trouble with the London censors, who were appalled by a scene in which a girl is raped and murdered while reciting the 93rd Psalm. Hitchcock shrugs. "I've been censored before, with the shower scene in *Psycho.* But if something is worth doing, it's worth doing well. The better you do it the more horrible it becomes. I fill up each scary scene with details. That's what sets my films apart—the details. In *Psycho* I had to show the blood running down the bathtub into the drain, but I did it in black and white, which took away from the violence on the screen and transferred the terror to the imaginations of the audience. That was much more horrifying than showing the knife plunging into the girl. Actually, I don't like violence for the sake of violence. I didn't care much for *Straw Dogs.* If you show too much, you don't scare the audience. You just nauseate them."

Alma Hitchcock, the charming wife to whom he's been married since 1926, interrupts with tea and there seems just time to ask one final question. "Yes," says the portly master of suspense, espionage and horror, who has received every major honor for movie directing and whose anthologies such as *Favorite Monsters* and *Stories to Play Russian Roulette By* have been translated into every language in the world, "I do have a sense of humor. I've been

scaring everybody to death for forty-six years. You have
to have a sense of humor to survive that."

And then the interview was over and he went back to
reading his afternoon paper. The headline read, "LON-
DON INFANT STABBED TO DEATH BY MANIAC IN BABY
CARRIAGE," and for the first time that day the stone face
of Alfred Hitchcock turned into something like a smile.

34

Alice Cooper

REACHING FOR MY VOMIT BAG, I watch a creature of puzzling gender hang himself from the top of a stage in Passaic, New Jersey, while the audience goes wild. A bulletin from the court of Henry the Eighth? Grand Guignol? No, just Alice Cooper, the hottest hard-rock music act in show business at the moment. Alice Cooper's *Killer* just won a gold record for passing the million sales mark. Alice Cooper touring the country is breaking house records everywhere. On stage or off, people are just wild about Alice. Well, not *all* people. Mostly those gullible freaks under sixteen. His fans. If one can call a hirsute mess of salivating teenagers people. Mothers and fathers are wild about Alice, too—wild with rage. They forbid their kids to play his records or attend his concerts. But the kids sneak off and do it anyway.

Lured on by radio commercials on which a teenybopper's voice peeps, "My mommy won't let me go to the theater tonight to see Alice Cooper, but me and my friends are going anyway," they stand in line by the thousands to see an act that is musically paramount in the ultraviolence kick of our current subculture. Alice loves it.

In the back of his limousine, Alice coils like a reptile in black-and-white dotted-swiss suit, tieless, and open-shirted to the navel. "It's frightening to scare parents half to death. That's what I love to do. It's great to widen the generation gap. Why shorten it? There are too many values already hardened. Sixteen-year-old kids live in fantasy. The older ones have too many rigid thoughts. No conclusions. They want just what we give them—an imitation of violence. I see violence as the answer to what's wrong with everything. I don't care about ecology like James Taylor—who cares? No one. Sex, death and violence is what folks care about today." Suddenly a throbbing throng of lumber-jacketed, gum-chewing youngsters spots Alice's gauntly emaciated head, with his long nose, high cheekbones and at least a foot of tangled black hair growing down toward his knees. He sinks as far back as he can, fingers twitching nervously. Almost in a whisper he mutters: "Go play with each other, babies, but don't touch me."

Face to face, Alice Cooper is a personable enough man who lives hippie-commune style with four members of his group in a large Connecticut house filled with groupies, dogs, babies and two Siamese kittens. They are a gentle, beer-drinking "family." No dope allowed, especially the hard stuff. Until six years ago they all studied art. They like to make you think one day it occurred to them they might better express their artistic urges in music rather than painting, but one secretly suspects the real reason is they are capitalists just like everybody else. Flower children is out, man, but there's money in violence and hard rock, and if you're clever, you might just create an act in which it's hard to tell the difference. So Alice Cooper was born.

They settled on the name Alice Cooper because it had such an all-American ring to it. "I mean, I could have called myself Mary Smith, but Alice Cooper just seemed to fit better," giggles Alice. Why a female name for five musicians? "People are both male and female, biologically," explains Alice. "I once studied under a hypnotist who taught me to become three equal parts—male for strength, female for wisdom and child for faith. We integrated this thought into the act: a feminine image, rough masculine music and the 'toys' we play with onstage."

When he started, Alice wanted to be like Barbarella. Then he changed horses in midstream. "I thought of all those fabulous villains of the horror movies. I love horror movies. I love violence. I love violence on TV. I think it's cathartic. The kids sit there and get their rocks off watching it. I don't think they are then as apt to go out and really do it. It's been done for them already. I just act as a mirror for them. I try to live Alice as Dr. Jekyll. That's me right now. Onstage, I become Mr. Hyde. I don't see any point in becoming political. Calling cops dirty pigs doesn't appeal to me. That's for the liberated James Taylor–Elton John–sophisticated–older–brainy group. I mean it's hard for me to imagine James Taylor getting it off. Rock music doesn't appeal to the brain, it gets you right in the crotch."

A gigantic blond ectoplasm with hair to his waist stomps into the dressing room backstage in Passaic, New Jersey. He's done up in a shabby costume of Flash Gordon comic strips. "Hey, didja see the line? Who's on the bill?" he jokes. Dozens of people are sitting on the floor, rolling and taping together Alice Cooper posters to later throw into the audience, and popping open Michelob beer by the gallon. The vibes in the room are kinetic. They are like a bunch of overgrown boys dressing up in drag for a campy performance of a college musical.

While technicians still in beardless puberty scramble all over the stage, setting up lights and microphones, old movies are running for the milling, chattering crowd of kids jammed into the auditorium. *The Destroying Ray,*

Serial No. 5. Some never-to-be-known starlet is locked in
a vault which is slowly filling with water. To the rescue,
Buster Crabbe appears with his ray gun . . . and, zippo,
she's free. The kids howl and jeer and stamp their feet.
Then, they start stamping and howling for Alice. "Come
on, Alice," they all yell, male and female. An announce-
ment is made that the city of Passaic is giving full coopera-
tion. "Smoke anything you are holding, but, please, *not* in
the auditorium. Thank you." Mothers, where are your
kids tonight? It makes you laugh when you think about all
these nervous parents worrying about X-rated movies,
doesn't it?

Darkness. An eerie crimson glow backlights a set of
drums elaborate enough to have given Gene Krupa a
breakdown. Brighter, brighter grow the lights, and
louder, louder grows the ominous hum of an electric or-
gan. Earwax runs with the vibrations the amplification
system sends out, as the first violence of the evening is
committed on the eardrums. Alice Cooper is there at last,
in torn black leotards, leather vest, leather buckles folded
into his groin, high black rocker boots and an evil
sadomasochist sneer painted in black on his face. "You can
be my slave and I'll be your master," he shrieks, setting
the scene for the first fantasy of the evening. A rapier,
used to accent the grotesque lyrics, slashes the long hair
of a child in the first row. A beer can is opened and
sprayed over everyone.

The audience strikes back. All kinds of things are
thrown at Alice—dolls, paper, marshmallows, popcorn,
cigarette butts. He nastily kicks them back. A boa con-
strictor is now around his neck, winding down his back
and between his legs. "I'm a killer," he continues. "I wear
lace and black leather. My hands are lightning on my
gun." The kids are in a frenzy now. Neal, the drummer,
is going bananas under his forty pounds of unwashed hair.
Dennis, on bass, is suffering from a hernia, so he's seated
for this performance in a chair to which is attached a
bottle of simulated blood plasma running into his trousers.
Bubbles are spurting in masses from several bubble ma-

chines. Alice bites at them. Smoke is filling the stage. Glass balloons are released and batted from audience to stage with hysterical venom. This is silly, the kids have had enough. They whimper, and start to move forward. They are crawling over the seats. Huge young men in football shirts link arms to keep them back.

This is it. This is what they've been waiting for all night, what they sneaked out of their homes and lied to their parents about spending the night at a friend's house to see. Alice Cooper, singing "Dead Babies" (a song claimed to have taken four years to write, and labeled a "psycho-drama"). Alice takes a golden-curled doll and rips its clothes off, piece by piece, throwing the pieces to the slithering, crawling children. An arm is then broken off and thrown to the screaming mob. The legs. Then an ax appears. Hysteria is cresting. The doll is decapitated on-stage, with red, inky juice running over its face. Four thousand kids who can't get into *A Clockwork Orange* are now screaming with pain, and yelling encouragement. Some have brought binoculars to see this unbelievable event in close-up. For his crime, Alice is punished. Out of the shadows emerges a real gallows. Spitting and hissing, Alice is hung—amid the unearthly, unimaginable shriek of hard-rock music that sounds like garbage-can lids being smashed together.

"That's it. People put their values on what they just saw, and their values are sometimes warped. They react out of insecurity. They consider it shocking, vulgar. But people who are really pure enjoy it for what it is, entertainment. The more liberated you become, the more you realize you are not just this or that, but everything. That's the future." So says Alice Cooper, creator of a new musical form— bubble-gum violence. Exhausted, he slumps grimly into a stuffed chair and pops open another Michelob. "I don't care what they throw at me, just so long as it's nothing worse than marshmallows."

Pray harder, Alice.

35

On Location: James Bond/Roger Moore

THE PUBLICITY SHOUTS: "Roger Moore *is* James Bond!" and I guess that's true enough. He certainly is playing him to the hilt. Sean Connery got sick of the role. George Lazenby lasted through one round, then went off to a monastery to meditate. Now there's a new 007 and Roger Moore says: "I don't know why they picked me, but the money is fantastic, so I think I'll stick around." Roger, who used to be prettier than his leading ladies, got roughed up a little for *Live and Let Die*, the eighth Ian Fleming novel about Bond to be filmed, but it wasn't all in the line of duty.

We were down in the Caribbean. About a hundred Jamaicans lined the cliff above the road in bright native costumes, some of them carrying baskets of bananas on their heads. Several toothless ladies stretched out a sign reading: "THE ROGER MOORE FAN CLUB IS HERE!" One woman didn't seem interested in the action at all. She was busy knocking breadfruit from a tree. Half an hour later, she reappeared with seventy pounds of breadfruit on her head. A nice day's profit. Where else can you watch a movie being made and make a living at the same time?

Suddenly James Bond, waving his Walther PPK38, came careening through a sugarcane field in a double-decker London bus. The villains followed in hot pursuit in a police car. The chase narrowed into a dirt road. *Oops!* There was a covered bridge ahead. No escape. Would he crash? Would this be the end of 007? The bus smashed into the bridge. There was an earsplitting explosion. The top of the London bus crashed to the ground. There was applause from the cliffs when Roger Moore emerged, safe and sound and ready for the next adventure. The whole thing will have to be reshot later with the top of the bus falling on the police car and killing the villains inside. When you see the final movie, you'll think it all happened at once. That's the magic of movies. What looks either accidental or deceptively simple onscreen actually takes weeks of careful preparation and painstaking coordination to accomplish.

In *Live and Let Die* there are more of these narrow escapes than usual. Roger Moore bursts into the mystical world of a black master-criminal, Dr. Kananga, who plans to bludgeon the Western powers with the way-out weapons of voodoo and hard drugs. Shooting started in New Orleans with a motorboat chase in which thirteen high-powered aquajets and fourteen other boats with 150-horsepower outboard engines roared to their destruction in a murky bayou. In another scene he destroys eight airplanes, flying through an airport hangar, ripping the wings off a plane, and hitting a DC-3 on the landing strip beyond. There's more. He crashes over a wall on a motorcycle and falls into the sea from which he is carried 800 feet into the air hanging onto a kite. Then the company moved to Montego Bay where Dr. Kananga's plantation for producing hard drugs is protected by a sea of crocodiles. Roger had to wrestle with live crocodiles in a pit surrounded by 1,000 crocs and alligators. At one point, while he's taking a bath, a poisonous snake comes out of the shower head and crawls into the bathtub. Add to that shark fishing, sea chases and scarecrows with TV cameras for eyes and mouths that kill off enemies while they are picnicking, and you have another dandy 007 concoction —with equal parts espionage, derring-do and high camp.

"They never kill James Bond, do they?" somebody asked.

"Would you, if you were Harry Saltzman?" answered Roger Moore.

Like Joseph E. Levine, Saltzman is a jovial, rotund fellow who can easily be classified as one of the last of the big-spender producers. In 1960, Saltzman bought up the rights to twelve James Bond novels and all of his short stories because Ian Fleming and he shared the same lawyer. Fleming had turned everybody else down. Alfred Hitchcock had tried to buy the Bond stories. William Paley of CBS-TV had tried to buy them. Fleming just wasn't interested. "He hated movies," smiles Saltzman, "and had only seen two in his life—*Gone With the Wind* and *Cavalcade*. He only gave me the rights because he wanted to set up a trust fund for his children. He hated the choice of Sean Connery, but otherwise he had no opinion of the Bond pictures." He died four years later and to date Saltzman has made $225,000,000. James Bond is here to stay, immovable and indestructible as the mainland of China.

"I don't think it matters who plays 007," says Saltzman. "There are theaterowners throughout the world who still think James Bond is the name of an actor. They never heard of Sean Connery. The Bond pictures have all made money and the grosses keep going up all the time on rereleases. Connery got tired of the image because he wanted to be a serious actor, but he did all right. He made six and a half million dollars alone on his percentages, not counting his salaries. We make 'em big and we make 'em expensive. This one has a budget of seven million dollars. The one with George Lazenby, *On Her Majesty's Secret*

Service, was the most expensive because of all the snow stunts and bad weather conditions that caused delays. But most of them cost around seven million. We've even got museums begging for all the James Bond cars and guns and gadgets. We have never lost money. Even the Lazenby one, which was the least successful film in the series, grossed twenty-four million. So it doesn't matter whether Roger Moore or Sean Connery or Joe Smith plays 007 and it doesn't matter whether they get good reviews or bad reviews."

No wonder the casts and crew members on Bond pictures live it up in the old Hollywood style. In Ocho Rios, Saltzman threw a Thanksgiving dinner party for 120 people and flew in the chef from Harry's Bar in Venice just to prepare the lasagna. He can afford it.

I asked Guy Hamilton, who also directed *Goldfinger* and *Diamonds Are Forever,* if anybody had ever been seriously injured on a Bond film. "Oh, yes, and the insurance rates are very high, especially for the stuntmen. But we nearly lost Roger Moore on this one. Not in the film, but in rehearsals. We taught him how to drive a speedboat for the water chase and he ran out of gas and hit a bank and it knocked him out of the boat and almost broke all of his teeth out."

Fleming's description of James Bond in the books was that of a skinny man with a scar on his face. His ideal choice was always Hoagy Carmichael. That's a far cry from Sean Connery, and even the boyish-looking, forty-five-year-old Roger Moore, but at least Moore is the closest yet. The son of a London policeman, he started out as a cartoonist and tea server in a publicity office. An extra job in a Shakespearean movie led to drama classes, modeling, and eventually a trip to America, where he was signed by MGM. He never got the roles and ended up as the pretty boy who lost Elizabeth Taylor to Van Johnson in *The Last Time I Saw Paris* or got upstaged by Ann Blyth's horse in *The King's Thief.*

"It's a period in my life I just laugh about now," he grins. "I remember my biggest part was opposite Lana

Turner in a bomb called *Diane*. *Time* magazine said,
'Lana Turner as Diane de Poitiers walked on the screen
in a clattering of heels and a fluttering of false eyelashes,
followed by a lump of English roast beef.' I was the English roast beef. Then they asked me to leave. 'Just check
in your wardrobe and clear out' is the way they put it. I
arrived in America on April Fool's Day, 1954. I should
have known that meant something. I made one picture
for Warner Brothers after leaving MGM and that was the
worst one I ever did. It was called *The Miracle* and I
played the Duke of Wellington's nephew who had an
affair with Carroll Baker that turned her into a nun. All
I remember was leading a parade of soldiers through the
streets of Brussels in Rosalind Russell's corset from *Auntie
Mame*. Don't laugh. It's true. I wore her leftover costumes."

It was *The Saint* on TV that finally made Roger Moore
more than just another pretty face. It ran for seven years,
was sold to eighty countries, and is still being shown in
reruns. Now, as the new James Bond, it could happen all
over again. "The first thing every journalist asks is 'How
will your James Bond be different from Connery's?' The
last time I said my teeth are whiter than his. Then they
ask, 'How do you feel being the third choice?' I say look
how many people played Hamlet. I mean, how do you
answer these questions?" Truth is, it's the best career
move he could make. He stepped down as managing director of Brut productions, the film division of Fabergé
perfumes, to do the picture. He's been signed for three
more, so like it or not, he's going to be James Bond for a
while. The only thing that disturbs his wife Luisa, an Italian temptress he met in a Yugoslav spectacular called *The
Rape of the Sabine Women*, is that she is now being called
Mrs. James Bond and Roger gets mobbed everywhere by
battalions of lethal lovelies. But when he's not working,
Roger is a family man. Luisa is now pregnant with their
third child. Besides, she makes great spaghetti.

"The only things I will not do are movies that have
anything to do with putting down the police or making

their job harder," he says. "We have enough trouble keeping law and order as it is. And I would never run around bare-assed. I've been in too many of those epics where they throw the pages of the script away and say, 'And now we do the South American version.'" He finds a joke in every situation and for an actor who is going to get a lot of ribbing about being James Bond, superhero, he has a gentle sense of humor. On the day I visited the set, he was sporting an ugly gash on his perfect forehead.

"Did you get that from the bus crash? Or the motorcycle crash? Or the motorboat crash? Or the battle with the deadly crocodiles?" I asked.

"Would you believe I cut it shampooing my hair in the shower this morning? I got out of the shower and there was blood on my hand. I fainted three times," said James Bond.

36

Peter Bogdanovich and Cybill Shepherd

THE ANCIENT RUINS of Rome have survived Nero, the Nazis, Mussolini, the American tourist and even the Italians themselves, who urinate on their statues, throw chewing gum into their fountains and are slowly eroding their national treasures with pollution and noise from their motorcycles. Now they are being invaded again by Hollywood. Peter Bogdanovich conjures memories of dusty reference libraries, screening-room pallor (he claims to have seen more than 5,000 movies), and the smartest boy in an all-Jewish Brown Derby. His girl friend, Cybill Shepherd, is like the prettiest Wasp at the Memphis country club, stirring visions of cheerleaders, vitamin C, crisp tennis togs on a summer afternoon and peanut butter and jelly on Wonder bread. Together, this unlikely duo has invaded the land of pasta and paparazzi to make a 1973 version of Henry James' pastoral 1878 short story, *Daisy Miller.*

After *Targets, The Last Picture Show, What's Up, Doc?* and *Paper Moon,* Peter has become the hottest director in the business. With only four movies under his belt (four and a half if you count *Directed by John Ford,* a tribute to one of his idols made for the American Film Institute), he's the one director in these hard-up times who can name both his price and his project. Success is tangible. His bank account has expanded and so has his waistline. Despite his annoyance at rumors that he has become nervous, egotistical and pompous since he made the transition from a journalist-critic (a few short years ago, he was eking out a living writing profiles for *TV Guide* with his wife Polly, whom he has since left for Cybill) to a big-time Hollywood director-celebrity, Peter shows only one sign of strain in the chaos of Rome. He's started smoking again. The Italian inefficiency runs rampant and to top off the problems of his first expensive costume epic in a foreign location, a cholera epidemic has broken out in Rome and the entire company might have to be vaccinated.

Right now he's pacing his suite at the Hilton, where he and Cybill are living. The chauffeur who will drive him to the set is late, as usual. He was staying at the Grand, where Elizabeth Taylor stays, but you couldn't order ice cream sodas and tunafish sandwiches there. Now both he and Cybill have caught colds from the Hilton air conditioning. She has just returned on an all-night flight from New York, where she appeared on another *Model of the Year* TV show. The room is a clutter of phonograph records, scripts people are begging Peter to direct, the Sunday New York papers Cybill brought back with her, a giant six-foot rubber penguin she gave him for his birthday because he reminds her of a penguin, three days of room-service spaghetti and such weird items as a drawer filled with sugarless gum. "I've got the best people on my crew and the same cutter who edited my other films and the man who designed the costumes for *The Go-Between* and the set designer from *Death in Venice* but it's still hard. Every-

thing is so expensive and they don't want us here and they
say no to everything out of habit. You can't even make a
phone call. That's why we moved to the Hilton, because
it has a swimming pool and dial phones. Now I'm going
to be late on the set again."

He phones somebody. "What do you mean, the driver
is downstairs? I was downstairs in the lobby and he wasn't
there. The guy is an idiot. What am I supposed to do, go
looking for the driver? He should be looking for me!" We
start out again. Cybill calls sleepily from the bedroom,
"I've got a bee in my bed." Peter laughs. "Cybill's got a
bee in her bed. Nothing fazes Cybill."

Nothing fazes him either on the set. Dark falls on the
Roman Colosseum, which is closed to even the tourists
now, because it is falling apart. A few feet from the spot
where the Christians were served for Sunday brunch to
the lions while Nero fiddled, Peter is setting up his cameras for night shooting. "This is the first time they've ever
let anybody inside this place to make a movie. You can't
believe the red tape. We only convinced them because
we said three or four people at the most would be tramp-
ing through the ruins." There must be 200 people at the
most and the Italian police are flapping about like bats.
Peter is nonplussed in his portable trailer. "I was going to
do a western with John Wayne, Henry Fonda and Jimmy
Stewart that Larry McMurtry and I developed. That
didn't work out because Wayne didn't want to do it. Then
Gavin Lambert did a script of Galsworthy's *Apple Tree*
that needed some more work. Then I did an original story
about an Italian who came to New York and got taken by
a girl from Texas—Cybill, naturally. None of these things
panned out. I was hung up on what to do next and I
wanted to do something this year with Cybill, so by accident I picked up *Daisy Miller* again and I saw her in it.
You'd think Henry James wrote it for her. I just decided
to do it."

Daisy Miller was written when Henry James was thirty-
four, the same age Peter is now. Larry *(The Last Picture
Show)* McMurtry's ten-year-old son, James, is playing Cy-

bill's little brother in the film. He was named for Henry
James. The coincidences keep cropping up like toadstools
around here. Peter is also using two other actresses from
The Last Picture Show, Eileen Brennan and Cloris Leach-
man, giving credence to the charge that he uses a kind
of repertory company in his films, like his hero John Ford
used to do. "It's true. Jean Renoir once said the important
thing in making a movie is gathering around a bunch of
friends as though you were preparing a prank. The more
friends, the easier it is to pull off the prank. That's why I
used Tatum O'Neal in *Paper Moon,* because I didn't want
to look for anyone else. I hate casting. My next film will
be an original story of mine built around twenty-four Cole
Porter songs and I'm using Ryan again, and Madeline
Kahn from *What's Up, Doc?* Cybill will be the star. I
always feel there are not enough musical numbers in
musicals. This one will have one song about every two
minutes. I'm shooting every foot of it in a Hollywood back
lot. I don't want any of it to look real. I was going to sing
and dance and star in it with Cybill, but Christ, the critics
would kill me, so I'm using Elliot Gould." Peter used to be
a critic himself in his struggling days. Now some of the
other critics he used to know murder his pictures, like
tomcats devouring their young. They accuse him of making homages to other directors. It makes him hopping
mad. "I'm a classicist. I like well-made films with begin-
nings, middles and ends, in which acting and writing are
important instead of camera angles. In that respect, I
prefer the traditional directors to the new ones. I like
Hawks, Welles, Ford, Hitchcock. But I'm afraid to say who
I like anymore because some stupid critic will write that
I copied them. I don't make homages or tributes to other
directors. I just make movies. It's my own damn fault
because I stupidly said on *The Last Picture Show* I was
inspired by *The Magnificent Ambersons* and they twisted
the words 'inspired by' to mean 'stolen from.' One Mid-
west critic wrote about *What's Up, Doc?* that it was stolen
from *Bringing Up Father!* I mean, they write the most
incredible nonsense! Pauline Kael said *The Last Picture*

Show was like *King's Row!* My God, what an insult! It
makes me wonder if these people even see the films they
write about."

He got into movies by writing about them. "I went to
see Roger Corman and he said, 'You're a writer, want to
write something?' and I said, 'Sure, what do you want me
to write?' And he said, 'I'm looking for a war picture—
something like *Bridge on the River Kwai* and *Lawrence
of Arabia* combined—only cheap.' " The result was a Peter Fonda motorcycle flick called *The Wild Angels.* He's
been in the business ever since and he still never touches
a script that says "dolly–zoom–pan–cut to close-up," all
that junk. I never plan out any scene until it comes up and
I never use a lot of cameras because I don't know where
to put them. I'm always in a severe fit of depression until
I see the movie on the screen. I work very fast, editing in
a room at the Hilton until the movie is finished. Until
then, I think it's awful. Somehow it all comes together in
the end. I say I won't read critics anymore, but my curiosity prevents it. I know them all personally and I know
how they think and I don't care what they think. I just
care about making the films I like and I hope the public
likes them, too. So far I've been lucky, but I know my turn
is coming. They build you up so they can tear you down.
I'm not immodest, I'm not humble, and the more success
I have the more the critics will resent me. The image they
give me is one of arrogance. They say I'm cocky and
audacious. But I just have enthusiasm for what I do and
that is not considered cool. They're just waiting for me to
have a flop. In a sense, that will be a relief—to have my
first disaster—because it'll make so many people happy.
But twenty years from now, I'd like to look back on a
career and see not just a bunch of pictures, but a bunch
of pictures that add up to something."

An Italian crone enters the trailer with roses for Cybill.
"Cybill started out as a whim, an instinct, a little voice in
my ear that I listened to. I had an itch and I scratched it.
I liked her face." He saw it on the cover of *Glamour* and
signed her with no acting experience for the petulant,

rich-girl jailbait called Jacy in *The Last Picture Show.* Whether she can play a turn-of-the-century heroine who dies of the plague remains to be seen. "She's very malleable," he says. "You can bend her in any direction." Hmm. "She does what she's told."

It's a gamble, but Peter likes risks. Giant scaffolds of light rise on the set, bathing the ruins in Hollywood moonlight. Peter surveys his location. "The critics will probably call this one my homage to George Cukor," he jokes.

Then he turns serious again. "I was walking around the Colosseum tonight, and I looked around and saw all of these technicians and actors and I said to myself, all of these people are here tonight in the Roman Colosseum because I wanted them here. It's a terrible responsibility and I felt, well kid, this has really got to be good because if it isn't, all these people are going to be disappointed. I'm very good at faking self-confidence. It's like a war and I'm the general and the whole army is waiting for me to tell them whether to retreat or attack. I'm a good bluffer. I think it's better to make a bad decision than none at all. I've made some wrong ones, but I've been able to pull them off so far." The cameras are ready for Cybill, the police are holding back the crowds, the cables are keeping the Roman rocks from falling on top of the actors' skulls and the lights are flooding the scene with a lemony glow. It is 1878 in ancient Rome. Peter takes his toothpick out of his mouth and bums another cigarette. "Lubitsch once said, I've been to Paris France and I've been to Paris Paramount. I prefer Paris Paramount."

Onward and upward with the arts!

Cybill Shepherd, looking more like a Memphis baton-twirler than an 1878 Henry James heroine, is nevertheless playing the title role of *Daisy Miller* in the crumbling ruins of Rome. She isn't the least bit terrified. Her boyfriend, Peter Bogdanovich, is directing and even though she has only appeared in two other movies (*The Last Picture Show* and *The Heartbreak Kid*), the fact that he is guiding her through every scene has given her enough courage to look right at me with periwinkle-blue eyes and say, "Henry James had me in mind when he wrote it."

There are similarities. Daisy was the epitome of irresistible American freshness and spirited innocence in an artificial world of European restraint. She flouted convention and died of malaria when she visited the Roman Colosseum at the time of a plague against everyone else's advice. It's a tragic love story with sumptuous sets and lavish costumes, and about as far removed from Cybill's real-life Pepsi Generation personality as the imagination can conceive. But Cybill is having a ball. "I always felt a desire not to fulfill what people expected of me, or expected me to be. Daisy was unpredictable, too—a victim of her own innocent gaiety in a crumbling era of decadence."

Right now the "victim" is eating a tunafish sandwich in her suite at the Hilton and listening to her new record album, *Cybill Does It—to Cole Porter!* It was produced by Peter Bogdanovich, who masterminds her far-from-liberated persona as well as her soaring movie career, and it is equipped with Cole Porter's sexy lyrics to his famous songs *(The most refined ladybugs do it when a gentleman calls/Moths in your rugs do it, what's the use of mothballs?)*. Peter sings on the album too, and his unreserved excitement seems to embarrass Cybill. She takes her sandwich and heads for the bedroom. "I called Frank Yablans," says Peter, hardly noticing she has gone, "and said I'd like to do an album. He said, 'You sing?' I said, 'No, of course not—it's for Cybill.' He said, 'She sing?' The whole thing was paid for by Paramount without any of them ever hearing one song. That's what happens when you have a couple of hit pictures."

The hardest thing about interviewing Cybill is getting her alone. Peter does most of her talking for her and even when he's out of the room the things she says often sound like Peter. The Hollywood wags are calling him a Svengali to whom she plays a willing, sexy Trilby. One gossip even refers to them as Edgar Bergen and Charlie McCarthy. It's only half true. Cybill is bright, loquacious and fun, but it is very obvious that she adores Peter and considers what he has to say much more important than anything on her mind. So she just lets him do all the talking.

It's not that she's dumb. It's just that she's been through all these incredible changes. First, there was the all-American high-school-girl period—city champion basketball team in Memphis, president of her sorority, most attractive in the senior class, winner of the Miss Teenage Memphis Pageant. Elvis Presley was her idol. Then there was the all-American model period, which is still not over —winner of the 1969 Model of the Year award, $500 a day as a magazine cover girl, TV commercials for everything from Coca-Cola to shampoo. (She still receives the highest fee ever paid for a thirty-second commercial for Cover Girl makeup.) Although she had never acted in films before, Peter wanted her for *The Last Picture Show*. Peter says: "She was the only one of the actresses I saw who didn't want the part. She came in and sat on the floor. I said, 'What do you like to do?' She said, 'Oh, I dunno, I read a lot.' I said, 'What have you read lately?' She said, 'Dostoevski.' I thought, 'Hmm.' So I said, 'Well, which one of his have you read?' Long pause. She played with a flower and sighed and finally said, 'I can't remember the title right now.' And I thought, 'That's the character.'" It started with a look. The look turned into love.

After *The Last Picture Show*, Cybill discovered literature and politics, and Svengali influence or no Svengali influence, under the tutelage of Bogdanovich she started giving out interviews about the Greek crisis, Camus, Sartre, sexual politics in advertising and *The Magic Mountain*. It began to sound like an Arthur Miller–Marilyn Monroe syndrome. The real Cybill Shepherd is more than that. She has her own identity, she is totally unimpressed by parties and glamour and publicity. ("I was hysterical when I read in Suzy's column that we were causing more of a sensation in Rome than the Burtons or Sophia and Carlo Ponti—we haven't been out of our suite at the Hilton once. At home in Los Angeles we never go anywhere, either. We lie around on the floor and watch old movies.")

She is also aware that a lot of people are expecting a lot in *Daisy Miller* and if she's lousy in it, they'll blame it all on Peter. "I'm very lucky. I know I wouldn't be in the movies if it hadn't been for him. Peter has always been there to look after me and that is a reality. But I look at girls like Katherine Ross, who are beautiful and talented, and I see how you can get sidetracked. I didn't become an actress because I needed the money. I had the Cover Girl commercials. The copy was bad but it was better than bad movies. Nobody reviews bad commercials. But I had to do something to keep my sanity. I was bored to death modeling and I never want to do it again. I've never taken acting lessons because I think choosing an acting coach is like choosing the right psychiatrist. The one who is right for one person can totally destroy another person. So I trust Peter totally."

Peter leaves the room so nobody will get the impression that he's Svengali, and she's on her own. "I guess people expect me to be dumb. But I really did read all those books. I went to school, taught myself, did all of it out of curiosity. I have a lot of energy and I have to channel it somewhere. I've always read a lot. I read *Gone With the Wind* in the sixth grade. I was a member of the Weekly Reader Book Club. It would be very sad if people thought I did all of this just to prove something." (Right now she's reading Isak Dinesen.) "All these articles that say I'm ambitious kill me because everyone who knows me knows I just walked into everything in my life by accident. The Cole Porter album was Peter's idea. I sang in a talent show at East High School in Memphis but I was so professional they wouldn't give me the prize. Then after *The Last Picture Show* I took singing lessons and sang opera with Eileen Brennan's vocal teacher. After you've sung opera, you can certainly sing Cole Porter."

She is very blasé about acting and still suffers from the nude scene in *The Last Picture Show*. She had done one previous screen test for Roger Vadim and it was such a painful experience she vowed she would never appear nude anywhere. "The night before I was to fly to California to begin rehearsals I was still trying to call Peter to tell him I couldn't do the movie if I had to do the nude scene. My ambition was to save enough money to go to the University of Florence and study art. But I couldn't reach him, so I went out to Hollywood anyway and he convinced me it would be done in good taste. Even the nude scene in *The Heartbreak Kid* was done by a stand-in. I just don't like nudity because it dissolves the mystery about people and I want to preserve as much mystery as possible.

"Then after all the worrying and almost not doing the movie, *Playboy* printed a grainy, blurred, pirated nude shot of me and the studio has no record of giving it to them. It wasn't even a photo—it's an enlargement of a frame from the screen that was cut out of the movie. They had been after me for years to pose as one of the sex stars of the Seventies. I kept saying no. They even called my mother and offered her $10,000 if I'd pose nude. Now this stolen photo appears. I'm going to sue Hugh Hefner personally, and also Playboy Enterprises and Arthur Knight, who reprinted it in a book called *Sex and the Cinema.*"

I tell her the people who saw the original nude will be minuscule compared to those who will read about the lawsuit. "You think so? I'll let Peter decide."

Peter reenters and says he doesn't care what the lawsuit costs, it will keep other innocent girls from being victimized in the same way. The discussion is ended. She is myopic and nearsighted. I ask if she has any other physical defects. Peter says, "That's a line from *The Trial.* Romy Schneider says it to Tony Perkins." I say that's nice but it doesn't answer the question. Cybill says, "I have a scar on my lip. I ran into a barbed-wire fence and had over two hundred stitches in plastic surgery when I was six. Also, my feet are too small for my body." She's 5 feet 8½ inches tall, big bones, 130 pounds (her father was a football player) and except for her face doesn't look like a model on close inspection. Peter laughs: "If you had feet the same size as your body, I wouldn't be around. I hate big feet."

Any girl who takes that kind of lip from her boyfriend is obviously not into Women's Lib. The question makes her squirm. She looks at Peter for help. "Well, I've read the three books on the subject, but the best is *A Room of One's Own* by Virginia Woolf," she says proudly. Sometimes it's better when he does the talking.

Later that night, at the Roman Colosseum, Cybill sits in her portable trailer while the crew tries to make a 2,000-year-old ruin look older. She is eating a banana in a hoop skirt, drinking black coffee, and trying not to cry over a box of hair Audrey Hepburn's hairdresser has just clipped from her shining cover-girl head. "I guess I'm a star now. I could have told her no, but I didn't have the nerve. I just don't like to upset people. I don't even give orders to my cook. I can't cook anything but an egg, but we have a housekeeper who worked for John Garfield and you can't argue with anyone who cooked for John Garfield." Women are flying at her with brushes, mirrors and curling irons and she has a pain in her stomach from the corset and the banana. "They did autopsies on Victorian women and discovered their hearts were pushed up into their chest cavities from these corsets. I used to think 1878 was very romantic, but now after this movie I think it was just uncomfortable."

She never goes home to Memphis anymore. "They expect me to be a freak there. They ask dumb questions like 'What is Ryan O'Neal really like?' Things like that. Or they expect me to be jaded or something. It's a big bore. None of them have ever met President Nixon or *anything*. I went to a party for him in San Clemente. I figured I helped pay for it, I might as well see what it was like. Everyone dressed in red, white and blue dresses. He took my hand and said, 'I've seen your name on many productions.' Geez, I only made two movies before now. Then he told Peter, 'Why don't you put her in a movie someday?' He was totally out of it. But you can't tell them that in Memphis. They'd think I was a Communist spy or something."

A crone is running a hot curling iron through her hair.

Cybill winces. "A hairdresser once burned a blister on my ear with one of those things. What else do you want to know? You wanna know my beauty secrets? They all ask for my beauty secrets. My only beauty secret is cucumbers on my face. That's right, cucumbers. Did you know they feed cucumbers to pigs in Yugoslavia? Or did I already tell you that? I read that somewhere. They feed cucumbers to pigs in Yugoslavia. Say, what are you gonna write about me? Just say I'm very dull and all-American and pure vanilla. My grandmother always says, 'Cybill, stay as sweet as you are.' Don't print that. Oh, go ahead and print it. I'll just tell my grandmother I didn't say it. Oh, God. They're ready for me on the set."

She emerges looking like a marshmallow sundae. Peter props her against a rock where she gets malaria. "Now darling, I know this is going to be very difficult for you, but you have to stand up." "What do I say?" asks Cybill. "This is your Mamie Van Doren shot—you don't say anything." The camera rolls. Peter yells: "Cybill, take the chewing gum out of your mouth!" They start again, and she goes home to bed at 5 A.M. Oh, well. It beats jerking sodas back home in Memphis.

37

Ann-Margret

ANN-MARGRET COLLAPSED next to a four-foot guitar made of carnations from Elvis Presley and ate a cheeseburger, a hot fudge sundae with whipped cream and pecans and a bowl of oatmeal with a diamond ring on her finger so heavy she could hardly lift the spoon. "Never mind a comeback," said Mama Cass Elliott, "you can just walk out onstage and let Peggy Fleming skate on your ring." But Ann-Margret did make a comeback. She can afford the hot fudge sundae, since she's down to 110 pounds ("I haven't weighed that since I was a cheerleader at New Trier High School in Winnetka, Illinois!"), and nobody complains. After what she's been through, she's lucky to get her mouth open.

Ten weeks earlier, she fell twenty-two feet from a stage in Lake Tahoe and suffered five facial bone fractures, a fractured left arm, a brain concussion and a broken jaw. The left side of her face was totally smashed. For a while, the doctors didn't know if she would live, and even if she pulled through, they warned, she would certainly never sing again. They didn't know Ann-Margret. Not only did she survive, but she went back to the Las Vegas Hilton with "Ann-Margret '73," an act so dazzling it turned Vegas into an MGM Technicolor musical.

After some insults from the comedy team ("She's got legs up to here, and wears a D-cup—that's not normal, a D-cup!"), on she came. The left side of her face has been miraculously restored except for one dent that will require more plastic surgery and some skin graft from her earlobe, but nobody noticed. She sang, she danced, she rode a motorcycle, and she was glad to be alive. The stage turned into a midnight masked Venetian, with a huge lighted clock replacing the near-lethal scaffold from which she made her near-fatal entrance ten weeks ago. She swept down a flight of Fred Astaire stairs in a floor-length white ermine and read her favorite telegram from "Mr. Warmth" himself, Don Rickles: "SINCE WHEN DO YOU DO A HIGH-WIRE ACT? HAVE BOOKED YOU INTO CIR-CUS-CIRCUS WITH FLYING WALLENDAS. NEXT TIME USE A NET, DUMMY!" Then she sang everything from Gershwin and Rodgers and Hart to "Saturday Night in Harlem" in fabulous costumes on sets that flew in and out from the wings like a Broadway show. There were dancers and an orchestra that could replace the New York Philharmonic next Tuesday, and when things slowed down to a roar she did a wild takeoff on "Kitten with a Whip" with a stage full of roaring Yamahas and whirling Hell's Angels and balloons, and confetti fell out of the ceiling. Sometimes it seemed as though she never took a breath, and when the show packs it in in Vegas, it hits Miami and then television and then a nationwide tour of the summer stock tents and . . . oh well, some people say she fell twenty-two feet and nearly killed herself just to get a rest.

"That's not true," she sighed in her suite after the show. "I read all kinds of things. The truth is there were four

wires like they used in *Peter Pan* attached to a scaffold for
my entrance. They were tested to support 1,700 pounds
each. Not even my thumpers weigh that much. What
happened was the wires weren't evenly rigged and the
platform tilted. The hotel told *Newsweek* I was weak from
dieting and fainted before I even fell. That's not true. I
don't remember a thing. I don't remember hitting the
floor, but I'm not a fainter. Naturally they would say that
because of the insurance company. I had rehearsed from
ten A.M. to six P.M. every day with time out only for lunch,
but I was in terrific physical shape. What they say against
me doesn't matter, but I don't like to see them blame
Roger."

Roger Smith, ex-teenage heartthrob from the old 77
Sunset Strip TV show and Ann-Margret's husband for the
past five years, gets blamed for a lot of things. They accused him of exploiting his wife, using her career to bol-
ster his own fading success as an actor, overworking her
to the point of exhaustion and all sorts of things. Now
there's a new criticism aimed at Roger. The day after her
opening, one of the Hollywood gossip columnists wrote
that she was a sick girl who should be in the hospital,
forced instead to return to work prematurely by a husband who was hungry for money. "Why don't they ask
me?" said the star herself, angrily. "It's not true. Roger
didn't want me to work again until February. This was my
idea. I don't cook or sew or have babies. I sing and dance.
Everybody said my career was over. Well, lying in that
hospital for ten weeks was no picnic. I was under such
heavy medication I didn't think about anything for a
while. I was in a coma for four days, then they rebuilt the
entire left side of my face in surgery. All my bones were
packed with white shoestring and then wired from inside.
The wires even went through my gums, so I couldn't even
open my teeth to drink through a straw. I didn't open my
mouth for seven weeks. I hope nobody ever has to go
through that nightmare. But lying there flat on my back
in indescribable pain, all I can tell you is that I couldn't
wait to get back on a stage. Roger had nothing to do with
it."

Between phone calls and visits from room service to feed the starving star who is making up for lost time, Roger Smith chimed in cheerfully: "Yeah, they've made me the villain. But they forget she's a very strong Swede. She once fell against a bed and went out like a light and it took twenty-two stitches in her head to get her on her feet and she went right back onstage and did her act. So she got the reputation for being a puppet and I get the reputation for pulling the strings. Listen. She could quit working tomorrow and we'd have enough money to live on for the rest of our lives. After *Carnal Knowledge* she decided she wanted to retire. She was sick of working, wanted to leave Los Angeles. I used to also have a reputation for being cheap, but I was really being frugal. We saved our money and we invested it in the stock market, real estate, other solid things. We could retire. But when the time comes, she gets interested in another act or a new film or something that delays it. The fact is, the girl just loves to work.

"The whole bit about working too hard started here in Vegas. We originally came to do a four-week engagement. The hotel didn't have an act to follow her, so they asked if she'd stay over and extend the run. We stayed on two more weeks, then Perry Como had an accident and they asked us to stay on even longer to replace him. She set a record for the hotel with ten solid weeks. So the reputation started. 'Why work that hard?' they said. It was a fluke. Listen, this girl is healthy as a bull. She's also a Taurus, so you can't get her to do anything she doesn't want to do. So they blame it on me. We don't have a sordid marriage, so they have to spice up their stories somehow. *Look* magazine said I had pornographic pictures in my bedroom. They just made it all up. She's no puppet."

Before Roger Smith came along, Ann-Margret was a joke in the movie industry. All those trashy sex-kitten movies had washed her up in the business. Eight years ago, when she met Roger, she was doing a B-picture in Europe that was never released. Since he took over her career, she has established a major reputation as one of the screen's finest dramatic actresses. For her work in

Mike Nichols' *Carnal Knowledge,* she was nominated for
an Academy Award in 1971, and her Vegas contract alone
will net her a cool million dollars in 1972. She has done two
other films, *The Train Robbers* with John Wayne and *The
Outside Man* with Jean-Louis Trintignant, and will next
star in a Timex television special of Arthur Miller's famous
play *After the Fall.* She's considering George C. Scott for
her leading man. Gossip aside, they must be doing something right.

"I've always depended on men," she says, licking the
hot fudge from her spoon like a dreamy kid. "I get my
stubbornness and determination and will to live from my
father. He was always the best man in my life. Now in
Roger I've found a man who is all the things I need rolled
into one—a father, a friend, a lover, a manager, a businessman. It's perfect for me. I couldn't exist without a strong
man." Her own father is now seriously ill and a lot of her
nerves and emotional instability come from worrying
about him. "I still don't have any self-confidence. Look at
all those silly films I did in Hollywood. They didn't exactly
inspire me to have faith in my talent. And all because I
had no man to shape my career. I had managers who had
signed me up for twenty-six pictures with no script approval when I met Roger. He taught me I didn't have to
do that. I was always too pretty to play meaty roles, too
sexy to play good girls or housewives, and I always ended
up as hard, tough-talking ex-topless dancers or vamps.
Carnal Knowledge was Roger's idea. I was impossible to
live with. I'd come home, have dinner, for the first time
in my life take sleeping pills, and go to bed. Roger was
fantastic. I let myself go, gained weight, never took off my
bathrobe and cried myself sick, and he put up with it. I
got all my strength from Mike Nichols and Roger. Otherwise, I could never have done it. I couldn't do one dramatic film after another or I'd be in an asylum somewhere. Now the thought of doing *After the Fall* in the
Marilyn Monroe part fills me with dread. When I saw the
play I started shaking all over and now thinking about
playing it frightens me. But if Roger thinks I can do it, I'll
do it. I let him decide."

Roger's three children live with them in the summer, but she's not your ordinary mother. She doesn't cook ("I don't have to, Roger is a gourmet cook, he makes fantastic chili from scratch") and her only current regret is that she's grounded for a year and can't ride her custom-built motorcycle. But she's making up for it by consuming a diet of Big Macs, Twinkies, Ding-Dongs and Ho-Hos. "I couldn't open my mouth but fourteen millimeters at a time for ten weeks. They finally rigged up a James Bond–type liquefier that could grind up anything and I could drink it through a straw. I had liquid pizza with anchovies, liquid fried chicken, liquid hot dogs. I still can't look a milk shake in the face. I don't recommend it as a way to diet. Now I'm grateful to even lick my lips," she says, licking her lips. "Let it spread. I'm lucky to be alive!"

Ann-Margret is one dish who has earned her day in the sun at McDonald's. If you ask me, she's just plain lucky, period.

38

Jack Lemmon

JACK LEMMON SLID into the leather booth in the Sherry-Netherlands bar, puffing on an imported Jamaican Macanudo, and ordered three bloody marys and some eggs. The lines under his eyes, the way his shoulders hunched slightly with fatigue inside his cranberry cashmere sweater, the sigh in his early-morning Jack Lemmon voice—it was all self-explanatory. He had been up late the night before showing his shattering movie *Save the Tiger* to the students up at Yale and they had hung around for four hours after the show was over asking him questions, understandably moved and charged by both the film and Jack Lemmon's honest, heartbreaking performance. It had been a long night, but the twinkle in his eyes said it had been worth the lack of sleep.

"This is the first time I have hit the road to publicize a film to this extent," he said, sipping and flicking cigar ashes. "But this is the first time I have ever truly loved any film of mine with this kind of passion. Once in a goddam blue moon you reach somebody or touch somebody and then your whole career seems worth it. I'm hitting the colleges, and let me tell you, these kids are bright, open, sophisticated. If you aren't honest, brother, look out. They'll nail you. Their questions are more offbeat than the ones you get from pros, and there are some idiotic questions, but mostly they are just plain astounding. They hit you directly between the eyes. We ran the film in pouring rain at Yale and then I went over to one of the college halls and rapped with the kids. Being a Harvard man, I didn't dare even ask the name of the hall. But the response to this film and the pride I feel in it have been like a big shot of adrenaline."

Save the Tiger is one of the most hotly discussed films of the year. It is one of the best films ever to come out of the Hollywood studios and it is unquestionably the summit of Jack Lemmon's acting career. Stripped to its bones, it tells the basic story of a dress manufacturer who must commit a felony to keep his business from going under at a crucial moment of truth in his life when the world is falling apart all around him. Colliding with his own moral values, Harry Stoner (the character Jack plays) is trapped midstream between the daydreams of his past—when baseball and music you could still identify and a lot of other nice things were still part of a world where there was still a place for heroes—and the ugly material realities of contemporary society, where the pressures of success make it too financially and emotionally expensive to survive with pride and dignity. The movie is about a lot of other things too, but even the audiences who cringe at its indictment of the way we live now come out of the picture raving about Jack Lemmon. *Save the Tiger* establishes him as one of the screen's most powerful actors, and even Jack Lemmon can't quite adjust to the idea.

"Listen," he says, "success means nothing to me. It's a

painful thing to say. I do not want fame. I love to hear
people say, 'That Jack Lemmon is a helluva actor.' I think
I'm good. I won an Oscar for *Mister Roberts*. I've been
nominated several times since. The respect I've got from
fellow actors and the other people in allied crafts is tre-
mendously satisfying. But fame for fame's sake means
nothing. I don't think I've been consumed with egotism.
I'm honest about my work. I don't play games. But I really
wanted to make a film that said something. I'm not knocking myself out over this picture just to goose up the box
office. It's become a part of my life I'm fighting for. The
alcoholic I played in *Days of Wine and Roses* was a dramatic role, but what could you do but feel sorry for him?
Harry Stoner is the whole middle-stream American proto-
type. He fought in World War Two and nobody even
remembers it. If we look at our society, there is nothing
left a young man coming out of that war can still believe
in. We accept Watergate. We accept Vietnam. We accept
cheating on our income tax and dancing around the law.
We accept junkies knifing us in the streets. We accept the
injustices in our courts. There are no rules, just referees.
We used to salute the flag, now they're making jockstraps
out of it.

"We live in smog and filth and pollution and we accept
it because we're worried about our own personal problems. We don't react until there's a disaster. Well, I hope
this film will make people more aware of what's happening. It's more than just a story of one man at the end of
his rope. It's a story about the materialistic society that has
made people the way they are. That's why college kids dig
it so enormously. It criticizes the society that turns decent
men into criminals. I'd better shut up or I'll be thrown out
of the country as a pinko hoo-hoo wah-wah or something."

Jack has already had trouble. Just getting *Save the Tiger*
made in the first place is a saga. "It made the rounds of
every studio in Hollywood. It was called a blasphemy
against America, anti-Semitic because of the Jewish types
it shows working in the garment center, and Communist
propaganda. One studio executive said nobody under

thirty-five would ever go see it. Another said it could not be made in English. He wanted to make it in Paris with Yves Montand and Truffaut and have the whole thing translated into French. But Steve Shagan, who wrote it and produced it, didn't want it in French. It's a movie about America, man. I tell you the crap you hear in Hollywood makes you wonder how the hell we ever make a decent film. By the time you finish, eighty-five thousand people get their hands on it. This movie is a miracle."

It finally got made because Jack worked for no salary, agreeing to a deferred percentage if the film makes a profit, and because of the enthusiasm of Frank Yablans and Robert Evans, two of the creative executive forces that have made Paramount the current success it is among the generally failing film studios. "I may not make a dime," says Lemmon, "but I've done something I care about. For years I made comedies that were just fluff. After a while, I was at the top of the popularity polls and riding, a crest. Reviews and public reaction were all beyond belief for *Irma La Douce, Some Like It Hot, The Apartment*—but people started saying 'Here comes Lemmon again' and my career lacked excitement. I was my own enemy. I didn't think I had the excitement to play serious roles. Success is always somebody else's opinion and not your own. I'm in an enviable position now. I've logged enough credits, and I've made enough money that I can afford to wait for the good things to happen. I don't have to do anything just for the sake of working. That, to me, is success.

"When I was walking along the East River wishing I had enough money to buy a new suit at the age of eighteen, I wanted to take Broadway by storm and become the biggest composer since George Gershwin. When I was in my thirties, I was still a self-centered baby. Now I just want to be the best actor I can be. There's a lot of difference. I've envied other people at times, but basically I'm happy with my life. I've had parts any actor would give his left ventricle for. And I've been in some real garbage, too. But mostly I played it safe, like a lot of actors do. And

I lost the capacity for excitement. That's the real tragedy. That's why I love Billy Wilder. He makes classics and he makes duds but his capacity for excitement is unequaled. I've never spent sixty seconds with him that I didn't find exciting."

Last year, Jack Lemmon turned out a movie for Billy Wilder called *Avanti!* that excited practically nobody. "It wasn't very good. It was my first nude scene. The first review I read said I looked like a dried prune. The second one said I looked like a dried peach. After that, I stopped reading. I thought it was handled with good taste, but I had no idea I was so ugly with my clothes off. Who the hell goes around looking at his own behind in the mirror? I got a shock when I saw the rushes." Most scripts with sex and nudity he never finishes reading. "I think all this going at it on the screen is boring and mechanical. I saw *Deep Throat* and thought it was the biggest piece of garbage ever made."

There's a scene in *Save the Tiger* where Jack and his partner (warmly and intelligently played by Jack Gilford) meet an underworld figure who promises to burn down their warehouse in order to collect the insurance. The meeting takes place in a seedy pornographic movie house. John Avildsen, the energetic and very talented director whose film *Joe* was such a cause célèbre a few seasons ago, insisted on realism, so the cast was dragged into a dirty movie palace and an actual grindhouse smoker was unrolled on the screen during the scene. "They turned the sound off, but left the picture on the screen," Jack blushes, "and the crook keeps saying to me, 'Look at the screen, Harry,' and I want to tell you, I couldn't remember what the hell I was supposed to be saying. There were these two girls making love to each other on the screen with a peach. They rubbed that peach on each other and went to town and it took us two days to get the scene. We kept breaking up. I don't think I'd be any good making porno flicks."

Jack Lemmon is forty-eight years old. Like the character in *Save the Tiger,* he says everything has changed

around him since he started his career. "I look back at my
old movies making the rounds for the five-hundredth
time on TV and I'm beginning to look like my own son on
the screen. I don't think everything was better in the old
days. I like the young directors coming out of college
because they don't follow patterns or serve institutions.
Today's kids think of film as an art form, and the young
administrators like Frank Yablans believe in the importance of a project, not the component parts. In the old
days, my generation thought of movies as escapist entertainment where stars would sell tickets even if the film
was lousy. That's no longer true. I can't make *Avanti!* a
success if it's no good. This is healthy. I no longer make a
million dollars a picture. *The Great Race* made
$25,000,000 and still hasn't broken even after they got
through paying Natalie Wood and Tony Curtis and me.
It's asinine to assume actors are that important. *Save the
Tiger* cost only $1,100,000 and it's all right there on the
screen. Some stars still hold out for the big money, but
they don't work much. I did *Save the Tiger* for nothing
and I'm prouder of it than all those movies I made millions
on all rolled into one. That's how the business is changing
and I'm happy to change. Billy Wilder says 'You are as
good as the best thing you've ever done' and if I never
make another movie that's good enough for me."

39

Jack Nicholson

I**T'S LIKE THIS:** Jack Nicholson is pacing nervously about his St. Regis Hotel suite eating a chicken sandwich, passing the time until he can go over to Sardi's and pick up the award the New York film critics have given him for *Easy Rider*. He moves softly. He has surprisingly tiny features, soft hands and thinning hair, and looks like a slightly seedy Eagle Scout who is always being stalked by a battalion of slightly aggressive field mice. He's eating the chicken sandwich because he's not sure if there will be any food at Sardi's and the other people in the room—a press agent, an agent from Creative Management Associates (CMA) and Nicholson's girlfriend Mimi— aren't sure either. He's nervous because, like most new heroes, he's a horse in midstream.

It's like this: Jack Nicholson, thirty-three, from Neptune, New Jersey, wanted to be a movie star. He had grown up watching Preston Foster movies and he knew how it was done, so he went to Hollywood, got a job in the MGM cartoon department, and eventually he became a movie star. Trouble is, nobody ever noticed him until *Easy Rider*. The movies he's been in have all been low-budget go-out-and-grab-a-movie B-flicks. Motorcycle flicks. Beach-blanket-bikini flicks. Horror flicks. The kind of trash only a mother or a *cahier* critic could sit through and love. Yet out of the anti-Establishment *Easy Rider* he has become a hero for two cults. The anti-Establishment B-flick underground digs him because he's the proof that something good can come out of all that American-International garbage. And the over-thirty crowd digs him too. When they saw *Easy Rider* they all said, "Oh wow, aren't Fonda and Hopper spaced out!" but Nicholson was the one they identified with. There was something so touching about his alcoholic southern aristocrat, searching for a philosophical grass-roots identity with the new hip and the new cool in his faded Fifties Ole Miss football jersey, that made them want to bathe in their own squareness. There's a nice-guy squareness about Jack Nicholson too, but he's trying to please both factions at the same time and the effort is taking its toll on his nerves.

Now he is shaking the ice cubes in his glass of Coca-Cola so loudly they are drowning out his voice on my tape recorder. "I knew *Easy Rider* was gonna be, uh, a big moneymaker right from the beginning, you know what I mean? I liked myself in it. If I get an Oscar, I won't feel like I've stolen anything. I got to edit my own part, so I picked the best shots and everything. I was the most sensible character in the whole movie. If you read it he was a real hick, saying things like 'Marijuana! Mercy!' . . . I still don't know . . . everybody was . . . the writing was confused . . . Dennis says the only thing Terry Southern wrote was the title. They just used Terry's name so people wouldn't think it was just another Peter Fonda motorcycle flick. I don't think they would've gotten the money just for a picture directed by Dennis Hopper . . . I mean,

if you know Dennis, you don't exactly just turn over some
money to him and say 'No problem,' you know what I
mean?" (Big laugh from Mimi.) "Hopper wrote most of
my part and I just added inflections here and there. I did
more writing on Peter's character. Yeah, there were
drugs around . . . you mean grass? Yeah. See, they came
in while I was writing and coproducing *Head* with the
Monkees and Annette Funicello and Victor Mature as the
Jolly Green Giant . . . did you ever see that?"

"No, I was out of town for the weekend. . . ."

"*Nobody* ever saw that, man, but I saw it 158 million
times. I *loved* it. Filmically, it's the best rock-and-roll
movie ever made. I mean, it's anti–rock-and-roll. Uh
. . . has no form. Unique in structure, which is very hard
to do in movies."

"Yeah, I can see that. . . ."

"I had also written *The Trip* for Roger Corman, which
Peter and Dennis were in, and which I had written a part
for myself to play and didn't get to because Bruce Dern
—Dernsie—played it. Dernsie is Roger Corman's favorite
actor. He was in Roger's biggest success, *Wild Angels,*
with Peter. Anyway, he was in *Will Penny* at the time and
didn't know if he'd be free, but Roger said, 'Look, if Dernsie can play it, man, I owe him,' so I wasn't in it, but I met
them all then and when they got ready to do their own
flick they came around again and you know how people
are always giving each other advice in California." (Big
shriek from Mimi.) "Well, uh, they came in with a bunch
of pages and I read it and knew it couldn't possibly lose
any money. The twelve pages looked terrific. Then they
came up with another idea called *The Queen* where we
were all dressed in white-satin ball gowns in a white-satin
room talking about the assassination of some queen.
Meanwhile, Rip Torn was supposed to play my part in
Easy Rider and he walked out and I got it, not because
Dennis wanted me, but because I just happened to *be*
there, you know what I mean? So he said, 'Great, go do
your number,' and that's how I got to be in the picture."

Now that he's walked away with *Easy Rider,* he's in hot

demand for big-budget prestige movies for the first time
in his life. The sky has opened and Chicken Little is getting rained on with pure gold. He just completed Vincente Minnelli's *On a Clear Day You Can See Forever*
with Barbra Streisand and when he talks about it he
speaks excitedly. Then he lowers his voice in case any of
his old buddies from the horror-flicks days might be listening. "I'm very frightened about it, I'll be perfectly honest.
I get nervous about this stuff. I wanted to see what it
would be like to be in a big Vincente Minnelli musical. It's
a radical departure for me, 'cause he makes a certain *kind*
of movie, you know? I didn't take a step in the whole thing
after I walked in carrying my suitcase. From that moment
on I'm either leaning on the windowsill with flower pots
or up against a chimney or something. Once he let me get
up to light someone's cigarette and I think my back went
crraccuncchh. You can probably hear it on the screen.
There was so little, uh, movement, you know what I
mean? I didn't have that much to do. You have to sort of
guess what he wants. One day I said, 'Look, Vincente, I
really don't *mind* being directed,' you know what I
mean? I sing. People will think that's funny, but I had my
own song. It wasn't a good song or anything, but I did it.
They didn't know if I could even carry a tune. . . . I think
I got it because Minnelli was looking at a film I did called
Psych-Out for some lighting effects and they saw me in it
. . . boy, I'd like to make a movie of Vincente Minnelli
watching *Psych-Out,* man . . . but I auditioned, just me
and him in the room, *a cappella,* me singing 'Don't Blame
Me' to Vincente Minnelli . . . it blew my mind!"

He grins and gulps his Coke. He looks innocent. "I don't
know how I come off, man . . . I just sort of drift around
in it. It was the clearest-cut job of acting for the money
I've ever done, you know what I mean? It was a financial
transaction. If I can bear that moment when I'll finally
have to sit there with my friends and watch myself sing
on the screen, then I think it will be worth it to be able,
uh, years from now . . . I'll have in my bio a Vincente
Minnelli musical along with the motorcycle flicks and the

horror flicks. Streisand treated me great, man. I don't
think she saw *Easy Rider* either, so it wasn't because of
that. She tried to help me in scenes, you know? She was
always telling me things to do."

Oops!

"I just recently went out there and rerecorded part of
the lyrics. Barbra, when we actually started shooting my
song, decided she would like to sing on the tail end of the
song *with* me, instead of making it a solo."

Did I say innocent? I meant *naive*.

It's like this: He's making Establishment noises now. He
shaved off his beard. There are no signs, in his hotel suite,
of sandals, hippie drag or funky shades. He hated *The
Wild Bunch*. He'd give anything to work for Orson
Welles. (On his first night in New York for the critics'
awards, he went out and saw *Citizen Kane*.) He admires
Jackie Gleason. And he hasn't been on an acid trip since
he and Dennis Hopper were on top of D. H. Lawrence's
tomb in Taos and he woke up the next morning in the top
of a tree.

He's a man with both feet planted firmly on the opposite banks of a generation gap. On one side the Establishment is offering him fame, glamour, hero-worship and big
money. On the other side the anti-Establishment writers,
grips, actors and friends who made it all possible are warning him that if he doesn't go one way or the other, he
could drown in the middle. The mud is deeper on the
anti-Establishment side and he can't get out. Not yet. He
just finished another low-budget flick, *Five Easy Pieces*,
directed by Bob Rafelson, who was responsible for *Head*,
and written by Carol Eastman, who wrote *The Shooting*,
a low-budget western he made once with Millie Perkins.
"I told them I would do it and I like to finish what I start,"
he says. "The only way I've been able to eat all these years
is through the help of friends. I figure ... uh ... I owe them
something."

"What's it about?" I ask.

"Uh . . . well, I'm this ex-child prodigy concert pianist
dropout who works in an oil field. Karen Black plays this

waitress and Lois Smith is a singer . . . very neurotic and all . . . we made it in Canada."

"Do they have oil wells in Canada?"

"Oh no, that part was shot in Bakersfield."

"Is it a comedy, or does it just sound like one?"

"Yes. I mean, it's not a comedy. I mean, it sounds like one, but it also plays very . . . heavily."

Next, he'll direct *Drive, He Said*, a film he wrote with Senator Eugene McCarthy's speech writer, starring Mike Warren, the UCLA basketball player, and Bruce Dern, his pal from the Roger Corman days. "What's *it* about?" I ask.

"An all-American basketball-playing college eccentric having an affair with a professor's wife who he also *likes*, you know what I mean? His roommate is, uh, trying to beat the draft to, you know, save his life. He's relating to it on a survival level although he's also very idealistic, very discontented, sort of a Quixotic character . . . like Don Quixote, you know? Mad but telling the truth a lot of the time . . . for instance, in the way that schizophrenics statistically with all their projections are, uh, right ninety percent of the time . . . you know, that's about average for a schizophrenic with all that withdrawal. This guy, in fact, says a line in there, as a non sequitur . . . he tells this character a schizogenic family is one which produces catatonia in its children because there are too many unspeakable things happening in the family structure, you know what I mean?"

I haven't the vaguest idea, but I can't help but ask how it all turns out. "He ends up in a straitjacket carted off in an ambulance . . . it's a very old-fashioned sort of movie . . . no zoom lenses or anything." I look closely to see if he's putting me on. He isn't. He turned down a fat role in Dennis Hopper's film, *The Last Movie*, which was shot in Peru. "Listen," he says, "my friend Hopper loves to act. He really wanted to play the part himself. He offered it to me really after he already knew I couldn't do it. He said, 'Well, Jack, you'd think you'd want to test.' I said, 'Now wait a minute, Hopper,' I said, 'I can't test. I've done that before and I always lose the part,' and he said, 'Well,

I'm gonna test.' " (Enormous roar from both Jack and
Mimi at the thought of Dennis Hopper testing for his own
movie.) "I've already overscheduled my work, because
I'm inexperienced at having so many offers. I did one
movie in two days. *The Little Shop of Horrors.* About a
guy who crosses a Venus's-flytrap with some other gigantic plant. This little Milquetoast starts out feeding it flies
and bugs and cats and dogs and eventually moves up to
people. We had one day's rehearsal. *Cry-Baby Killer* was
shot in six days. The people who never saw my movies are
better off in life than I am, man, but like all other actors,
I needed the work. I did all those horror flicks because
they were the only jobs I could get, man. Nobody wanted
me. Now it's different. In June, when I finish directing my
film, I'm going into Mike Nichols' new film. Acting is no
longer a vacation."

It's time to go pick up that award. He's worried. "Will
they let me in at Sardi's without a tie?" Mimi says yes. "Will
I have to give a speech or anything? I think I'll just say 'I
accept this award in the name of D. H. Lawrence.' " Mimi
laughs. She met him when she acted with him in *Hell's
Angels on Wheels* under the name I. J. Jefferson, but her
real name is Mimi Machu. It sounds like the name of a boat.
("Or a mountain," adds Mimi.) He takes off his tie, throws it
on a chair, and heads for the elevator, followed by the press
agent, the agent and Mimi. Will success spoil Jack Nicholson? "Anybody in the world can get me on the phone."

Mimi interrupts. "Some people called up last night
from downstairs wanting autographs. I wouldn't let them
come up."

Nicholson laughs. "I went down when she wasn't looking. The main difference now is money. My price is pretty
much . . . uh . . . theoretically, the same . . . whatever's fair.
I got scale on *Easy Rider* and no percentage . . . I always
say 'whatever's fair' . . . I mean, you know what I mean?
I go for whatever's fair." The agent shoots him a despair-
ing look. He straightens his cuffs. "Only at this point *fair*
is a little bit different." Then he climbs into his limousine
and drives into the Sunday-night traffic to conquer the
world, with a brief stop at Sardi's.

40

Adolph Zukor's 100th Birthday Party

ETTE DAVIS SWEPT into the Beverly Hilton hotel like a ravishing barracuda, took one look at Adolph Zukor's 100th birthday party, and laughed: "Same old faces in the same old places!" So many movie stars in one room, in fact, that Bob Hope called it a "living wax museum."

Mae West was in bed with the flu, Dean Martin canceled when he heard Jerry Lewis was coming, Gloria Swanson was doing a play in New Jersey, Bing Crosby got sick at the last minute and nobody could find Veronica Lake. But practically everybody else was there. I mean, how many times do you get to see a 100-year-old man? Certainly not in this town, where most people die of ulcers before they can count their first million-dollar gross. Adolph Zukor, the last founding father of the motion picture industry, has counted several and lived to tell about it. The furrier's apprentice who arrived as a Hungarian refugee with $25 sewn into the lining of his pockets stayed on to lay the cornerstone by sponsoring Cecil B. De Mille's *The Squaw Man* in a stable that later became Paramount Pictures. That was 1913. "It cost him $40,000," quipped Bob Hope. "Today Ryan O'Neal spends that much on hair spray."

Yes, the business has changed. But it hasn't forgotten. So Paramount took some of those grosses from *Love Story* and *The Godfather* and threw a party for the grand old man who made it all possible. I guess you could call it the party of the year. If they made it into a movie, you wouldn't believe it. The limousines started arriving at 7 P.M. "I don't know why I'm here," said Barbara Stanwyck. "By the time I got to Paramount, Zukor was already gone." After which Stella Stevens whispered: "By the time I got there, Barbara Stanwyck was already gone." It was that kind of night. Bette Davis, who never worked at Paramount at all, shook hands with Dorothy Lamour. Jim Aubrey, of MGM, shook hands with Ted Ashley, of Warner Brothers. Buddy Rogers, in a fire-engine-red dinner jacket and fire-engine-red lipstick, shook hands with everybody for himself and Mary Pickford, who was all alone in Pickfair watching the whole thing on television. And Zsa Zsa Gabor, who didn't get the lead in *Forty Carats*, said: "I don' vant to be bitchy, dalink, but that Liv Ullmann looks dreadful." Well, after all, it *is* Hollywood.

Armed with champagne, they marched through a giant replica of the Paramount gate and mounted the dais. One hundred movie greats (count 'em) cheek to jowl. Alfred Hitchcock, Edith Head, Fred MacMurray, Anne Baxter, Jack Benny, Peter Bogdanovich, Michael Caine, Frank Capra, John Gavin, Gene Hackman, Gregory Peck, Rock Hudson, Danny Kaye, Gene Kelly, June Haver, Groucho Marx, Jack Oakie, George Raft, Diana Ross, George Stevens, Jimmy Stewart, King Vidor, Hal Wallis, Jack Warner, William Wyler, Laurence Harvey, Bette Davis, Barbara Stanwyck, and on and on until nobody could applaud anymore. Lisa Kirk sang the National Anthem and

Jack Benny said if Adolph Zukor had listened to him he'd only be seventy-five years old now and Bob Hope said he had never seen so many "A" people in a "B" hotel. Everybody laughed.

It was some party, all right. There were no invitations and at $125 a plate it was sold out the day it was announced. It took a year to prepare, but it was worth it. The waiters were dressed by the Paramount wardrobe department, and the prop men dug up 100 champagne buckets, 300 boxes of confetti, 5 tons of rose petals, 500 balloons, 900 yards of material for tablecloths and 1,500 napkins, 108 blowups of Paramount stars on 800 square feet of paper, 3,000 stills from old movies, 101 candles wired to light up at once with a flick of one central switch and a 14-foot-high birthday cake built in three sections that took ten days to make and four days for the Hilton pastry chef to decorate. It took four moving vans to haul it and 125 men to set it up. Paramount paid the bill and they still raised $100,000 for charity. Don't tell me they don't know how to do something right in Lotus Land.

There were a few complaints. Hollywood's idea of dressing up is to wear a gold brocade caftan with the top button unbuttoned. Agent Sue Mengers, in a black sequin Donald Brooks gown, gazed ruefully at Francis Ford Coppola, director of *The Godfather,* looking rather scruffy on the dais in an orange suit, and sighed: "I feel like Babe Paley at a bar mitzvah in the Bronx." And some of the young stars didn't know who the old stars were. (Cybill Shepherd kept asking, "Who is Regis Toomey?") But it was a good public relations night for an industry badly in need of some cheer.

Charlton Heston made a fine emcee. Tommy Tune and twelve dancers dressed up like Paramount stars did a lively production number while Nelson Riddle's orchestra sounded like a Frank Sinatra recording session. Dorothy Lamour came out with two monkeys called Bing and Bob and sang a song from *Jungle Princess.* Bob Hope did his thing. Jack Benny did his thing. And Diana Ross sang songs from *Lady Sings the Blues.* At ten minutes to midnight, Adolph Zukor called down from the Presidential Suite where he was supposed to be resting, and said he was bored and going home. That called for emergency action, so the Paramount executives rolled him out in his wheelchair and everybody stood and sang "Happy Birthday" while a cake lit up as high as the Hilton ceiling. Somebody read a telegram from the President of the United States and Zukor, in a cracked, frail voice, said: "God bless the President." (Somebody at my table said, "He thinks it's President Hoover." Somebody else said the only way they could top off the evening was to have a 100-year-old naked woman jump out of the cake.) I do think they got a bit carried away when they compared Adolph Zukor to Moses, but Hollywood has always been nothing if not excessively enthusiastic.

It wouldn't be a movie party without a movie, so they showed a twenty-five-minute tribute to the last movie mogul, linking the movies with their historic past. Flashing across the screen were the names who couldn't be there—W. C. Fields, Cecil B. De Mille, Clara Bow—but were part of it all just the same. A lot of people cried. Then they bought Mr. Zukor's birthday candles for $1,000 apiece, the night was over and Bette Davis was the first one on the street in the traffic jam, looking for her limousine.

Yes, Virginia, there is still a Hollywood.